earthly
encounters

SUNY series in Gender Theory
Tina Chanter, editor

earthly encounters

sensation, feminist theory, and the anthropocene

stephanie d. clare

"Feeling Cold: Phenomenology, Spatiality, and the Politics of Sensation" was originally published in *differences* 24, no. 1: 172–93. Copyright 2013, Duke University Press. All rights reserved. Republished by permission of the publisher. www.dukeupress.edu.

Published by State University of New York Press, Albany

© 2019 State University of New York

All rights reserved

No part of this book may be used or reproduced in any manner whatsoever without written permission. No part of this book may be stored in a retrieval system or transmitted in any form or by any means including electronic, electrostatic, magnetic tape, mechanical, photocopying, recording, or otherwise without the prior permission in writing of the publisher.

For information, contact State University of New York Press, Albany, NY
www.sunypress.edu

Library of Congress Cataloging-in-Publication Data

Names: Clare, Stephanie D., 1980- author.
Title: Earthly encounters : sensation, feminist theory, and the anthropocene / Stephanie D. Clare.
Description: Albany : State University of New York Press, [2019] | Series: SUNY series in gender theory | Includes bibliographical references and index.
Identifiers: LCCN 2018045645 | ISBN 9781438475875 (hardcover) | ISBN 9781438475899 (e-book) | ISBN 9781438475882 (pbk.)
Subjects: LCSH: Senses and sensation. | Feminist theory.
Classification: LCC BF231 .C53 2019 | DDC 305—dc23 LC record available at https://lccn.loc.gov/2018045645

10 9 8 7 6 5 4 3 2 1

Theory can be a dew that rises from the earth and collects in the rain cloud and returns to earth over and over. But if it doesn't smell of the earth, it isn't good for the earth.
—Adrienne Rich, "Notes toward a Politics of Location"

I am not burying myself in a narrow particularism. But neither do I want to lose myself in an emaciated universalism. [...] My conception of the universal is that of a universal enriched by all that is particular, a universal enriched by every particular: the deepening and coexistence of all particulars.
—Aimé Césaire, "Letters to Maurice Thorez"

Contents

          Acknowledgments   ix

          Introduction   xv

ONE   Feeling Cold: Phenomenology, Spatiality, and the Politics of Sensation   1

TWO   Locating Affect, Swimming Underwater   21

THREE "Being Kissed by Everything": Race, Sex, and Sense in Bessie Head's *A Question of Power*   45

FOUR   Psychic Territory, Appropriation, and "Geopower": Rereading Fanon, Foucault, and Butler   65

FIVE   Location, Sensation, and the Anthropocene   85

          Notes   113

          Bibliography   149

          Index   173

Acknowledgments

"Day after day, and all day long," Simone de Beauvoir writes in her *Memoires d'une jeune fille rangée*, "I measured myself against Sartre."[1] In this calculation, Beauvoir finds herself ultimately lacking: "I was simply not in his class. [...] My reasoning was shaky and my ideas confused."[2] Yet Beauvoir concludes this ranking of herself with an indirect jab at Sartre. She explains, "I was by nature curious rather than imperious and preferred learning to shining."[3] In a reading of this passage, Michèle Le Doeuff points out that philosophy is precisely not about shining, but rather about learning. It is not about being imperious, but rather about being curious. In this way, although Beauvoir claims that Sartre will always be the philosopher, not herself, at the same time she suggests that something in Sartre's mode of arguing, thinking, or presenting himself is both not properly philosophical and yet often constitutive of the field.

When I began this project, I thought that writing a book had to be about shining, not learning; an author had to be imperious, not curious. As a result, I did not believe that I could actually finish this project. My feelings of insufficiency were familiar to me. As a white woman, I often feel confident in my role as a teacher (especially in smaller classrooms). Privileges of race and class significantly support that confidence. Yet it is hard to see myself as a writer and researcher. As a result, I often give up, write less, and remain altogether silent, trying to hide. This is not a personal failing. Feminists and critical race scholars have made it clear that epistemic confidence is structural.

Within this context, I especially want to thank those who made institutional, intellectual, and personal space for me to write and those who helped me to understand that I could write even if I preferred learning to shining. I am grateful to Elizabeth Grosz whose joy, humility, care, and brilliance carried me through my PhD, and inspires me still today. Amber Jamilla Musser provided crucial feedback and emotional support necessary for completing this project. She continues to model how to approach intellectual work with resolve, creativity, and pleasure. I am also beholden to the feminist scholars at the University of Oxford, especially Ros Ballaster and Deborah Cameron, who donated their time to run the

MSt in Women's Studies and who applied for the funding that became my postdoctoral fellowship. The support of Ranjana Khanna and Priscilla Wald came at a crucial period for me; it was under their guidance that I realized this material could become a book. Finally, although my time at the University at Buffalo was brief, Ewa Plonowska Ziarek's palpable love of feminist theory coupled with her decision to work with me ("*Me?*," I remember thinking) propelled me to complete this project. Each of these feminist scholars is known for publishing many important works; their support of emerging scholars is less widely visible, but I am incredibly grateful to have benefited from it. Thank you.

It feels as though I wrote this book on the road, packing and unpacking suitcases and boxes, scavenging for furniture, forks, and friends. As I traveled from Montréal to Oxford, from Highland Park to New York City, Durham, Buffalo, Syracuse, and finally to Seattle, I found many whose support has become invaluable. At Rutgers University, I was lucky to learn from many dedicated, passionate and brilliant scholars and students, especially, but not only, in the Department of Women's and Gender Studies: Agatha Beins, Ashley Glassburn Falzetti, Anahi Russo Garrido, Jodie Barker, Leigh-Anne Francis, Laurie Marhoefer, Andy Mazzaschi, Anel Méndez Velázquez, Stina Soderling, Sonja Thomas, Shakti Jaising, Nimanthi Rajasingham, Elizabeth Grosz, Carlos Decena, Jasbir Puar, Harriet Davidson, and Carolyn Williams. From my time at Rutgers, I am especially grateful to Agatha Beins, inspired by her attention to detail and to the seemingly mundane yet fundamental elements that sustain us.

The University of Oxford twice took me in and built me up, literally feeding me when I needed it. Over many cups of tea and across endless conversations, the Oxford polymorphous perverts, Amber Jamilla Musser, Niamh Duggan, Marcie Bianco, Joanna Cupano, Irene Revell, and, when she visited, Sophie Green, recalibrated the world for me. They showed me that I had value, and they gave me vision. I would not have written a book were it not for their support. When I returned to Oxford almost ten years later, I once again found sustenance. Many thanks especially to Pelagia Goulimari, who told me to keep my eye on the ball; to Pamela Sue Anderson, from whom I was lucky to learn about the politics of confidence just before she passed away (far too early, far too quickly); to St. Hilda's College, which fed me (an extra thank you!); to Idalina Baptista; and to my students, especially Lilith Acadia, Kate Turner, Mel Stewart, and Julia Tanner.

As I moved between New Jersey, Oxford, North Carolina, and Buffalo, Syracuse, NY became my home. I am now based in Seattle, but I am grateful for all the love that was granted to me in that Central New York town, especially as I weathered the academic job market and decided to continue to pursue academic work. Thank you to Susan Branson, Lori Brown, Peter Couvares, Julie Gozan, Mary Hagemann, Paul Hagenloh, Kate Hanson, Chris Hanson, Mark Heller, Samantha Kahn Herrick, Martin Hogue, Tom Keck, Laurie Marhoefer, Gladys McCormick, Erin Rand, and Diane Williamson. Thank you also to the four-footed crew: Tigger, Biscuit, Stache, and Zoe, especially for their (albeit uneven) companionship across icy trails, and to the little ones—though quickly no longer little: Sasha Gozan-Keck, Ruby Gozan-Keck, Amelia Couvares, and Lucia Couvares. You have reminded me to be playful, even in my writing.

At Duke University, I was incredibly lucky to be part of the then-named Women's Studies Department—never before have I had the privilege of attending so many wonderful talks and seminars. Thank you to everyone who made them happen! Thank you especially to Martha Kenney, Ranjana Khanna, Priscilla Wald, and Ara Wilson for your generous thought and care.

Were it not for the Department of Comparative Literature at the University at Buffalo, I doubt this book would exist. I have already thanked Ewa Ziarek, but I am also grateful to Rachel Ablow, Krzysztof Ziarek, Sergey Dolgopolski, Rodolphe Gasché, and Kalliopi Nikolopoulou for their attentive engagement with my work. The Gender Institute at University at Buffalo also provided helpful funding for the completion of this project. Such institutional hubs, even if they have no official walls, are critical to the support of feminist scholarship, and I am grateful to all those scholars and administrators who have worked hard to forge space for cross-disciplinary and interdisciplinary feminist work.

I completed this project in Seattle at the University of Washington. Many of my new colleagues have granted me generous support that has been especially crucial to sending this book out into the world. Thank you especially Carolyn Allen, Nancy Bou Ayash, Anis Bawarshi, David Crouse, Gillian Harkins, Habiba Ibrahim, Deborah Kamen, Charles Laporte, Sarah Levin-Richardson, Colette Moore, Jesse Oak Taylor, Brian Reed, Juliet Shields, Alys Weinbaum, and Bonnie Whiting. Many thanks as well to the wonderful undergraduate and graduate students who have helped me think through some of this project's final arguments: Katherine Cavanaugh, Thaomi Michelle Dinh, Tyler Kipling, E. J. Koh, Kathleen Reeves, Maxine Savage, Elise Stefanou, and Sam Wooley.

This work was funded by the Social Science and Humanities Research Board of Canada, the University at Buffalo's Gender Institute, les Fonds de Recherche du Québec, Rutgers University, and the Andrew W. Mellon Foundation. Thank you especially to Canadian and Québecois taxpayers and voters for their support of education, research, and the arts. Thank you also to the people of New Jersey for funding Rutgers. I was lucky to finish this manuscript with the support of the University of Washington's English Department and the Office for Faculty Advancement. They paid for me to complete the National Center for Faculty Development and Diversity's Faculty Success Program, which helped me to get words on the page and worry a little less. Although we spoke just a few times, I am especially grateful to Aimee Carrillo Rowe for her mentorship throughout the program.

It has been a pleasure to work with Rebecca Colesworthy, Andrew Kenyon, and Chelsea Miller at SUNY Press. Thanks, too, to Wendy Lochner at Columbia University Press for reaching out to me several years ago. The anonymous reports Lochner solicited significantly helped me to revise the manuscript.

Je suis Montréalaise. J'espère que l'esprit créatif, ouvert, généreux (mais imparfait) de ma ville est présent dans ces pages. From Montreal, though certainly beyond the island as well, I am beholden to my sister, Carolyne Clare, who generously and brilliantly played the role of my younger sibling, forever granting me the position of a legitimate knower. Thank you. Now, especially as we both have young children, our roles are often reversed. Every day, I benefit from Carolyne's insights. My parents, Charlotte Pinsonnault and Richard Clare, have supported me in every way they can. Their love for the arts and interest in politics inform these pages. Over and again, I am floored by my mother's kindness and my father's abundant energy. Also from Montreal, I want to thank Lindsay Drennan, who has helped me to practice confidence, and Julia Carbone Gold, Jennifer Cutler Berzan, and Margaret Gales for all those years of fun. My New York City crew also deserves thanks, especially Des Almoradie and Niamh Duggan. Niamh is gifted in building people up. She has always made me believe that I can accomplish what I set out to do.

Laurie Marhoefer has stood by me as I have written each and every one of these words. Without her ambition, her feminist commitment, and her unwavering support of my career, I doubt that I would have completed this project. Thank you. Together, we now have what once felt unimaginable: a household with, first, two PhDs; then, two Mellon postdocs; followed by two tenure-track jobs; and, finally, two books (soon to become more!). I am proud of what we have accomplished together and eager to see what else we shall do.

This book is dedicated to our daughter, Harriet Lavoie Marhoefer Clare. "My eyes are wide-opened and I'm asking so many questions," she told me last night, at 10:00 p.m., long past her bedtime. But Hattie, at two years old, wanted to find out what, precisely, is a sky, and whether it is only creatures with eyes that sleep. She wanted to know what pirates are (they feature in one of our favorite lullabies). "Where we went?" she asked. "Where are we? Where will we go?" Hattie almost always wants to learn. She is curious, creative, playful, and caring. But also, critically, she is confident. "It's okay, Mama, I can climb this lifeguard chair. I'm big enough." I opened these acknowledgments with what I cannot but read as Simone de Beauvoir's own gendered lack of confidence. Such a "lack" might, of course, be reframed as a fruitful presence, a form of questioning that need not be overcome in writing but is productive of something better, more just, more thoughtful. Nonetheless, I hope that Hattie continues questioning *and* never loses her confidence, a confidence guided by curious aspiration. There is so much to do and far too little time in which to do it.

Some of this material has appeared in "On the Politics of 'New Feminist Materialisms,'" in *Mattering: Feminism, Science and Materialism*, edited by Victoria Pitts-Taylor (New York: New York University Press, 2016). An earlier version of chapter 1 appeared as "Feeling Cold: Phenomenology, Spatiality, and the Politics of Sensation," *differences: A Journal of Feminist Cultural Studies* 24, no. 1 (2013); and a version of chapter 4 was published as "Geopower: The Politics of Life and Land in Frantz Fanon's Writing," *Diacritics* 41, no. 4 (2013), 60–80. Reprinted with permission by Johns Hopkins University Press. Copyright © Johns Hopkins University Press.

Many thanks to Will Wilson for granting me permission to reprint his photographs, *AIR: Confluence of Three Generations*, *AIR (Auto-Immune Response) #4*, and *AIR (Auto-Immune Response) #5*.

Introduction

Ta-Nehisi Coates ends his unflinching account of living as a black man in the United States with the weather. He recounts driving through Philadelphia.

> Through the windshield I saw the mark of [...] ghettos—the abundance of beauty shops, churches, liquor stores, and crumbling houses. [...] Through the windshield I saw the rain coming down in sheets.[1]

At first, this rain—which appears as the subject of the final sentence of *Between the World and Me*—seems like a "natural" phenomenon, unlike the phenomena of race and racism that Coates navigates, a social production materialized, in part, in and as this urban space. The rain appears to have nothing to do with the American, historical coconstitution of race and space. So why conclude with the weather?

My reading of this passage captures *Earthly Encounters*' central arguments. This book seeks to understand how gender and race, or gendered racialization and racialized genders, inform and are informed by sensations of the more-than-human world, such as the rain. My analysis of sensation allows for an understanding of gendered, racialized subjectivity *as it exists on this planet*, a more-than-human world that is material, mediated, and by shaped by politics, as well as by more-than-human forces. The book also elaborates on the concept of "geopower," the force relations both between humans, and between humans, nonhumans, and more-than-humans, that transform the surface of the earth. It shows how this concept is relevant for rethinking gendered and racialized subjectivity on this planet, including in the context of the Anthropocene.[2]

I borrow the phrase "more-than-human world" from Nancy Tuana, who uses it to index a world that is "neither 'fabricated' in the sense of created out of human cultural practices, nor [...] independent of human interactions of a multitudes of forms, including cultural."[3] The concept "more-than-human" is powerful because it allows for an externality without hiding the entanglement of nature, culture, and power. This entanglement is clear in Coates's description of the rain. The rain is "more-than-human," because human practices have not created it. However, at the same time, the rain is not independent of such practices, either. First, the burning of fossil fuels has increased global temperatures, which has melted ice caps, leading to an increase of moisture in the air and a more volatile weather system. Climate scientists agree that violent storms will become more frequent in many places in the world; there will be more sheets of rain.[4]

Coates is clear about this connection between climate change and the rain. He recounts sitting in his car thinking about climate change, thinking about how the "Dreamers," those who believe themselves to be white, have plundered not only "the bodies of humans but the body of the Earth itself."[5] He builds a continuity between the violation of black bodies and the pillage of the earth.[6] His reading of the Anthropocene joins the many others who argue that the transformation of the earth is not separable from structural inequality. "Uneven distribution," as Andreas Malm and Alf Hornborg argue, "is a condition for the very existence of modern, fossil fuel technology."[7] In this context, the rain that comes at the end of *Between the World and Me* cannot be understood as a "natural" phenomena independent of human practice. It can instead be read—at least in part—as the materialization of modern fossil-fuel capitalism, which is itself integrally linked to histories of racial inequality and racism. To be very clear: this is not to deny that the rain is often experienced as something exterior from or other than these social, economic, political relations. It is also not to reduce the rain to the creation of (some) human beings. This is why the concept of the "more-than-human" is powerful: it allows for an externality while highlighting the entanglement of nature-culture-power.

But the rain is more-than-human in a second important way, as well: it is not actual rain that appears in the writing, but rather a description of the rain; this rain is a linguistic event. Some might want to read this description as a metonymy for tears or as a form of imagery representing sadness. The weather matches or expresses Coates's mood. Indeed, it would not be surprising had this scene described Coates crying. While he is sitting in his car, the text explains, he is thinking about an acquaintance of his, a black man, who was shot dead by the police. Coates explains that he himself became "hard" to survive on the streets of Baltimore and in the family of his youth. Because this toughness gives form to his body, he cannot easily dispense with it. Thus, one might argue that at the end of the memoir, the *I* who tells the story comes to match the *I* who has lived through that same story: Coates displaces the sadness. In this performance of racialized masculinity, Coates does not cry. Instead, he describes the rain.

However, to understand racialized and gendered subjectivity in a more-than-human world requires that we not simply interpret descriptions of that world as, primarily, metaphor. This is certainly not to say that such descriptions do, indeed, function as metaphor. It is also not to forget that these descriptions appear in language and thus are linguistic. My purpose here is not to "redeem" language's referentiality, to insist, in the words of Lawrence Buell, on texts' "outer mimetic function."[8] Such an approach has been important in the history of ecocriticism, which, moving away from deconstruction and poststructuralism, has sought to understand how literature actually describes the world, pointing our attention to it, awakening us to something natural beyond human conceptualization and production. Following this line of thinking, many ecocritics have upheld nonfiction and realism.[9] This approach, however, is limited, especially since the identification of what counts as real or realistic tends to naturalize and prioritize postenlightenment, secular perspectives.[10] Language does not capture the real so much as, potentially, produces a sense of reality. This sense is political, cultural, and social. The job of a critic is to understand how that sense of reality is produced, to analyze its ideological underpinnings, and to consider its effects.[11]

Yet an ideological, interpretive approach is not sufficient either, because it tends to reduce the analysis of the more-than-human world to the analysis of cultural politics, and thus treats the more-than-human solely in the realm of human representation. My approach to language, literature, and the aesthetic is therefore different. While I do consider the cultural politics of representation, I also draw attention to the sensory underpinnings of language. That is, I do not understand language as separate from the sensory. The two are intertwined (which also means that they are not reducible to one another). By considering the sensory underpinnings of language, I am able to recognize that language is not a transparent medium while, at the same time, considering human, embodied beings in a more-than-human world.[12]

An example can help to make this approach clear. How is it that the rain in *Between the World and Me* can function as a metaphor of sadness? Which sensory experiences and contexts subtend the figure of speech such that it is meaningful? What is it about the rain, and the experience of the rain, that allows it to stand in for sadness or tears in this context? It is not merely literary convention that connects the rain to the tears. It is, rather, that both are wet. It is that, in certain circumstances, both can feel like a form of defeat, can feel uncomfortable. It is, finally, that one experience can be lived through the other.

This approach is especially powerful in reading other passages of *Between the World and Me*. Directly addressing his son, Coates writes, "You have been cast into a race in which the wind is always at your face and the hounds are always at your heels."[13] This wind and these hounds are metaphors for the hardship and violence of racism.[14] But these metaphors make sense because something in the lived experience of racism is similar to the lived experience of the wind and the attacking dogs. Even more, these experiences share a continuity, such that the experience of one comes to be lived through or is even productive of the other. This is not a difficult argument to accept when thinking about the hounds, for instance. During the American civil rights movement or the movement for black liberation, police departments employed dogs to attack and breakup demonstrators.[15] The hounds in Coates's text evoke this history. In other words, the rain is more-than-human in that it is perceived from the perspective of a living being, and history effects that perception.

Overall, the rain is more-than-human in at least three ways: first, since we no longer have access to a climate that has not been shaped by modern fossil-fuel, racial capitalism, the rain cannot but be read as an effect, in part, of climate change. Next, the rain appears in language and can be read metaphorically, yet this does not mean that it is "only" linguistic. Even as metaphor, the rain points to an embodied experience in the more-than-human world. Finally, that embodied experience is situated. A living being's perception of the world depends on his or her social and cultural position, a position on earth that is not static and not necessarily singular, but is nonetheless informed by embodied, historical memory, habit, and affective associations.[16] James B. Haile III, in a reading of Coates, argues that "the issue is not so such what exists *for* consciousness but the ways in which consciousness is influenced by embodiment and the historicity of embodiment."[17] I would put it a bit differently: what exists for consciousness is important—in fact, what exists for consciousness shapes embodiment—but the historicity of embodiment likewise comes to affect future perception. The rain is more-than-human in that it is sensed through that history. Building on this analysis, *Earthly Encounters* interprets a series of specific sensations: feeling cold, the touch of the wind, the sense of being immersed under water, and the feeling of containment. These sensations index a more-than-human world, one constituted by the thermal energy of particles, by currents of water, and by the earth's axial tilt. And yet sensations are lived by particular people in particular places. They emerge in social and political contexts that cannot be abstracted from them. My analyses are located in the twentieth century. I write about feeling cold in Canada, of the warm embrace of the wind in rural Botswana, of the sense of being immersed in the North Atlantic Ocean, and of the feeling of containment in Algiers. While I focus on *descriptions* of sensations and *descriptions* of the more-than-human world often (though not always) in aesthetic form, I consider the sensory underpinnings of these descriptions to identify traces of the more-than-human, traces of earthly encounters within linguistic representation itself. Across this analysis, my aim is to build a fuller account of the lived experience of racialized gender as it exists on this planet, earth.

My approach features some important points of overlap with Gayatri Spivak's more recent writing about what she calls "planetarity"; however, I also depart from Spivak's vision, as well. Beginning with her 1999 "Imperative to Re-imagine the Planet," Spivak has published a series of essays that calls for the elaboration of a form of "planet-thought."[18] At its most basic, this form of thought begins with the recognition that we live "on, specifically, a planet."[19] This "planet" is not to be confused with the "globe." The globe has been mapped: it is an "abstract ball covered in latitudes and longitudes, cut by virtual lines, once the equator and the tropics and so on, now drawn by the requirements of Geographical Informational Systems."[20] The globe, in other words, is known. It is inseparable from the modern and postmodern system of knowing that has been placed on it, forms of knowing entangled with globalization, imperialism, and colonization. Indeed, the globe, in Spivak's reading, is inherently connected to globalization with its "imposition of the same system of exchange everywhere."[21] It is found "on our computers. It is the logo of the World Bank."[22] Thus, this "globe" is knowable, striated yet smooth in its connection to global capitalism, and, Spivak argues, uninhabited: "No one lives there."[23] This image of the globe figures the human (or at least particular humans) in control, as agents of charge, even sovereign because it does not imagine us as living in this space but rather as knowing it and managing it.

In contrast, planetarity, Spivak insists, "cannot deny globalization," but it provides an alternative vision to this globe.[24] We "inhabit" the planet, "indeed are it."[25] We are part of the planet on which we live, and while we "inhabit it," "we inhabit it, on loan."[26] The planet is not ours. In fact, we are "planetary accidents."[27] We are derived of the planet and from the planet. We are part of the planet rather than agents above it. And yet the planet did not constitute us knowingly. We remain but accidents. The planet, however, ought not to be thought simply in opposition to the global. Spivak insists that it provides no "neat contrast with the globe."[28] This is because planetarity in Spivak's view consists in a radical form of alterity: "Its alterity," she writes, "is mysterious and discontinuous—an experience of the impossible."[29] The planet is "not our dialectical negation," which is to say is it not the other through which we come to define ourselves. The planet is also not "a self-consolidating other as the self's mere negation."[30] It is neither simply our negation (in part, because we are derived of and from it), nor is it self-consolidating. The planet remains indefinite in Spivak's writing. It is not formed; it is neither "continuous with us," nor is it "specifically discontinuous."[31] One way to understand this argument is to recognize that to grant the planet a specific, definite form would be to position it as an object that is known by us. However, by "planetarity," Spivak seeks to decenter the human, to posit an outside from which we derive. Thus, to consider the planet as mysterious, as a radical form of alterity is, in effect, to honor this decentering.

While my approach to earthly encounters is likewise skeptical of global imaginaries and is likewise insistent that we are part of and derive from this planet, my turn to sensation offers a different approach than Spivak's. Because of planetarity's radical alterity, Spivak does not "offer a formulaic access to planetarity. No one can," she insists.[32] In contrast, without claiming that sensation offers a formulaic point of access, the book considers sensation as a point of encounter with elements of the planet. For instance, in the sensation of feeling cold, in the touch of the wind, and in pull of a wave, we are affected by that which is beyond us, even though we inhabit and depend on it. Planetarity might not be known, but it affects us daily. The analysis of various sensations offers one lens through which this becomes clear.

Why Sensation?

This book's analysis of sensation and the more-than-human addresses a central problem in contemporary critical (and especially feminist) theory.[33] On the one hand, the past ten years has seen a wave of scholarship arguing for ontological, new materialist, nonrepresentational, object-orientated approaches in the humanities and interpretative social sciences, approaches that claim to move beyond poststructuralism's focus on signification, representation, and discourse.[34] Although this scholarship is clearly diverse, it is characterized by repeated influential and compelling refrains: agency need not be figured primarily as human;[35] materiality is open to becoming and effective of change;[36] relations captured in the analysis of affect rather than signification better attend to our imbrication in the material world and allow for an understanding of movement.[37] And yet, on the other hand, questions about signification, representation, and discourse have not simply disappeared. Accounts of materiality are themselves representations, and this new scholarship is itself a discursive formation that legitimizes some accounts of materiality over others. What are the politics of the ontologies that this new scholarship posits? Who is the implicit subject who comes to know materiality in the way described in this literature? How can we understand this ontological turn in light of prior, rich analyses of "situated knowledges," to use Donna Haraway's phrase?[38] And finally, matter might always be something more, but it is also appropriated and transformed into property, territory, and the nation-state. How might new materialisms engage with *these* material politics (which is to say, what is the relationship between so-called new materialisms and old materialisms)?

Much of the literature in new materialism frames the revelation that matter is open to transformation and in a state of perpetual becoming as somehow liberating. This makes sense in the context of feminist debates concerning the distinction between nature and culture, sex and gender. Rather than understand "sex" (and, with it, "nature" or "the body") as deterministic and closed, new materialisms offer a way to understand gender as materialized or embodied and yet also transformative and transforming. In other words, this scholarship provides a model for thinking through the sex/gender binary in a way that neither reduces gender to signification nor treats sex, nature, matter, and the body as inert, meaningless, or essential.[39]

However, when thinking in the context of climate change, the becoming of materiality is not inherently liberating. In turn, new materialisms might be helpful for thinking about how racial logics become embodied, or how racism is materialized—yet this thought is not inherently liberating in the way that it is in a (nonintersectional) version of feminism. In fact, one might point out that such an understanding of materiality or the body was key to eugenics and concerns about degeneration.[40] Finally, the question about how materiality is represented is especially critical in the context of settler colonialism where the stories we give of materiality, land, and the earth have real effects on the ways territory is formed and materiality is appropriated.[41] Faced with these arguments, it might be tempting to return to representational analysis, considering the politics both of whose representations count and of what counts as a representation. However, such an approach is insufficient as well. A focus on representation often precludes an analysis of the more-than-human world, reducing that world to its conceptualization by humans.[42]

Thus, in response to, on the one hand, approaches that analyze primarily the *representations* of things and places, objects and bodies, and, on the other hand, ontological approaches that insist on creating new understandings of matter as "an excess, force, vitality, relationality, or difference,"[43] *Earthly Encounters* begins in-between, in the analysis of the sensible.[44] "Sensations," as Amber Jamilla Musser puts it, "reside at the border of reality and consciousness."[45] The study of sensation allows for a middle ground between new materialism and idealism.

My approach builds on scholars such as Mel Chen, Banu Subramaniam, Deboleena Roy, Angela Willey, and Neel Ahuja, who have reworked new materialist scholarship to consider how social, political, and economic relations give form to bodies, contributing to the materialization of social difference and inequality.[46] Roy and Subramaniam, for instance, argue that "there can be no decontextualized generic body or matter, be it human or nonhuman, organic or inorganic."[47] In an analysis of the Bhopal disaster and the contemporary practices of surrogacy in India, they trace how "global inequities mounted by global circuits of capital, or practices of reproductive tourism ... become manifested in the materiality of sex, gender, sexuality, and the body."[48] This important scholarship highlights the traffic between meaning and matter; it contributes to a reworking of feminist, queer, postcolonial, and critical race studies in a more-than-human world, one that engages science, while recognizing its entanglement in colonialism, imperialism, and patriarchy. I am inspired by this research, but ultimately, my approach is different. I seek to highlight the encounters through which the material world, which I frame here as "more-than-human," is perceived in the first place by focusing on sensation.

Phenomenology of Perception

Feminist phenomenology and the phenomenology of race, especially as influenced by Merleau-Ponty's *Phenomenology of Perception,* inform my approach to the sensory.[49] My contention is that first-person, phenomenological approaches have been too quickly dismissed.[50] More precisely: these approaches are useful in the attempt to attend to the more-than-human.

There are many ideas in Merleau-Ponty's writing in particular that are helpful in the context of new materialisms. The first—and most central—is Merleau-Ponty's argument for what he calls "the primacy of perception." Merleau-Ponty explores how science and reason, even human self-understanding and ethics, are grounded in perceptual experience. His goal in *Phenomenology of Perception* is to "return to the world of actual experience which is prior to the objective world."[51] In other words, instead of starting with things in themselves or with the more-than-human as given and forceful, and instead of starting with science or ethics, his work brings attention to the perceptual experience through which the world comes into being for a person. "All my knowledge of the world," Merleau-Ponty highlights, "even my scientific knowledge, is gained from my own particular point of view, or from some experience of the world."[52] Science is built on "the world as directly experienced," and Merleau-Ponty claims that "if we want to subject science itself to rigorous scrutiny ... we must begin by reawakening the basic experience of the world of which science is the second-order expression."[53] To be clear, Merleau-Ponty is not against science. His goal, though, is to describe the sensible world—the world as it presents itself to us rather than the world as it is—independent of us. Merleau-Ponty's phenomenology is an attempt to get at experience from the perspective of the lived. "Experience" here is not imagined as something in the past tense, something that happened and is being recalled. Rather, the aim is to describe experience as it is being lived, in the first person. This starting point is useful in the context of new materialisms because it begins with the location or point of view from which the more-than-human world is sensed.

From the outset, however, it is crucial to recognize that Merleau-Ponty is critical of the term *sensation*, advocating for the analysis of "perception" instead. This is because he argues that when we think about "sensation," we imagine an external world impinging on us, resulting in a sensation. This model, Merleau-Ponty contends, is retroactively produced when we think about perception after the fact.[54] Perception, in contrast, as it is experienced in real time, does not posit an external world that is separate from us. Rather, it entails a sense of immersion in the world. In addition, unlike the notion of sensation, perception, Merleau-Ponty argues, is laden with meaning that is culturally and historically informed. "The *person who* perceives," he explains, "has a historical density, he takes up a perceptual tradition."[55] In contrast to Merleau-Ponty, I use the terms *sensation* and *perception* throughout this book. In fact, we can argue that *Phenomenology of Perception* does not advocate turning away from the concept of sensation so much as reimagining it. This is, notably, Simone de Beauvoir's reading. In her review of Merleau-Ponty's text, she writes, for instance, that "sensation is neither a quality nor the consciousness of a quality; it is a vital communication with the world."[56] Here, then, while understanding the limits of how sensation has been conceived, Beauvoir holds onto the term. I follow suit, using Merleau-Ponty analyses of perception to reimagine sensation because "sensation," unlike "perception" more clearly invokes embodiment.

This clarification introduces the second crucial idea that is important in the context of new materialisms. Merleau-Ponty's analysis of perception insists that the world is more than ourselves, more than our representations of it.[57] Perception is not a collection of my own thoughts, he writes. "The world is not what I think."[58] Instead, the world is "what I live through."[59] To describe perception is to consider how "I am open to the world.... I am in communication with it, but I do not possess it."[60] Merleau-Ponty gives the example of perceiving the sky: "As I contemplate the blue of the sky I am not *set over against* it as an acosmic subject; I do not possess it in thought, or spread out towards it some idea of blue. [...] I abandon myself to it and plunge into this mystery."[61] In this example, I do not constitute the blue of the sky. Instead, I am summoned by it, open to it, and it becomes determinate in me as I give into it. The sensible beckons the sensor and the sensor responds, opening to the sensed.

David Abram evocatively develops this aspect of Merleau-Ponty's phenomenology. He explains how Merleau-Ponty describes "the sensible world ... as active, animate, and, in some curious manner, alive."[62] That which we perceive calls out to our bodies, and our bodies respond to this call. There exists "a reciprocal interplay between the perceiver and the perceived."[63] Dualistic divisions between subject and object, active and passive, animate and inanimate fall away. When attending to the sensory, Abram argues that one only finds "relative distinctions between diverse forms of animateness."[64] He continues, "[T]he things and elements that surround us" are not "inert objects but [...] expressive subjects, entities, powers, potencies."[65]

This too is useful in the contexts of new materialist, feminist thought, which is invested both in interrupting the objectification of people and things and in reaching beyond discursive analysis, beyond the analysis of how things are conceived. To bring attention to the sensible is to consider a point of contact with that which is beyond ourselves and to reject the transformation of the world into inert, passive objects.

This approach also departs from prominent poststructuralist approaches to exteriority, which often consider the exterior to be a constitutive other, formed in the production of an interior. In this topology, if there is an "outside," this "outside" is framed as always already within. Take, for instance, Spivak's "Can the Subaltern Speak?" In this essay, Spivak calls for deconstruction, its "sustained and developing work on the *mechanics* of the constitution of the Other" and its attempt to render "*delirious* that interior voice that is the voice of the other in us."[66] Within this framework, otherness is positioned as within; it is an "interior voice." Similarly, in Judith Butler's *Bodies that Matter*, there exists no absolute outside to discourse: the nondiscursive is posited within discourse as that which stands before it. She insists that there is no "absolute 'outside,' an ontological thereness that exceeds or counters the boundaries of discourse"; instead, the outside "can only be thought—when it can—in relation to that discourse, at and as its most tenuous borders."[67] Here an epistemological limit becomes an ontological argument. In the field of geography, we find similar statements. Geographers have long been critical of the idea that nature is somehow "external" to culture. David Harvey argues that "nature exists in an 'internal' relation with society," and Bruce Braun argues similarly: nature is not external but rather is produced through struggles of power/knowledge. "Nature's *externality*," he writes, "is merely an effect produced through the discursive and material practices of everyday life."[68]

However, there are both ethical and political reasons that rejecting notions of externality is not sufficient. It is not quite Fredric Jameson's diagnosis of the "prison house of language" that concerns me.[69] Neither is it, exactly, the argument that such a framework makes it difficult to speak of the material world, including the body—an assertion that was key to the development of new materialisms.[70] It is, rather, that this topology limits ethical and political questions from the start. If otherness is always already inside, if the ethico-political move is to find otherness within (as Spivak has described it), if nature is never outside but produced as such from within, then an engagement with that which is not already internalized, with that which is not an effect of an internalization, is never staged. The issue here is partially one of human conceit: as long as interiority or the inside is figured as consciousness or discourse, and as long as these entities (rightly or wrongly) have been tied to the human, the topology that figures the outside as an effect of the inside or as always already inside forecloses thought about how humans engage with that which is veritably outside us, more than us. This frames the world as one of our own creations and suggests that we never engage with that which we have not constructed.[71]

Even more, reading what are now classics in poststructuralist feminist, queer, and postcolonial theory, I am struck by the faith placed in finding otherness within.[72] The belief often seems to be that unearthing how the self, identity, or even the national body are dependent on that which they exclude, and hence constructed in relation to a constitutive outside, is an ethical, important step toward justice. Such faith in uncovering is hard to maintain—and not simply because it depends on what Eve Sedgwick has diagnosed as paranoid reading, which insists that exposure or uncovering is a good in itself.[73] Rather, I am unsure what follows from the revelation that the other is in effect within, or the outside is in effect a constitutive exteriority, especially with respect to the more-than-human world, and especially, as well, in this age of climate change. The goal was to deconstruct colonialism and patriarchy to show how they are dependent on that which they devalue or foreclose. However, humans, for instance, can be violent toward themselves. To recognize an other within might only lead to more of such self-directed violence. Further, echoing Jameson in a different register, I question whether this familiar move of finding the other within can be understood as an entrapment, internment, or even colonization of otherness. I do not use the term *colonization* figuratively. I am rather thinking of the rich scholarship in indigenous studies that calls into question the framework of inclusion. Positing indigenous nations as a racialized minority within the U.S. (for instance), and seeking to find justice for this "minority" erases indigenous nationhood from the outset, placing the indigenous within.[74]

In other words, to figure an "other" as, in effect, within or as a constitutive exteriority might unhinge the self, imagined as self-same. It might also unhinge the belief in a pure, untouched nature that ought to ground social organization;

it might unhinge models of national purity. But it does not provide a framework for thinking about encounters with that which is different. In contrast, Merleau-Ponty's *Phenomenology of Perception* describes how in perception, we are opened up to that which is not ourselves. By focusing on human sensation of the more-than-human world, phenomenology starts from the outside without insisting that this outside can be known for itself, which is to say, while recognizing that sensation takes place on the border between the interior and the exterior.

That said, while Merleau-Ponty figures perception as externally directed, he argues that it is nonetheless meaningful and historically contextual. Borrowing from Gestalt psychology, Merleau-Ponty highlights how something is only ever perceived within a context, and therefore as a distinction between a figure and a background is drawn. This distinction is, in part, formed as a result of partaking in a particular "perceptual tradition." This does not imply that our perceptions are what we project onto the world. Instead, perception is constituted, as Gabrielle Bennet Jackson aptly summarizes, by the "demand placed by an object on the body and the body's reply to the object's demand."[75] In other words, Merleau-Ponty asks us to reimagine sensation as a form of entanglement between the inside and the outside, a meeting or conjunction that does not reduce one into the other. He neither imagines sensation as the simple impingement of the world onto ourselves nor as our projection onto the world. The world is something we live through, and a significant part of that living involves sensing, which comprises a dynamic encounter between the world as it calls out to us and our bodies as we respond to it.

Finally, perception, in Merleau-Ponty's writing, is clearly embodied. That is to say, perception is always located from a particular, incorporated point of view, the point of view of a lived body. It is bound up both with our sense of space and potential mobility. Merleau-Ponty famously replaces phenomenology's focus on the intentionality of consciousness (which is the recognition that consciousness is always consciousness *of* something) with an intentionality of the body or motor intentionality. The lived body, he argues, "appears to me as an attitude directed towards a certain existing or possible task."[76] My perception of the world—and especially of spatiality—is tied to this sense of being able to move through, in, and with the world. Merleau-Ponty takes the example of the "sensation" of red. He considers how viewing the color becomes associated with a bodily response: "When we say that red increases the compass of our reactions, we are not to be understood as having in mind two distinct facts, a sensation of redness and motor reactions—we must be understood as meaning that red, by its texture as followed and adhered to by our gaze, is already the amplification of our motor beings."[77] In other words, he argues that perceptions "present themselves with a motor physiognomy, and are enveloped in a living significance."[78] In addition, since Merleau-Ponty treats the body not as an inert object but rather as lived, this body also becomes situated in time. This implies, as Jorella Andrews argues, that perception "remains irreducibly open to the 'unfolding of experience.'"[79] The lived body as point of view is located, but not fixed. It is not an object but a responsive gearing to the world.

This is the final, insightful starting point that I draw from *Phenomenology of Perception*. Sensations are entangled with how we move and act in (and with) the world. They are embodied and "the body" is not fixed. Overall, Merleau-Ponty is helpful in that he provides a model for analysis: rather than begin with things-in-themselves, we can begin with the lived body's sensory experience of the world. This starting point does not reduce the world, however, to our conception of it; it rather has us attend to the lived body's encounters in the more-than-human. It also highlights that sensations of the more-than-human are always already laden with meaning, attached to one's sense of spatiality, and connected to potential action.

Lived Bodies: Nature-Culture-Power

I return to phenomenology notwithstanding the widespread critique of it, and while recognizing that many difficulties arise when drawing on Merleau-Ponty's phenomenology in the context of feminist and critical race studies.[80] One central problem concerns the politics of knowledge. Why ever feature another white, European, male philosopher? Feminist continental philosophy's attachment to a particular canon (including my own attachment) appears at times to work against its very project. I address this problem below. But for the moment, let me consider the relatively easier difficulty: while Merleau-Ponty writes of embodiment, he treats the lived body as undifferentiated and unhindered by power relations. More precisely, predominant throughout *Phenomenology of Perception* is Merleau-Ponty's belief in an anonymous, prepersonal body. It is on the basis of the existence of this body that Merleau-Ponty argues that our perceptions are shared. According to Merleau-Ponty, we similarly embody this anonymous body; we therefore share a world.

A brief investigation into feminist phenomenology and the phenomenology of race shows the limits of such an undifferentiated and foundational understanding of the body. For instance, in "The Lived Experience of the Black," Frantz Fanon shows how what he terms the "historico-racial schema" comes to inform the ways that racialized bodies are lived.[81] Fanon writes, "In the white world the man of color encounters difficulties in the development of his bodily schema.... The body is surrounded by an atmosphere of certain uncertainty."[82] The man of color experiences himself through the white man, through "a thousand details, anecdotes, stories" that make him take himself "an object" and leaves him feeling "dislocated."[83] In this example, the body as it is lived cannot be separated from its social, cultural, and political intersubjective constitution; "alongside phylogeny and ontogeny," Fanon writes in the book's introduction, "there is also sociogeny."[84] This argument overlaps with Iris Marion Young's classic essay, "Throwing Like a Girl," which shows how feminine bodily comportment, self-image, and sense of spatiality are affected by sexism.[85] Young argues that "the lived body has culture and meaning inscribed in its habits, in its specific forms of perception and comportment."[86] Reading such accounts, one can conclude, with Gayle Weiss, that it is "impossible to distinguish a 'pure' sense of proprioception or a postural schema from . . . racialized, gendered, religious, ethnic, and able-bodied body images."[87]

I do not want to claim, however, that culture, power, and politics only inform embodiment at the level of the body image. Rather, the constitution of the anonymous body is itself historical and shaped by nature-culture-power.[88] In as much as I follow Merleau-Ponty's approach, I am influenced by a particular reading of the anonymous body—and with it, a particular reading of the "phenomenological reduction." The phenomenological reduction, or the process of bracketing (also known as the *epoche*) is key to the phenomenological method, though not uniformly understood. Husserl begins the phenomenological enterprise by bracketing the "natural attitude," which posits that there exists a world outside of ourselves that causes perception. He instead focuses on the world as it is known by the subject. He frames this retreat into consciousness as guaranteeing some sort of transcendental truth to phenomenological claims. Merleau-Ponty, in contrast, reworks phenomenology as an existential philosophy, developing a critique of Husserl's idealism. He insists that consciousness is in the world and embodied. Since we are in the world, we can never stand outside of it to understand it; we can never bracket it as Husserl suggests. "The most important lesson which the reduction teaches us," Merleau-Ponty writes, "is the impossibility of a complete reduction."[89] And yet some form of a reduction is necessary, in his view. He writes: "The best formulation of the reduction is probably that given by Eugen Fink, Husserl's assistant, when he spoke of 'wonder' in the face of the world."[90] Phenomenology in Merleau-Ponty's version begins not by withdrawing into consciousness but rather by defamiliarizing that which is taken for granted, by reawakening ourselves to the richness of perceptual experience.

This reworking of the reduction has been important to the attractiveness of Merleau-Ponty's writing in feminist thought because often feminist concerns are seen as empirical, having to do with the world. If phenomenology begins by bracketing that world, retreating into consciousness, feminist interests would then become bracketed. Thus, as Johanna Oksala notes, "Many feminist phenomenologists discard the transcendental reduction. They usually turn to Merleau-Ponty and reiterate his view on the impossibility of complete reduction."[91] However, Bryan Smyth argues that the incompleteness of the reduction leaves the project tenuous, since it is on the basis of this reduction that phenomenological insights become differentiated from subjectivist, personal views. Smyth asks: if the reduction is incomplete, then what is the status of the claims that Merleau-Ponty's phenomenology describes?

Smyth develops an important reading of Merleau-Ponty that solves this problem. He argues that Merleau-Ponty holds onto an understanding of phenomenology as transcendental, and yet reconceives transcendental phenomenology as a "human practice that never really leaves the empirical world."[92] Although the reduction is partial, this does not tarnish the completeness of phenomenology's philosophical insights. Rather, Merleau-Ponty draws on a philosophy of history from Marx and Lukács, one that asserts that the prepersonal or anonymous body, the body that cannot be left behind or transcended, consists in a historical, universal incarnate. This impersonal, habituated body is "the repository of the general form or structure of past experience," or the "concrete locus of historical apriority."[93] The anonymous body is "prepersonal," but as Sara Heinämaa argues in a recent reading of *Phenomenology of Perception*, this does not mean that it is "self-less."[94] By "anonymous" and "prepersonal," Merleau-Ponty is pointing to aspects of the bodily nature of perception that are often hidden, but that "include the sedimented accomplishments of earlier acts, some of which are not our own acts but acts of others unknown to us and preceding us in time."[95] This means that while the organism cannot be bracketed, and while the organism is influential, its effects do not undermine phenomenological inquiry but rather contribute to it. Smyth writes, "[R]eduction cannot be seen simply as an act of freedom, a kind of heroic detachment, but rather must be understood in incarnational terms as a matter of 'living my time ... by plunging into the present and the world.'"[96] In this sense, phenomenology remains transcendental, not by detaching itself from the world but rather by losing one's self in one's organism, which crucially is conceived as historical.[97]

Smyth's powerful reading of Merleau-Ponty, along with Heinämaa's analysis of the prepersonal body, provides an opening for how I draw on phenomenology in this context. To be clear: I am less interested in producing a faithful interpretation of *Phenomenology of Perception* than in articulating a useful approach to phenomenology in the context of feminist, ecocritical, and critical race studies.

The anonymous, prepersonal body can be understood as the corporeal materialization of history or nature-culture-power, and this understanding makes room for the analysis of how difference and power give shape to that body.[98] In other words, one's body image is not "just" an idea, but is incorporated in habit and patterns of affect. The process of bracketing then becomes an analysis of the production of the body-subject.

Several scholars working both in the phenomenology of gender and race consider how these social positions become embodied. For instance, Linda Martín Alcoff argues that "race and gender consciousness produces habitual bodily mannerisms that feel natural and become unconscious after long use."[99] She argues that the materialization of bodies emerges within contexts of power differentials and inequalities that shape those very bodies. "The body itself," she writes, "is a dynamic material domain, not just because it can be 'seen' differently, but because the materiality of the body itself is, as [Elizabeth] Grosz puts it, volatile."[100] Similarly, Emily Lee, making a case for the relevance of Merleau-Ponty's phenomenology for the study of race, examines how the meanings ascribed to particular bodies shape individual experience, such that "the subject develops certain emotions, knowledge, ethical/moral postures, and sense of being-in-the-world."[101] While recognizing that race (and, I would add, gender) are socially constructed, Lee considers how the ways that embodiment is lived suggests that these forms of social difference do "not lie as a superficial cover over the primary layer of common humanity."[102] She continues, "[I]n a profoundly intimate sense, one lives race through the immediacy of the particular differences of one's embodiment."[103]

Such an argument emerges in *Between the World and Me*, as well.[104] Coates explains, over and again, that race is a fiction—a biological narrative invented to legitimize exploitation and violence, invented to create a feeling of superiority and invulnerability amongst those who believe themselves to be white. Whereas many scholars in critical race studies recognize this fiction, but argue that racialized identities are nonetheless important sites of contestation, meaning making, and community, Coates insists that the language of race is never far enough removed from the essentializing biology narrative. " 'Race,' " he writes, "is just a restatement and retrenchment of the problem."[105] At the same time, however, Coates writes extensively about how racism and racial stratification shaped and shapes his body and senses. "Racism," he states, "is a visceral experience. . . . It dislodges brains, blocks airways, rips muscle, extracts organs, cracks bones, breaks teeth."[106] Within this context, Coates calls himself "unoriginal."[107] He feels frightened; he learns to make his body hard. He incorporates—at least in part—his social position. He learns "rules that [. . .] have you contort your body to address the block, and contort again to be taken seriously by colleagues, and contort again so as not to give the police a reason."[108] Coates explains how hard it is for him not to pass on these habits and this fear to his son. For example, when his toddler jumps right in and plays with others at a preschool, Coates finds himself wanting to run after him, and stop his playing: " 'We don't know these folks! Be cool!' "[109] In short, Coates shows how one develops habits, forms of movement, and affective connections that materialize the experience of racialization and racism in and as the lived body.

And through these bodies, as Jeremy Weate argues in a reading of Fanon, "we belong to relatively different worlds."[110] In other words, the phenomenology of race pluralizes the "conditions of possibility for experience."[111] This argument is also central to *Between the World and Me* where racializing experience shapes perception itself. "But oh, my eyes," Coates writes. "When I was a boy, no portion of my body suffered more than my eyes."[112] Coates explains how he had a limited sense of the world, and could not imagine any place beyond either the Baltimore of his youth or the white suburbs on television. Following a phenomenological approach, we can read this passage as a statement about his lived eyes, his eyes as they are seeing in the world. In other words, "his eyes" are neither a metonymy for his sense of the possible, nor is he writing about his physical eyes. It is not that his retina suffered. His eyes as they are lived suffered.

Yet while gendered racialization shapes both the body and perception, it does not determine it. Merleau-Ponty writes: "I am not the outcome or the meeting-point of numerous causal agencies.... I cannot conceive myself as nothing but a bit of the world, a mere object of biological, psychological, or sociological investigation."[113] Instead of seeing the lived body as determined, Alcoff argues that Merleau-Ponty both recognizes the "importance of social influence" while also allowing "for meaningful intentionality."[114]

In short: a problem with phenomenology, as Michel Foucault influentially argued, is that "it gives absolute priority to the observing subject, ... which places its own point of view at the origin of all historicity—which in short, leads to a transcendental consciousness."[115] Yet Merleau-Ponty does not give priority to the observing subject as an origin or transcendental consciousness, if that consciousness is understood as standing above or apart from the field being perceived.[116] "There is no inner man," Merleau-Ponty writes, "man is in the world, and only in the world does he know himself."[117] "Man," in Merleau-Ponty's understanding of perception, is not reflecting on the world, standing apart from it, but rather living in it—apart of it. At a minimum, this immersion in the world takes form in and as the body itself, a historical materialization of nature-culture-power (and therefore not "man" at all). This implies that perception of the more-than-human world is what phenomenologists call "intersubjective," which is to say constituted (and not only situated) through nature-culture-power and affected by the production of social difference.[118]

Such a rendering of phenomenology, however, is still not sufficient. I've argued that Merleau-Ponty's *Phenomenology of Perception* provides a useful method for considering the more-than-human world in a way that does not erase the embodied locations from which that world is perceived and yet that also points to something beyond us. I've also focused on how the anonymous body is not universal, and have argued that this body is best understood as the historical materialization of nature-culture-power in (and as) us. Analysis of the more-than-human world, however, need not simply consider the differential production of lived bodies. It also requires a historical rendering of the nature-power-cultures that shapes what comes to be sensed.

This is clear, again, in Coates's and Fanon's writing. For instance, in *The Wretched of the Earth*, Fanon describes a colonial world, divided in two along racial lines: the indigenous colonized sector, which is cramped and hungry, and a white, colonist's sector, which is satiated and spacious.[119] Violence and its threat separate these worlds; violence surrounds the colonized, transforming him into a "man penned in."[120] As I argue in chapter 4, Fanon's writing sheds light on geopower, the force relations that transform the surface of the earth. Geopower physically transforms the earth through techniques such as urban planning, architecture, engineering, agriculture, and surveying—but also through digging, logging, and marking territory. In this context, the description of someone's perception of the more-than-human world requires not simply the analysis of the differential production of lived bodies but also an analysis of the production of the places and spaces in which these bodies move.

In short, *Earthly Encounters* develops a historicized phenomenology of the embodied subject, one that shows how such a phenomenology requires not simply an account of the production of the lived body but also of the production of the spaces and places we inhabit. It draws on phenomenology to provide a fuller account of the lived experience of racialized gender as it exists on this planet, a more-than-human world, and it offers the analysis of sensation as one lens for getting at that experience.

"Philosophy" and Feminist Theory

While highlighting phenomenology, this book is not a detailed study of this philosophical tradition or of any philosophy, for that matter. This book is not tethered to a philosophical canon. While I argue for the relevance of phenomenology to contemporary critical theory, I also turn to a series of texts that blend autobiography with philosophy, poetry, fiction, and politics. This form of writing is a key genre in feminist theory. I read, for example, Bessie Head's *A Question of Power* and Rashmika Pandya's "The Borderlines of Culture and Identity." Written from particular historical and geographic locations, locations shaped by colonialism and settler colonialism, these texts archive earthly encounters in explicitly political contexts, contexts that demand attention to territory, appropriation, and belonging. The locations from which the texts are written do not remain unchanged through the writing process; they are not essential, and yet the texts highlight the embeddedness of accounts of materiality, as well as the power to affect and be affected by words, storms, and places.

My sideways treatment of philosophy responds to the political constitution of the discipline's boundaries; it is both symptom and statement. The book leans toward philosophical questions, but the philosophers who have most influenced me have not been primarily located in philosophy departments. Therefore, as symptom, this book is only partially philosophical, because philosophy has rejected those philosophers who most captured my political, creative, and conceptual imagination. But the book's treatment of philosophy, as well as its archive, is also statement. I do not engage in close analysis of any one canonical philosopher so as to widen philosophy's archive, to show the conceptual relevance of voices outside the discipline without subsuming these voices within it. I work not in the name of diversity, which assumes that differences can be named, known, even consumed, but rather for the purposes of humility.[121] This humility refuses to universalize my own (white, Western) position that is tied to a particular canon, and seeks to challenge the privilege of ignorance entangled in that position, though it will never rid itself of it.[122] This means that I take the risk of working with texts such as Head's. I recognize that I am in danger of appropriating such work, using it for the purposes of a theoretical tradition with which their writing is not explicitly engaged—Head, for instance, did not consider herself a feminist. She was not explicitly concerned with phenomenology. This book nonetheless takes the risk of appropriation, attending to this danger by paying attention to the contexts and intellectual debates that the books I refer to themselves engage. I want to show that philosophy comes in different forms and from different places; I want to show the relevance of voices not considered philosophical to philosophy. I take inspiration here from Chela Sandoval's *Methodology of the Oppressed* in its vision of ending what she calls the "apartheid of theoretical domains" that divides "academic endeavors by race, sex, class, gender, and identity."[123] If the problem in the end remains that the book's central theoretical question emerges from a Western tradition and thus recenters the West, I propose that the method for addressing this question nonetheless unsettles this tradition as well.[124]

Earthly Encounters' turn to first-person creative and political nonfiction (often written by women) follows a long history of women's studies scholarship that brings attention to women's voices. Such an approach has been deemed suspect. The claim is that the "evidence of experience," to use Joan Scott's phrase, or the autobiographical, in Nigel Thrift's version, spuriously treats the subject as foundational.[125] Scholars argue that such genres cannot account for how subjects are constituted; they provide a false sense of oneness, presenting the world retroactively within structures that appear always already there. These criticisms overlap significantly with the critique of phenomenology. And yet I argue that autobiographical writing can also explore and can be read to explore these very problems. Still more, autobiographical texts put pressure on philosophical traditions that are indifferent to difference, a problem that Luce Irigaray and Adriana Cavarero have made central to feminist philosophy.[126] Cavarero argues that the voice, emanating from deep within the body, captures a uniqueness, an "unrepeatable singularity" that philosophy has mistakenly, dangerously, treated as superfluous.[127] Although *Earthly Encounters* focuses on written rather than spoken words, I am influenced by Cavarero's claims. I analyze a range of texts, including autobiographical texts, paying attention to their location so as to refuse philosophy's tendency to ignore the materiality of singular bodies. This continues a long history of feminist thought.[128]

Most recently, Mariana Ortega has challenged problematic distinctions between literature and philosophy, arguing that the writing of women of color, and Latina women in particular, has been relegated to the realm of literature as opposed to philosophy, because it often attends to "personal stories" having to do with "gendered and racialized selves" rather than "metaphysical inquiries" that attend to the "nature of selfhood and subjecthood in general."[129] Ortega argues, however, that these "personal stories" have theoretical, philosophical relevance. They incite us to rethink "the self." They show us how too often that which is taken to be universal or general is in fact white and masculine. They highlight how selfhood is situated. Following Ortega, one can argue that this book does not explore autobiographical or creative nonfiction, but rather expands the philosophical archive itself.

In short, *Earthly Encounters* brings attention to sensation in order to develop thought in more-than-human worlds. I draw on the work of Merleau-Ponty, all while considering the limitations of philosophy and its canon. I often analyze sensations within the contexts of settler colonialism, for it is within these contexts that the politics of what counts as matter and who is appropriating matter is most clear. I consider how sensation informs and is informed by race and gender, especially as we understand how these structures give shape to bodies, spaces, and places. And, finally, I develop a philosophical method, one that reads philosophy alongside autobiography to make space for difference.

The Turn to Affect

Scholarship on affect provides the final, critical context for this book's argument. Beginning in the 1990s, in both cultural studies and feminist and queer studies, some theorists argued for a new, affective approach to the analysis of culture. In 1995, Eve Kosofsky Sedgwick and Adam Frank, for instance, introduced the work of Silvan Tomkins to humanists, arguing that Tomkins's writing on affect productively disrupted prevalent assumptions in the field. Tomkins understands affect as a biological system that structures human motivation.[130] Also that year, Brian Massumi published "The Autonomy of Affect," arguing that bodies respond to media not simply according to its meaning, but also according to its intensity. Massumi claimed that affect, this second form of responsiveness, is nonrepresentational, nonconscious, and even prepersonal in that how we understand ourselves and who we are is incidental to how we respond.[131] Sedgwick's and Massumi's approaches to affect were significantly different, yet both sought to address the antibiologism that had become prominent in the humanities. Both developed an understanding of biology as dynamic and nondeterministic. In this way, their work overlaps with new materialist scholarship.

This turn to affect has been accompanied by an overlapping interest in "structures of feeling," a term coined by Raymond Williams in his 1977 *Marxism and Literature*.[132] Building in part on Sedgwick, but also turning away from Tomkins's approach to affect, scholars such as Lauren Berlant, Ann Cvetkovich, and José Esteban Muñoz, to name just a few, have considered how feelings are neither "simply" personal nor subjective.[133] Instead, they are shared across populations, and they give form to particular historically constituted subject positions. Public feelings find expression in political decision and in popular culture, literature, art, and film. These feelings can be indicative of social and political problems, just as they can become an important political resource around which to build social movements.

My analysis of sensation offers a place between these two approaches.[134] On the one hand, I am inspired by approaches to affect that highlight embodiment, but I develop a sustained argument that embodiment cannot be accessed as prior to meaning. The book's approach to sensation likewise moves away from considering structures of feeling—those realms of responsiveness that are more clearly tied to the self and sociality. Instead, I read sensations, such as feeling cold or sensing water. I argue that these sensations are informed by nature-culture-power such that they too come to shape racialized, gendered subjectivities.

In addition to tracing a pathway between these two approaches, my work on sensation addresses a problem that reoccurs in contemporary scholarship on both affect and structures of feeling: the relationship between the past, present, and future. How does the materialization of the past in (or partially as) the present shape affective response (and thus the future)? This question touches on an associated problem concerning the relationship between affect and the structural or affect and "identity." Many scholars have tied affect if not directly to the future then at least to a potentiality or virtuality that can bring about change. For instance, Massumi posits affect as autonomous; its effects are virtual, though certainly real. For Massumi, affect offers the possibility for change, whereas structure and identity are fixed. In a different context, Jennifer Nash traces a black feminist political tradition, a "love-politics," in the work of Audre Lorde, June Jordan, and Alice Walker. Nash convincingly shows how this tradition, which predates the affective turn in queer and cultural studies, mobilizes affect toward social and political ends. Love-politics, Nash details, is quite different to the framework of intersectionality, which has been so widely institutionalized as black feminism. Rather than seek state recognition of existing, which is to say, present intersectional identities, love-politics aims to cultivate communal feeling that pushes the self beyond its current formation. This love-politics, Nash shows, "is staunchly utopian," departing from "the presentism of a visibility politics like intersectionality, which calls for legibility and recognition in 'the here and now.' "[135] In the place of the now, love-politics looks to the future.

Yet it is from the position of black feminism and womanism that this love-politics emerges. What then is the relationship between the location of love-politics' illocution and the affect it posits? Though future-oriented, love-politics emerges in a present (no matter how fleeting), from a particular position. Similarly, returning to Massumi's framework, could we not understand affect less in opposition to structure and identity, and more as a reworking of these concepts? In such a framework, identity might be understood as a form of affective becoming rather than affect's capture. Throughout this book, I argue that distinctions between the past and the future, between structure and affect, and identity and affect have been too rigidly imagined. I contend that affect is shaped by (though not determined by) historical memory and habit. I argue that nonetheless affective response can change through, for example, critique, the built environment, and social and political organizing.

Chapter Outline

Chapter 1, "Feeling Cold: Phenomenology, Spatiality, and the Politics of Sensation," makes a case for phenomenology, most especially Merleau-Ponty's *Phenomenology of Perception*. Against approaches to emotion and affect that have become prominent in the humanities and interpretive social sciences, the text develops an analysis of sensation. I focus, in particular, on the sensation of the cold in twentieth-century Canada through a reading of Rashmika Pandya's phenomenological, autobiographical essay, "The Borderlines

of Culture and Identity." The chapter examines how Pandya's claim that she takes the cold within is a gendered, racialized assertion of national belonging within a context of Canadian immigration policy. This policy used racist understandings of the supposed unique suitability of Northern European bodies to the Northern climate to legitimize itself. The chapter neither focuses on popular representations of the cold nor on the biology of the cold: rather, I write in the space between, the space of sensation.

Chapter 2, "Locating Affect, Swimming Underwater," examines how this turn to phenomenology allows for an approach to affect does not cleave the affective from the social. Here, I address work in cultural studies and feminist, queer, and critical race studies that often draws on Gilles Deleuze's understanding of affect to posit a form of embodied, autonomous responsiveness to the world, a response that, they claim, is preconscious, prediscursive, nonsubjective, and even presocial. I too understand affect as an embodied form of responsiveness to the world, one that transforms the affected body-subject itself. However, through the analysis of the practice of swimming, I argue that affect is not independent or autonomous from social and cultural forces. To make this argument, I examine both the production of the swimmer's body and the spaces and places where the swimmer swims. I also make a renewed case for the potential of autobiographical writing.

Chapter 3, "'Being Kissed by Everything': Race, Sex, and Sense in Bessie Head's *A Question of Power*," explores whether and how the elaboration of particular sensations can foster forms of belonging apart from identity and the nation-state. I show how although Head's autobiographical novel, *A Question of Power*, is disparaging of sexuality, the text upholds sensual relations such as the touch of the wind or the feeling of the earth. I demonstrate how Head understands this sensuality as the basis for the recognition of a common humanity that exists across racial and gendered divisions. However, reading against the grain, I argue that gender, race, and nation nonetheless give shape to these sensations, especially when we read the text in relation to the history of agriculture in Botswana, which Head cannot but engage.

The next chapter departs from the discussion of sensation per se, moving toward an analysis of what I term *geopower*, the force relations that transform the surface of the earth. Chapter 4, "Psychic Territory, Appropriation, and 'Geopower': Rereading Fanon, Foucault, and Butler" draws on Fanon to introduce geopower. I analyze writing by Fanon alongside Judith Butler and Michel Foucault to show how while Foucault studied geography and architecture, he did not see the transformation of elements of the earth as a form of power relation itself. Fanon's approach to settler colonialism and decolonization differs from this. For Fanon, a central feature of settler colonialism involves the shaping of the earth. And still more, decolonization involves not simply a reappropriation of land, but also its physical manipulation. Through my reading of Fanon, I build on Darieck Scott's compelling interpretation of muscular tension in *The Wretched of the Earth*, arguing that a spatial reading of this tension reveals an important ontological argument in Fanon's work: life or vitality does not exist simply within bodies but between bodies and the earth.[136]

Finally, chapter 5, "Location, Sensation, and the Anthropocene," draws together the book's arguments concerning both sensation and geopower within the context of the Anthropocene thesis: the thesis that the earth system has been transformed by human action. Although the Anthropocene requires a model of the earth as a singular, whole system, I insist that we do not live on such an earth. From the perspective of life, we live in differentiated, multiple places, places that are sensed. It is in such locations that the Anthropocene is effected; it is there that it is a danger, and it is there that we cannot but respond to it. Understanding the Anthropocene at multiple scales is necessary. Through an analysis of Will Wilson's photography, specifically, his series, *AIR* I show how it is only by focusing on the scale of inhabitation that we can see how addressing climate change goes hand in hand with addressing the continuing effects of colonization and asserting indigenous sovereignty.

Overall, the book develops a simple theme: we are not angels. We live on this planet, earth. Human subjectivity, relationality, power, identity, and difference: these take shape on this planet. They are the result, in part, of earthly encounters.

one   **Feeling Cold**
Phenomenology, Spatiality, and the
Politics of Sensation

I am bodily, I am earthly, and sometimes, I feel cold (even if I am inside). As bodily beings, we are differentially exposed and vulnerable to the thermal energy of particles. We sense temperature as the earth's atmosphere touches skin. Sometimes we heat or cool the atmosphere, but no matter, the air that surrounds us remains part of the air that surrounds the earth. For this reason, the sensation of temperature connects us to our earthliness; it highlights our lives' dependence on the planet, a more-than-human world that is neither a human product nor an entity that exists completely apart from humans. Feminist scholars have built models of embodiment and subjectivity that highlight our dependence on others; however, we have yet to understand how earthly, temperate existence implicates differential experiences of subjectivity and objectification.[1] This chapter begins to do this work by focusing on the sensation of temperature, especially feeling cold.[2]

Though rarely centered, the sensation of temperature appears in philosophical, phenomenological writing about race and gender. For instance, in his much-cited account of racial objectification, Frantz Fanon draws attention to the weather. Fanon describes a scene, in the first person, where a man on a train finds himself the object of both curiosity and fear. A little boy points the man out to his mother: "Look, a Negro!" the boy exclaims, and later, "Mama, see the Negro! I'm frightened!"[3] As he overhears these comments, the man's "corporeal scheme crumble[s]."[4] He comes to experience himself in the third person; he is "completely dislocated" and makes himself an object.[5] He comes to feel cold. In effect, the day is suddenly given a season: it's a "white winter day."[6] And as the narration transforms from the first to the third, derogatory person, the black man starts to shiver: "[L]ook, a nigger, it's cold, the nigger is shivering, the nigger is shivering because he is cold. [...] The nigger is shivering with cold, that cold that goes through your bones."[7]

1

This account of objectification finds resonance some forty years later. In *Femininity and Domination: Studies in the Phenomenology of Oppression*, Sandra Bartky describes the experience of being sexually objectified: "It is a fine spring day, and with an utter lack of self-consciousness, I am bouncing down the street. Suddenly I hear men's voices. Catcalls and whistles fill the air. These noises are clearly sexual in intent and they are meant for me; they come from across the street. I freeze."[8]

It might be tempting to read each of these passages as metaphors. In this case, one would insist that the philosopher is not describing the lived experience of actually freezing, but rather using the term *frozen* symbolically. Yet to conclude that these passages are only about the ways that sensations appear in language as opposed to sensations themselves misses an analysis of how this metaphor becomes meaningful in the first place. What is it about the lived experience of feeling cold that is akin to the lived experience of racialized and gendered objectification? In other words, why describe the experience of objectification in terms of the bodily sensation of temperature? And still more, how do the experiences of each of these come to be lived through one another such that the sensation of temperature contributes to the experience of social difference? It is significant that while Bartky does not literally freeze, the sensation of temperature remains part of the story. She begins her scenario with a "fine spring day" and ends it feeling frozen. Especially since Bartky includes the weather in her description of the experience, her text suggests that the experience of being subjected to catcalls has her experience the environment differently.

A particular challenge emerges when writing about the sensation of temperature, however. On the one hand, it is tempting to argue for a form of universalism: no matter the person, all humans sense temperature similarly (which is not to say identically). Postulates about bodies' supposed differential capacity for sensation—especially pain—have legitimized violence, especially racialized violence. Faced with this historical context, assertions of universalism seem crucial.[9] However, at the same time, arguing that there exists a universal lived sensation of the cold can repress difference. To take a specific example, for Inuit families traveling to the United States at the turn of the century, what counted as a harsh environment was relative, dependent on cultural knowledge and local biologies. The United States might have been warm, but it was also the place of potential disease.[10] In this context, the cold might be sensed differently; rather than function as a metaphor for objectification, it could be figured as a site of comfort and ease. And yet perhaps, returning to an argument for sensory universalism, we can maintain that at a certain cold enough temperature, everyone would agree that it is cold. Could we say there exists a temperature that is so cold that any human exposed to it would not survive? Or do we want to follow Baruch Spinoza's much-cited statement, "We do not know what the body can do"?[11] A final issue has to do with body temperature: live human bodies give off warmth, and a corpse is cold. Is this suggestive, then, of a universal experience of temperature, one that links the cold or, at least, the very cold to the deathly?

These issues are at play in the passage of Fanon's *Black Skin, White Masks* that I quoted above. The language moves from the first, to the third, and finally to the second person: "that cold that goes through *your* bones." In this transformation to the second person, we can read a call for universalism. The man might be "other," he might experience himself in the third person, but he feels the cold that goes through *your* bones. In the original French, this passage refers to a "froid qui vous tord les os."[12] *Vous* is either the formal second-person singular or the second-person plural, and therefore Fanon's language reaches toward a shared experience of the cold, one that touches your (either singular or plural) bones. In other words, Fanon's language seeks to implicate the reader through empathy. You too can feel the chill. It is significant that this cold reaches the skeleton, that calcium or stone inside of each of us, which, when laid bare, is suggestive of mortality.[13] The skeleton also brings attention away from racialized skin. The phrase, "the cold that goes through your bones" highlights a shared, universal human vulnerability.

My goal here, however, is not to develop a form of humanism grounded in the precarity of life, even though one could argue that Fanon is pushing for such a conceptualization here.[14] My focus instead is on lived experience. It is only ever in particular contexts that the cold is sensed. One is never cold in a vacuum because one does not exist in a vacuum. In other words, my analysis of the cold is not an attempt to extract a universal experience of the sensation so much as to highlight how the sensation is lived in particular contexts. Nonetheless, I use the analysis of the cold in one location to shed light on the sensation's lived experience in another. This is not to argue that the sensation can be extracted from the contexts it enfolds. This is also not to claim that there exists a universal experience of the cold. It is rather to notice how some contexts wherein the sensation appears share similar features.

I take my lead here from feminist phenomenology, which draws attention to lived experience. For instance, in her discussion of Simone de Beauvoir's *Old Age*, Penelope Deutscher concludes that "biological facts (for example, the shortness of breath which makes one 'unable' to climb mountains any more) are always already synthesized with historical, social, and psychological factors."[15] Sonia Kruks seemingly agrees: "Biological 'facts'—similar to 'social' facts—do have a 'reality,' but as *lived* phenomena, as real experiences to which we should be attentive."[16] Drawing on these arguments, we can conclude that the "fact" of the sensation of the cold is only ever lived. As lived, the sensation only ever emerges within particular contexts. It is such located sensations that this analysis considers.

This chapter begins by arguing that phenomenology provides a useful framework for thinking about feeling cold. I then turn to an analysis of the sensation in twentieth-century Canada, focusing on Rashmika Pandya's phenomenological essay, "The Borderlines of Culture and Identity."[17] I consider how a sense of self may be defined, in part, through an attachment to particular sensations, and I explain how drawing attention to the sensation of temperature transforms Merleau-Ponty's understanding of spatiality. Finally, I return to Fanon and Bartky, considering the sensation of temperature within their accounts of subjectivity and objectification. Ultimately, I show how a phenomenological approach to the bodily sensation of temperature makes visible the intertwining of the symbolic and the sensory as well as the connections between subjectivity, spatiality, and territoriality, connections that push us to consider what it is to be social, cultural, and biological beings on this planet, earth.

Phenomenology, Affect, and Emotion

My approach to the sensation of the cold departs from contemporary critical scholarship on emotion and feeling, which often subsumes bodily sensations into emotion. Take, for instance, two influential and important works by José Esteban Muñoz and Sara Ahmed. Ahmed's reading of Fanon folds feeling cold into the emotion of fear, passing quickly over the specificity of the sensation: for the black man she writes, "fear is felt as coldness."[18] The rest of her discussion considers the contours of fear. Thus, while Ahmed claims to avoid "making analytical distinctions between bodily sensation, emotion, and thought as if they could be 'experienced' as distinct," her reading of Fanon prioritizes emotion over sensation, passing over coldness to fear, examining the contours of fear, but not of the cold.[19] This approach involves a continued movement away from embodiment toward more clearly subjective realms.

A similar tendency is at work in Muñoz's "Feeling Brown: Ethnicity and Affect in Ricardo Bracho's *The Sweetest Hangover (and Other STDs)*." Muñoz risks seizing, rather than refusing, the stereotype that Latinos and Latinas are " 'hot'n' spicy' or simply 'on fire.' "[20] "Spics," he explains, "is an epithet intrinsically linked to the question of affect and excess affect."[21] To be "hot and spicy" is to be "over the top," to have an excess of feeling. This stereotype is used to stigmatize Latinos and Latinas, but at the same time, it demonstrates how Latina/o affect "puts a great deal of pressure" on the affective norm of majoritarian, white public culture. It makes visible how "the affect of whiteness" is framed "as underdeveloped and impoverished."[22] Muñoz argues that bringing attention to Latino/a affect can help to make visible how "historically coherent groups 'feel' differently and navigate the material world on a different emotional register."[23] Here, like Ahmed, Muñoz treats bodily sensation as emotion: he reads the feeling of being hot as a metaphor for an excess (in reference to white, majoritarian culture) of emotion. And though such a reading is certainly valid, it likewise misses an opportunity for centering bodily sensation, for thinking about temperature and earthly existence. What it is to *feel* hot? Is this related to Latino/a identity?

To be clear, my goal here is not to produce a simple distinction between bodily sensation and emotion. Neither is it to deny that bodily sensations are emotional nor that emotions involve bodily sensations. My argument concerns emphasis: rather than transpose sensations of temperature immediately into emotions, I suggest that we slow down and consider these sensations themselves. When coldness is read simply as fear and when heat is read as an excess of feeling, we miss an opportunity to think about feeling cold or hot as productive sensations in themselves, sensations that index a relation to the earth or to a more-than-human world: the thermal energy of particles.

It may seem as though this approach resonates with scholarship in affect studies that, rather than thinking about emotion, has turned to the work of Gilles Deleuze to posit a form of impersonal feeling: affect. Brian Massumi, for instance, insists on a distinction between emotion and affect, a distinction that could be useful for classifying feeling cold as an affect. He frames emotions as "subjective."[24] They are the result of a "sociolinguistic fixing of the quality of an experience which is from that point onward defined as personal."[25] Emotions are a putting into language, which is at the same time a putting into the personal, experiences that are "irreducibly bodily and autonomic."[26] In fact, to name such experiences "experience" is not quite right, because, as Massumi writes, "something happening out of mind in a body directly absorbing its outside cannot exactly said to be experienced."[27] Whereas emotion can be narrated, put into language and owned by the self, affect, for Massumi, impinges upon the body, uncaptured by meaning, happening autonomously outside the mind.

Yet there are many limitations to such an approach.[28] As Jasbir Puar argues, while Massumi attempts to move beyond poststructuralism's focus on representation, in the end, he cannot but produce a representation of affect, one that begs to be analyzed.[29] Still more, this framework for thinking affect reintroduces a reductive distinction between the mind and the body. Doesn't "the mind" affect how "the body" senses? Ruth Leys makes a similar point in her analysis of the "new affect theorists," which focuses particularly on Massumi's writing.[30] Leys critiques his conceptualization of affect as separate from intention, meaning, and cognition.

She contends, for instance, that Massumi's argument that the body reacts to its environment before the mind interprets neuroscience to posit an unconvincing separation of "mind" from "body."[31] Finally, Massumi's text raises the question of whether this affective body is unmarked by, for instance, categories of race and gender. Massumi's account of racial and gender identities argues that cultural studies has trapped the body in a freeze frame: it has located bodies on ideological grids, positions brought down to earth. Within this model, Massumi argues, we miss a sense of how bodies move and how because of movement, the body does not coincide with itself. But is this body, moved by, through, and with affect not gendered? Is it unmarked by race? Are gender and/or race simply a retroactive telling of the body, a capturing of the body in freeze frame? Or could gender and/or race be materialized through such movement? Gender and/or race would then become not only questions of ideology, signification, meaning, representation or recognition, as Massumi posits them, but also (or perhaps instead) an affective becoming of the body. In the end, while Massumi's framework is provocative, I am skeptical of his undifferentiated body, and I wonder whether it can "directly" absorb "its outside."[32]

For these reasons, my approach to feeling cold turns instead to the phenomenology of race and gender as influenced by Maurice Merleau-Ponty. As this book's introduction explained, I recognize that turning to Merleau-Ponty in this context may appear to raise more problems than solutions given that many feminist scholars and scholars interested in race and racism have argued that his concepts of the body-subject, intentionality, the flesh, and visuality are phallocentric and repress difference.[33] But Merleau-Ponty has something specific to contribute. His work gives us tools to think of bodily sensations in a way that neither reduces them to ideal states nor to the effects of external agencies. That is, bodily sensations, such as the sensation of temperature, belong neither to an inner self and its emotions nor to an automatic bodily response.[34] Instead, these sensations index encounters with the world as we live and act in it. This framework allows me to think through the sensation of feeling cold without falling into idealism, simply understanding the meaning of the sensation, and without falling into objectivism, simply arguing that the cold has an objective, automatic effect on human bodies. Merleau-Ponty's phenomenology provides a useful middle ground, a method, in other words for thinking about exteriority in a way that does not cover over the position from which that exterior is being encountered; a method that elucidates the intertwining of the symbolic and the sensory, making the divorce of "pure sensation" and symbolic meaning impossible.

A Cold That Goes through Your Bones

Rashmika Pandya was cold. She was "struck with terror" as she faced "a wild howling whiteness."[35] The cold made it difficult for her to control her bladder. She "felt trapped" because it was "too cold to play outside," and she was trapped not simply indoors, but "trapped" within her "own body."[36]

What was this cold that she felt? It was, in part, Saskatoon's winter, with its average temperatures in January of zero degrees Fahrenheit. It was also, in part, that she may not have had sufficient winter clothing for the weather. It could have also been that she felt socially isolated, or that she was used to Kenya's climate. In any case, she felt cold. This feeling belongs neither to an inner self and its emotions nor to an automatic bodily response. The feeling exists, rather, in Pandya's encounter with the earth as she lives and acts in it.

Pandya includes this description of feeling cold in "The Borderlines of Culture and Identity." In this text, Pandya draws on Merleau-Ponty alongside personal narrative about her family's immigration from Kisumu, Kenya, to England, and finally to Saskatoon, Canada, where she arrived, a young girl, in November 1969.[37] Pandya intervenes in Merleau-Ponty's philosophy of language, specifically his claim, in *Phenomenology of Perception*, that "we only 'live' in one world at a time."[38] In contrast to Merleau-Ponty, Pandya explores how the experience of immigration does not necessitate "choosing" between cultural worlds. Instead, she describes a space *between* worlds where the memory of the past infuses a difference in the present, the creation of an in-between.

Pandya's analysis connects to Mariana Ortega's work in Latina phenomenology. Ortega argues that through the experience of border crossing, the self described by Gloria Anzaldúa and María Lugones experiences "ruptures in her everyday existence."[39] These ruptures lead her to become "more reflective of her activities and her existence."[40] Similarly, Pandya's experience of the cold—and her analysis of the philosophy of language—suggests a life "of not-being-at-ease," a life in-between, one that, however, leads to greater reflection.[41]

But implicit in Pandya's essay are two other arguments. First, we identify with sensations; that is, sensations constitute part of our sense of self. Second, space is not something we simply move through; rather, we are immersed in ambient conditions, and this ambience affects our sense of spatiality. I develop each of these arguments in turn.

Throughout her essay, Pandya's emphasis on bodily sensations is striking. Toward the beginning of the text, Pandya asks the question, "Who am I?" To answer this question, she recounts memories, and each of these memories features bodily sensations. Thus, it is through recalling sensations that Pandya builds a picture of who she is. Pandya offers her first memory of "rocking back and forth in a cloth cradle."[42] She explains, "I recall clearly the feel of swinging back and forth and the comfort this induced in me."[43] She then turns to her memories of "the warmth of African summers, the sweet smell of dung and fires."[44] She includes the sound of her siblings and cousins' shrieking, "the feel of a stolen mango and the muted colors of an arid landscape."[45] These memories are less about occurrences than about sensations: the feel of swinging, the warmth of the summers, the touch of a mango. This "stolen mango" may carry a narrative with it, but it is its feeling Pandya recalls. Pandya's response to the question "Who am I?" suggests that "I" am made up (at least in part) of how I have felt, of the sensations I have had. I can give a sense of who I am to an other by recounting these sensations.

To write about these sensations transforms them from the felt to the linguistic. The resultant statements construct at least a grammatical separation between the I that feels and the feeling being felt. "I" come to feel "X." Yet feeling itself is a form of entanglement or coexistence. When I write "I feel hot," it is not that there is hotness and there is I separate from the heat. It is rather that the heat comes to inhabit the subject, and the subject, the heat. The English language produces a separation between the sentence's subject and its direct object, yet Pandya's essay invites us to consider how the *I* emerges through the sensory.

These sensations index that the self is relational. As Adriana Cavarero argues, "the sensory faculties place us in relationship."[46] Cavarero explains, "each of us is practically in relation to those with whom—here and now, in a specific physical space and in a specific definite time—one is exposed."[47] Yet we emerge not simply in relation to that which is denoted by "who," but also in relation to physical spaces. Our relations are not "in" these spaces, as Cavarero suggests; space, as Merleau-Ponty argues, is not an empty container within which we relate. Rather, we are engaged in material, corporeal relations with the environment around us; we are exposed and vulnerable to the physical places within which we exist, and these physical places affect and are affected by our relations with other humans (and nonhumans).

Thus, Pandya's memories of sensations index a relation to specific physical places (as they exist in a given time). An obvious example is her statement that her memories are "filled with the warmth of African summers."[48] Here she narrates who she is through the memory of a sensation, and this sensation indexes a relation between the warm African summer and her body. This warmth is not simply a warmth of the summer outside of her, but a warmth that she felt; her environment was warm and she, too, was warm. She comes to identify with this warmth; feeling this way is who she is. Her identification with this sensation means that when she arrives first in England and later in Canada, the cold initially leaves her fearful and uncomfortable. Her body "abandon[s]" her. The sensation makes her feel that her body is "an alien thing."[49] The new sensations are unfamiliar to her, and thus she does not recognize the body sensing them as her own, or at least she feels that this body is unfamiliar or even unearthly, alien.

In this context, coldness is perceived as impersonal. Though reverberating through my bones, coldness does not come to inhabit the well of selfhood and identity. Instead, it is other to me; I am uncomfortable. Something must happen so that it is no longer inside me. I will be cold when I am no longer, and thus this cold that invades me, this cold that reaches the bones to which I will decompose, does not make me but cuts through me, freezes me; it is the bit of death inside of me that I struggle to guard myself from. It prevents my mobility, making it difficult for me to use my muscles and to go out into the world. (And indeed, when Pandya first feels the Saskatoon wind, she "cannot move").[50] The cold is an other, not welcomed inside. It makes my insides other to me.

Coldness comes also to be linked with losing contact with another body or with leaving the womb. Pandya first feels the Canadian winter wind when she disembarks from a plane. She writes of this moment, "my father with my younger brother in his arms pushes me forward."[51] It is her father who pushes her into the cold, and unlike her brother, she is held neither by him nor by her mother. Whereas the ideal maternal is often represented as a space of warmth, the cold is that space in the world that the father pushes the girl child toward. This analysis suggests that although the cold may be experienced as an otherness inside, warmth can index a sociality: bodies can find warmth touching one another, thus in their relation to one another. That which feels like me, then, is not something separate from others, but rather something created through my contact with others.

Social exclusion may actually feel cold. This too resonates with Pandya's account. She explains that when she first arrives in Canada, she makes no friends. Public school feels like an assault on her dignity: her brother is regularly beaten; a teacher suggests that Indians lack "control *and* intelligence."[52] As a result, her family develops an identity as African East-Indians, differentiated from "them," that is, "Canadians." At first, Pandya embraces her role as a dutiful daughter in training to become a "good Indian wife."[53] She writes, "After all had I not already begun to learn that it was infinitely wiser to accept my role than to reject it in favor of a Western ideal individualism? Look what it had got me so far, cold, bitterness."[54] Pandya is cold—embracing a "Western" ideal leaves her, for the time being, isolated.

Pandya explains that she eventually comes to identify with the cold. She now carries "the cold Canadian prairie landscape within."[55] She exists in the cold; the cold comes to exist within her even when she is no longer in it. This statement could be understood as a form of identification: I come to assimilate an attribute of the other and am transformed "after the model the other provides."[56] This suggests that I can identify not simply with other humans or things but with climates or atmospheres, and their sensation.

The argument that I can identify with the sensation of climates intertwines the phenomenological with the psychoanalytic. In psychoanalytic discourse, identification, as Diana Fuss summarizes, "is the detour through the other that defines a self."[57] Identification "inhabits, organizes, instantiates identity," but it likewise points to the otherness at the heart of the self.[58] That is, it is through identification that the self comes to recognize and define itself, then the self comes to self-recognition only in relation to and through the assimilation of that which is outside of itself, that with which it identifies. For the most part, psychoanalytic theory considers identification with human others: the other that the self identifies with is, if not a person, then a body part (e.g., the breast) or a social position (e.g., a woman). But Pandya's essay suggests something different. The self also defines itself as that which is subject to particular sensations. This formulation highlights a movement between quality or adjective and object and noun. That is, Pandya at first feels cold. She is cold. Here, *cold* is an adjective that qualifies the self. However, Pandya then comes to "carry the cold within." Cold becomes an object and a noun, something outside of the self in the very same moment that it comes within, becoming a feature of the self itself. This demonstrates the gap entangled in identification; that is, we identify with something that is outside of ourselves, all while coming to internalize that other. We become attached to sensations and identify with them as we transform them into entities that exist apart from us. Pandya's identification with the cold, however, is not only psychic. The cold literally gets inside Pandya by inciting her to retrain her muscles. Pandya explains how when she first arrives in Canada, she finds it difficult to control her bladder. Later, she becomes acclimatized: the cold gets inside of her such that her muscles come to work in a range of climates. The sensation comes inside; it shapes the body-subject.[59]

This body-subject, however, is not universal; the sensation of the cold is infused with the politics of race, class, gender, and citizenship. Within Canadian culture, notwithstanding changes across time in Canadian immigration policy, a particular pernicious discourse about race and climate remains consistent. The contention is that while, on the one hand, the Canadian northern climate is productive of a particular Canadian identity, on the other hand, only particular bodies are open to becoming "properly" affected by the climate. This discursive knot navigates between two ideas: the first, a claim that race is produced through exposure to a particular climate, and the second, a claim that race determines one's suitability to a particular climate. In the first case, race is open to transformation, but in the second, race is fixed, determining of social belonging.[60]

A recurrent theme in settler-colonial, Canadian nationalist thought is the idea that the severe Canadian winter produces an ideal national character: self-reliant, strong, prosperous, and free. These traits have been coded as masculine and seen as constitutive of a "northern, white race." For instance, in 1869, *The Globe*, an English-language Canadian national paper, explained how northern winters "will preserve us from the effeminacy which naturally steals over the most vigorous races when long under the relaxing influence of tropical or even generally mild and genial skies."[61] Members of the Canada First Movement, a post-Confederacy, Toronto-based nationalist group, argued for a vision of Canadian independence from both Britain and the United States and consistently imagined the cold as producing a vigorous Canadian national identity. For instance, Robert Grant Haliburton, an associate of the Canada First Movement, addressed Canadians in 1869, claiming that although long winters may harm the economy, "our snow and frost give us what is more value than gold or silver, a healthy, hardy, virtuous, dominant race."[62] In 1875, Charles Mair, who helped to found the Canada First Movement, wrote, "whilst the south is in a great measure the region of effeminacy and disease, the north-west is a decided recuperate of decayed function," and in 1871, William Foster, a cofounder of Canada First, suggested, "We are a Northern people, as the true out-crop of human nature, more manly, more real, than the weak marrow-bones superstition of an effeminate South."[63] The cold, so the story goes, produces a strong, masculine race. Here we are far from the seventeenth-century discourse of the humors, which the French physician Marin Cureau de la Chambre aptly summarized in 1665: "[T]he Temperature of Man is hot and dry, and that of the Woman cold and moist."[64] Instead, one becomes manly in being exposed to the cold. It is as though the cold, unlike the heat, incites the contraction of muscles in the hope of remaining warm; this contraction produces hard bodies, bodies that are said to be manly because of this response. The relationship drawn between these "Canadian" masculine bodies and the cold is a movement that is central to settler colonialism wherein the settler, as Marie Lo writes, seeks to establish a "national and autochthonous claim to the land"—one that displaces the native and imagines a natural connection to the land, and one that covers over colonial violence.[65]

On the one hand, then, the Canadian climate is seen as productive; it shapes its inhabitants. On the other hand, dominant Canadian discourse about race and climate suggests that only certain people are suited to the Canadian climate. In this case, the climate does not produce gendered racialization; rather, only a particular race belongs within a certain climate. Such a framing of the cold is part of the archive of what scholars such as Aileen Moreton-Robinson have described as possessive whiteness: the logic that naturalizes the nation as a white possession.[66] Tracing the discourse of the cold, however, clarifies how not all who arrive in the settler colony are in the position of the settler because, as Lorenzo Veracini writes and Iyko Day quotes, "not all migrations are settler migrations."[67] In other words, not all who arrive (whether through willing migration, forced displacement, or anything in between these poles) have access to the "proprietorial logics of whiteness" that frame the land as both symbolically and literally one's own.[68] For example, Sir Robert Alexander Falconer, president of the University of Toronto from 1907 to 1932, asserted in 1908 that "the rigour of the northern climate has been, and will continue to be, a deterrent for the peoples of Southern Europe," and George Parkin, principal of the elite Upper Canada College in the 1890s, wrote that the climate protects the country from "lower races," who are "squeezed out by that 30 or 40 degrees below zero."[69] In 1947, Prime Minister William Lyon Mackenzie King argued that people from India should not immigrate to Canada. This was, he claimed, for their own good, because "accustomed as many of them are to the conditions of a tropical climate, and possessing manners and customs so unlike those of our own people, their inability to readily adapt themselves to surroundings entirely different could not do other than entail an amount of privation and suffering."[70] The claim, quite simply, is that those who have lived in tropical climates are supposedly unsuited to Canada, and will not be able to adjust to the climate. Thus, the racial makeup of Canada was framed less as a political than natural effect of the weather, and what constituted Canada was a climate that attracted what was understood as a desirable race, one that would only become increasingly superior and masculine as a result of the climate. The inconsistency here is obvious: on the one hand, the Northern climate produces a strong, Canadian race, and yet, on the other hand, race is already fixed, not changeable according to the climate. This inconsistency is central to the triangulation of settler colonialism, which is best understood not simply with the dichotomy settler/native but rather with the differential positions of the settler, native, and alien.[71]

This apparent conflict between these different understandings of the race and climate was resolved, if unconvincingly, in Immanuel Kant's 1775 "Of the Different Human Races."[72] In this text, Kant argues that humans were first created with the "seeds" of four original races, and that, as the result of existing within different climates, certain humans came to actualize particular seeds. However, those living between the thirty-first and fifty-second latitude in the "old world" did not have to significantly adapt, and therefore were most similar to what Kant considers the original human form. This means they were "well-prepared to be transplanted into every other region of the earth."[73] This suggestion implies, by comparison that "the Negros," for instance, acclimatized to hot weather, were not suited to migrate. Kant's contention is that the effects of climate on human races are irreversible.[74] He legitimizes European colonialism and settler colonialism, since he suggests that Europeans are biologically capable of moving across the earth. His story provides one mode of making sense of the seeming incoherence in the Canadian discourse of race. For some, climatic effects made them unsuitable for the Canadian winters; for others, living within the preferred latitudes, they still had the capacity to adapt.

Canadian immigration policy shifted drastically in the 1960s, with Ellen Fairclough's reforms, the 1966 White Paper, and the establishment, in 1967, of the Points System. These reforms made race less explicit in immigration law.[75] Nonetheless, the effects of the discourse about climate, race, and gender did not simply disappear. The idea of the Canadian climate continued to be framed with racist and often sexist ideologies in the thought of George Grant, Charles Paradis, Vincent Massey, W. L. Moreton, and Margaret Atwood.[76] In addition, vulnerability to the cold is distributed along class lines. Poverty makes it difficult not simply to pay for shelter and heat, but also to buy warm coats, sweaters, hats, mittens, scarves, socks, boots, and long underwear, as well as to procure access to cars, taxis, and public transportation. Within a culture that deems comfort in the cold as a sign of belonging, poverty, in its resultant exposure to the cold, takes on additional stigma.[77] Quite simply: the feeling of comfort in the cold is central to the Canadian version of possessive whiteness.

Thus, when Pandya feels the cold upon arriving in Canada in the 1960s, and when she writes about this feeling forty years later, she feels and writes within a context where feeling cold is riven with the settler-colonial politics of race, class, gender, and citizenship. Her claim that she takes the cold inside her is a claim to Canadian identity; she is Canadian. This might be understood as an attempt to partake in white settler colonialism and adopt its logic of possession. The cold has become a part of her no matter how she has been racialized and gendered. This is a claim of belonging and of citizenship within a context of racial exclusion based on notions about the climatic effects on humans.

And yet Pandya's phrase that the cold gets inside her is striking, for although it is a claim on citizenship and belonging, it likewise reverses the white, masculinist discourse of Canadian nationalism. In this way, I argue that, in fact, her claim to the cold is better understood not simply as a reiteration of Canadian white-settler logics, but rather as a navigation of the position of the "alien," as described by Day. The alien arrives in the settler colony but is excluded from hegemonic understanding of who belongs, who owns, and who has sovereignty over its territory. The positions of the settler and alien are, in part, articulated through gender. Both Pandya and the nationalist discourse admit that the cold affects its inhabitants. However, in the white masculinist version, the men are not said to carry the cold within; instead, because they are a supposedly masculine, hardy race, they are only deemed more strong and manly through their exposure to the cold. In contrast, Pandya suggests that the cold enters her and she carries it within. We can read this as a feminizing response to the climate. Otherness, in the form of the cold, enters the self, and the self harbors this other and defines itself in relation to it. The men do not claim to be inhabited by something that is other to them. They have been strengthened by the cold; the cold does not inhabit them. There is no otherness within. Through the introjection of the sensation, an introjection that likewise transforms the sensation into a thing, Pandya defines herself in relation to something that remains other or alien to her. In contrast, the nationalist discourse disavows the particular tangle that is identification.

In short, Pandya's essay demonstrates how bodily sensations are integral to identity. Her writing also points to how we make sense of sensations within discursive contexts that frame sensations' experience. Most centrally, she shows how our sense of self even as it is narrated is not only developed in relation to other humans or even other objects, but rather in relation to atmospheres, climates, and temperatures. Relations to these more-than-human entities can help us understand lived experiences of settler colonialism where relationships to territory and the land are key. The Spatiality of the Cold

But "The Borderlines of Culture and Identity" also makes space for a second insight. Its discussion of coldness mounts an implicit critique of Merleau-Ponty's understanding of spatiality. Though beginning from the body, Merleau-Ponty misses the role of the temperature, climate, and the weather. As a result, his analysis implicitly assumes temperate conditions.

Phenomenology of Perception contends that the "experience of spatiality is related to our implantation in the world."[78] Merleau-Ponty seeks to describe the origin of oriented space, the idea that space has an up and down, left and right. He shows how both empiricism and what he calls "intellectualism" (or idealism) fail to account for orientation, and through this reasoning, he comes to the conclusion that orientation emerges not in relation to "my body as it in fact is, as a thing in objective space, but as a system of possible actions, a virtual body with its phenomenal 'place' defined by its task and situation."[79] I have a sense of what my body can do, of the actions it can take up in the world; spatiality is organized around these possibilities, in the projection of a virtual body.

One of the reasons phenomenological investigations of the sensing body were largely abandoned, as Massumi explains, is because they downplayed the structuring capacities of culture and power relations on the human body.[80] But although *Phenomenology of Perception* does not focus on the effects of power and culture, there is a place in the text's account of spatiality to elaborate these effects while centering the analysis of sensation. The virtual body that Merleau-Ponty introduces in his understanding of spatiality makes room for the place of culture since orientation emerges as I project an imagined, virtual body onto the world. My imagination of what I can do is entangled with cultural and social understandings of my body.[81]

Merleau-Ponty's discussion of space makes room for, but does not elaborate on, how temperature might affect our sense of spatiality. Whereas our bodily being always touches the ambient—that is, temperature, weather, humidity (even indoors)—Merleau-Ponty's work on spatiality focuses primarily on our sense of vision, passing over ambience's touch.[82] Nonetheless, his contention that "there will always be a primary spatiality for each modality" of "our implantation in the world" suggests that, if I were implanted in a cold world, my experience of spatiality would change.[83] Specifically, my projection of a virtual body acting in the world could be significantly affected by different weather conditions. For instance, in Pandya's case, the cold leaves her feeling as though she cannot move and as though she is trapped. In other words, her sense of spatiality contracts because she feels cold; we might say that from Pandya's perspective, in the cold, spatiality lacks depth as the body turns into itself for warmth. Or perhaps this is not quite right: the cold might give Pandya a sense of an expansive space, one in which she cannot survive, one without place. In response to this expanse, she turns inward; the space of livability becomes small.

Pandya's experience of a contraction of spatiality in the cold might point to a "prejudice in favour of being," where being is certainly spatial, but being also requires that spatiality have a particular temperature so that I can continue to exist in it or continue to think I can exist in it.[84] When it is cold and when I sense that this cold poses a danger to my being, I turn into myself, I seek shelter; I look for a contracted space within which I can continue to be.

Canadian national discourse may be read as a response to this spatiality. That is, faced with the winter's chill, faced with the expanse of the cold, white settler masculinity reasserts its possession of the world by framing the cold as strengthening the white, masculine constitution and projecting this white, masculine body through the cold. That is, this settler national discourse posits white, masculine bodies not only as naturally suited to the cold climate, but as fortified by it. This discourse has the effect of making it more difficult for others to project their bodies within this climate because white, masculine virility is built on the suggestion that those who are not white men cannot move so effectively in such a climate. The experience of this climate becomes informed by culture and lived in one's bodily mobility and sense of spatiality.

Feeling cold can thus be linked with an expansive spatiality from which one might seek shelter. This sense can be mitigated or intensified through cultural discourses and practices that are saturated with power relations. In addition, we identify with sensations such as feeling cold. These sensations index a relationality between our sense of self and the earth.

Territory and "The Subject"

Given these arguments, why do Fanon and Bartky describe the experience of being objectified in terms of the bodily sensation of temperature? What does feeling cold have to do with feeling objectified?

One might argue that the cold Pandya feels is quite different from the cold described in *Black Skin, White Masks* and *Femininity and Domination*: the train in *Black Skin, White Masks* might not literally become cold, whereas Saskatoon's winter is certainly chilling. In this case, whereas Pandya's feeling may index relationality to the earth, the sensation in *Black Skin, White Masks* is primarily psychological, social, or cultural. However, insisting on this distinction misses an opportunity for analysis: both Fanon and Bartky describe feeling objectified in terms of the bodily sensation of temperature. That is, although it may not literally get cold on the train, the black man comes to experience this space as if it were cold, or like it were cold. Even if I were to insist that these passages are merely *descriptions*, that the man in Fanon's text is but a character and therefore does not actually experience anything—even in this case, it would then make sense to attend to the use of figurative language in Fanon's and Bartky's work. They describe objectification in terms of the sensation of temperature. Why?

Most often, critical analysis of Fanon's scene draws connections between his work and Jean-Paul Sartre's existential phenomenology, which figures the objectifying gaze of another as a threat to the subject's defining capacity for transcendence. In this reading, the boy in Fanon's text does not address the man as a subject, but rather sees the man's body and speaks to his mother, as though the man could not hear him. The man is then objectified in the boy's gaze. A similar dynamic is at play in Bartky's writing: she is "bouncing down the street" but then finds that she is being looked at from afar.[85]

This reading prioritizes vision in the relation between the boy and the man, or the woman and the men. Indeed, Fanon begins the chapter by repeating that the man of color becomes black in relation to the white man through the white man's *gaze*. Fanon writes, for instance, that racial difference becomes a problem only when a man of color meets "the white man's *eyes*";[86] he claims that the "black man has no ontological resistance in the *eyes* of the white man";[87] and he explains that the "movements, the attitudes, the *glances* of the other fixed [him into objectivity]."[88] Drawing on these passages, we may want to argue that Fanon imagines the relation between the white boy and black man as a visual relation: the white boy *sees* the black man, fixing him in his gaze, and the black man *sees* himself seen, finding himself objectified.

Yet this reading misses another aspect of Fanon's and Bartky's text: it is not simply vision that mediates the encounters they describe. Sound also plays a role, and paying attention to sound draws out the spatiality of their encounter. Indeed, Fanon's chapter begins with speech: " 'Dirty nigger!' Or simply, 'Look, a Negro!' "[89] Later, when Fanon describes the encounter between the man and boy, again, he repeats, " 'Look, a Negro!' "[90] Although these exclamations reference the act of looking, they remain acts of speech. Both the speaker and the man *hear* the phrases. The same is true in Bartky. She "suddenly" hears "men's voices. Catcalls and whistles fill the air."[91] In comparison to the boy's comment in Fanon's scene, the catcalls are actually directed to Bartky. Perhaps the hope is to gain her attention, to make her know that she is being looked at, or to assert a particular form of masculinity that takes up space and denotes women's bodies as objects to be looked at.

That sound figures in both scenes is significant, because whereas vision locates that which is seen in discrete places that are separate from one another, hearing fills a space that is shared by those who hear (or feel) sound. Hearing involves sensing that which imbues a space, and to exclaim aloud is (at least temporarily) to fill a shared space with one's voice. In this model, to make a sound could be understood as an enactment of power or the production of a territory, since it involves the creation of something, a space, outside of one's self that refers back to the self.[92] In addition, the experience of hearing can be contrasted to the experience of sight, which requires opened, directed, and focused eyes. Unless he were deaf, the man in the train could not but hear the song that imbues the territory; he could not but hear the boy's phrase, "Look, a Negro!" Therefore, the man becomes momentarily, unavoidably immersed in the boy's territory.[93] The same is true for the woman walking down the street. Rather than experiencing the "fine spring day" as a space within which she can act and move in the world, the space becomes the territory of some others.

In both cases, objectification works not simply as subjects are made aware of their bodies as objects to be looked at, but also as they come to experience the space in which they exist as another person's territory. Being in another's territory feels, in both Fanon's and Bartky's accounts, cold. Perhaps this is because objectification halts motion. Bartky writes that her "motions become stiff and self-conscious."[94] Fanon explains how a "circle" draws tight around the man.[95] Spatiality shrinks as each subject finds it difficult to project a virtual body onto the world. This shrinking spatiality is akin to the sense of space sought when faced with the expanse of the cold. Another way to say this is that the cold is experienced as a force in itself, one that marks space as the territory of another, the territory of the cold. The result is that one turns inside. This analysis suggests that to feel objectified is to feel as though the earth is uncomfortable; it is to sense the temperature and to imagine the difficulty of surviving within it. To feel like a subject is to feel as though the earth is temperate, to sense that one can act in the world and survive in it.[96]

Thus, even if we read Fanon's and Bartky's descriptions of the cold as metaphors, some important conclusions hold. That is, the figuration of the cold is effective to the extent that it speaks to a particular lived experience. The cold functions as a metaphor for the spatialization of objectification, because the two experiences of spatiality are similar. These similarities do not simply explain why we might use one (which appears more concrete) to describe another (which appears more abstract). Such an argument would cleave language from lived experience as though the former does not affect the latter. Instead, it is not simply that the metaphor expresses or indicates a similarity of two separate things, it is also that this figuration expresses something true of lived experience. The cold is experienced as objectifying, and objectification is experienced as inducing an experience of the spatiality of coldness. Merleau-Ponty argues that "the predominance of vowels in one language, or of consonants in another, and constructional and syntactical systems, do not represent so many arbitrary conventions for the expression of one and the same idea, but several ways for the human body to sing the world's praises and in the last resort to live it."[97] Likewise, we can argue that the use of the cold as metaphor is not an arbitrary literary convention, but rather expressive of a mode of living in the world; it is expressive of sensory, lived experience where intersubjective objectification and the feeling of the cold are lived through one another.

A More-Than-Human World

In short, Fanon and Bartky describe scenes of objectification that produce and reproduce particular social positions. The incursion of the sensation of temperature within their accounts indexes a more-than-human world within which subjection occurs. Feminist theorists have already developed rich accounts of human subjectivity that highlight our dependence on others; this chapter builds on such accounts by insisting that we are not simply dependent on the humans around us, but also on the places and spaces within which we live. Judith Butler, in *The Psychic Life of Power*, argues that the child is passionately attached to those who secure the possibility of its continued existence, and the adult emerges as she or he comes to deny this prior attachment. This accounts, Butler writes, "in part for the adult sense of humiliation when confronted with the earliest objects of love—parents, guardians, siblings, and so on—the sense of belated indignation in which one claims, 'I couldn't possibly love such a person.' "[98] And yet our continued existence does not simply depend on human caregivers. Our life is also dependent on the earth, including its atmospheric temperature. To argue that it is simply human others who make this earth livable is to frame the earth as that which is endlessly malleable and providing. Yet our relations with the earth are not unmediated by our relations with others. Objectification, for instance, shapes one's experience of being in place.

Living in Oxford, UK, during the second decade of the 2000s, I was confronted, over and over again, with how women's clothing often contributes to our feeling cold, our feeling of being in a space that is not properly our own. And yet, at the same time, many of us choose this dress.

Oxford students are used to being photographed. They are required to wear academic gowns for their exams, making them particularly photogenic. Many smile for the tourists' cameras. In 2012, female students were first allowed to wear pants (or *trousers*, to use the English word) under their robes. This change of dress code was framed as accommodating transgender students—as though there are no female-identified students who would rather wear pants.[99] But perhaps this framing was correct: skirts remained the norm among women. In Oxford, gender normativity is all the rage.

In the strange mix of academia, gender, empire, and class-consciousness that is Oxford, I was struck by a postcard being sold in many tourist shops: "Oxford by Night." The card was a cartoon of young, white people, presumably students, queuing outdoors to get into a club. It was cold. But the male clubbers wore their academic gowns and trousers. Some had scarfs. The women, on the other hand, wore short skirts and bras—no shirts. The cartoon made it clear that many of them were shivering. Stupid girls, one might think, noting their lack of the dignified gown. Were they even Oxford students? Why not wear appropriate clothing for the weather?

This horrid postcard reinforced the idea that the archetypical Oxford student is white and male.[100] It also seemed to revel in the sexual availability of white, young women in the city. The cartoon did not emerge from nowhere. The scene may have exaggerated Oxford by night, but it captured some kind of truth. On Fridays and Saturdays, Oxford becomes a party city. Students attend college "bops," drink at pubs, and go dancing at various clubs. Queues do form outside these clubs. Women often wait outside, not dressed for the weather.

The women, both in the postcard and on the streets, feel cold and yet valuable, according to the postcard and its culture, to the extent that they expose themselves to the temperature. I cannot but read this as a defeating undress that presumably women choose because they think it gets them further than the robe. Their sensation of the cold highlights how they are in the territory of an other, Oxford. Their presence is welcome as long as they play a deal: they will get ahead as sexual-objects-to-be-looked-at; they will feel cold; they will show how this space is not quite theirs; they will remain sexually available. I wonder if many of the women became frigid.

two   Locating Affect, Swimming Underwater

At first, there is the cold—for let us assume that the body entering the North Atlantic Ocean was used to the warm summer day. And with this cold comes a sharp inhalation. Hairs stand on end; adrenaline rushes through her body. She goes under. And there, she is suspended in another world. Her face is illegible. Her emotions are not read; she need not attend to the emotions of any other. Moving with the water, she pulls herself through, then up: she uses her arms to breathe as she pulls herself to the surface. She dives back in, reaching the ground with her hands. She presses up. Flips over. She feels alive in this world—a world that is not her own but which she is now part of. Could this sense of liveliness exceed her? In the water, her body becomes, moving with the water, becoming-fish, becoming-water itself. It is for this reason that swimming in the ocean is best; it is there that the water moves her. She is transported by the current, becoming part of the current itself.

But who is this swimmer? Where did she learn to swim? Where is she swimming? If the practice of swimming takes her beyond herself, if the sensation of being in water touches on a liveliness that is beyond the lived body, beyond the personal or the social, how can we account for the practice's location?

My previous chapter troubled the distinction between the symbolic and the sensory. I showed the relevance of phenomenology to developing thought between idealism and objectivism. Here, I continue this project, but I focus more squarely on an overlapping problematic: the argument that affect is autonomous or asocial, an argument that, following Brian Massumi's reading of Deleuze, has become prominent in some versions of feminist, queer, critical race, and cultural studies scholarship.[1]

In much of this scholarship, a curious dichotomy often appears between affect and the social, affect and the structural, and affect and identity. Over and again, affect is imagined as existing apart from or before these entities. It is this idea that

I challenge here. I argue that the social is sensory; positionality produces and is productive of sensations, and structures moves.

The chapter makes this case both through the study of scholarship on affect and through an analysis of the sensation of swimming. I show how this sensation might feel like an undoing of personhood, an escape from the social and from structural relations, but in effect, the social informs the practice, both making it possible and giving it shape. This is especially evident when we consider the production of the spaces and places within which we move and the differential production of lived bodies. The chapter begins by explaining how swimming can be understood as inciting affect. I then show the limitations of this framework to finally consider an alternative: critical autobiography.

Affect Underwater

It is tempting to write a Deleuzian-inspired description of swimming, because his understanding of embodiment seems particularly attuned to the activity. Deleuze critiques phenomenology's reliance on a "lived body" as that which naturally synthesizes perception. There may be a unity of the senses, he writes in his book on Francis Bacon (which itself can be read as a rejoinder to Merleau-Ponty's analysis of Cézanne), but this unity is not a result of natural perception, the lived body, or intentional consciousness.[2] Rather, sensory domains, such as the visible and the audible, invoke one another because each overflows with a vital force, a rhythm that is more profound than each domain.[3] This rhythmic unity, Deleuze is clear, has nothing to do with the lived body. In fact, it can only be discovered in surpassing the organism, moving toward the limits of the body. Painting, for instance, liberates the eye from its organization in the organism. It "gives us eyes all over: in the ear, in the stomach, in the lungs."[4] Painting transforms the eye into a polyvalent and provisional organ, all while placing a body before us, a body free from organic representation.[5] To really sense a painting, to be affected by the forces that constitute it, one departs, at least momentarily, from one's organization as an organism with defined organs. Instead, one responds to the world, resonating with its vibration.

We might say something similar of ocean swimming. Underwater, feet are no longer feet on which we stand. The whole body becomes a lung, in that to breathe, the body must come to the surface. There is an undoing of the terrestrial body, which involves a remaking and reworking of muscles and organs. One becomes part of the current, the wave. And the senses become engaged: sight, sound, smell, and taste—all are different underwater; all are overwhelmed by the water.[6]

Following Deleuze, we might argue that these senses do not invoke each other so much as index a vital responsiveness that is more than each taken individually.

Something affective also haunts the description of swimming with which I began. Although affect, as Elizabeth Grosz explains, is "not readily identifiable," what is clear is that it is "closely connected with forces, and particularly bodily forces, and their qualitative transformations."[7] Grosz elaborates: in Deleuze's view, lived bodies can never directly experience forces of chaos or the earth itself. This is because as soon as affect enters the realm of language, cognition, and experience, it becomes captured in the personal and the subjective; its effects are actualized. Nonetheless, with affect, the body's immersion and participation in these forces become clear. That participation incites virtual change. It creates a sense of potentiality, an intensity. Affect incites (as Kathleen Stewart elaborates) a feeling that something has happened.[8] More precisely, affect instigates potential becoming. In Deleuze and Guattari's words, affects are the "nonhuman becomings of man," becomings not from one state to another (this would freeze movement into two steady states), but rather continual becomings or movement itself.[9] Through affect, "something or someone is ceaseless becoming-other (while continuing to be what they are)."[10] While we cannot actually experience affect, Massumi argues that we can access the "continuity of affective escape."[11] When that escape "is put into words," Massumi continues, "it tends to take on positive connotations. For it is nothing less than the *perception of one's own vitality*, one's sense of aliveness, of changeability."[12]

Although the swimmer with whom I began does not actually experience affect, the sense of vitality and the feeling of transformation that emerge underwater can be read as indexing that something affective has occurred. In other words, swimming can incite affect, which is to say that the practice creates a form of responsiveness that connects the virtual body to the forces of the earth. Swimming can transform the swimmer to become one with the moving water, part of the water; at the same time, the swimmer continues to be what she or he is. In being in the water, one senses this escape, this vitality, this potentiality, even though affect itself is never exactly experienced.

That said, finding affect in the practice of swimming may seem strange to many readers. This is because in Deleuze and Guattari's writing, affect is directly tied to art and the aesthetic. For instance, in *What Is Philosophy?*, Deleuze and Guattari develop a nonsubjective and nonrepresentional theory of art. They argue that a work of art does not represent anything. Instead, it preserves sensations, which they understand as blocs of "affects" and "percepts." A lived subject experiences, owns, or has affectations (such as joy) and perceptions (such as blue), but art captures sensations, independent of the subject. In Deleuze and Guattari's view, although living, phenomenological subject cannot directly experience affect, a work of art captures forces that entice embodied transformation. "Life alone," Deleuze and Guattari contend, "creates such zones where living beings whirl around, and only art can reach and penetrate them in its enterprise of co-creation."[13]

While Deleuze and Guattari link affect to the aesthetic, this connection falls away in the scholarship in both cultural studies and feminist, queer, and critical race studies that I address here. The connection is also not obvious in all of Deleuze's writing. For instance, in her summary of affect in cultural studies, Clare Hemmings convincingly explains how affect is understood as a form of embodied responsiveness that interrupts "social logic."[14] Hemmings draws some examples of affect from Deleuze's reading of T. E. Lawrence's *Seven Pillars of Wisdom: A Triumph*. Lawrence, for instance, describes how he had an erection while he was being raped. Hemmings writes, according to Deleuze, such "instances index the unpredictable autonomy of the body's encounter with the event, its shattering ability to go its own way."[15] Indeed, in his reading of Lawrence, Deleuze explains that the text shows how "the body has autonomous external reactions," acting and reacting "before the mind moves it."[16] Affect, however, is not necessarily this independent, bodily responsiveness: Deleuze continues to explain that after the mind coldly witnesses the body, it then becomes "affected, [. . .] an impassioned witness, that is, it experiences for itself affects that are not simply effects of the body, but veritable critical entities that hover over the body and judge it."[17] In this passage, the mind experiences affects; affects are not simply an embodied response, independent from the mind. Instead, affect appears immaterial—which is not to say unreal—in this account. Deleuze adds, "Spiritual entities or abstract ideas are not what we think they are: they are emotions or affects. They are innumerable, and do not simply consist of shame, though shame is one of the principal entities."[18] Deleuze offers us "affect" and "emotions" as synonyms in this passage, and while this is a reading of an autobiographical text, that is to say, of literature or of an aesthetic composition, Deleuze is not concerned with how affect is held in the aesthetic. Instead, he claims that the character's mind experiences affects. These affects are incorporeal entities that are neither in the body nor in the mind. They appear as the mind comes to witness the body and transform as a result of bearing witness.[19]

Thus, while swimming is not aesthetic, the practice might nonetheless incite affect. Having established this argument, I now turn to describe a problem that emerges in contemporary scholarship on affect, which I then address.

Affect and Positionality

In much of the scholarly literature in cultural studies and feminist, queer, and critical race theory that draws on Deleuze, affect is cleaved from positionality, identity, and the social. Connected to this vision of affect is the claim that both the autobiographical and the phenomenological provide a false sense of oneness that entraps sensation as though it only always belongs to a located self, with its personal memory. This approach contends that it is only through affect, from an impersonal, virtual yet embodied and nonsubjective form of responsiveness that transformation, autonomy, freedom or change are possible. But these are, I argue, unnecessarily rigid distinctions.

Take, for instance, Jasbir Puar's arguments in *Terrorist Assemblages*. This text puts pressure on feminist understandings of intersectionality, which have become prominent in the field of women's and gender studies. Puar contends that "intersectionality demands the knowing, naming, and thus stabilizing of identity across space and time, relying on the logic of equivalence and analogy between various axes of identity."[20] Intersectionality accounts for "positionality ... locality, specificity, placement."[21] Its understanding of identity "colludes with the disciplinary apparatus of the state—census, demography, racial profiling, surveillance."[22] In the place of intersectionality, Puar turns to Deleuze's understanding of "assemblages," arguing that rather than understand subjects as positions on grids, we might see them as corporeal events, the temporary coming together of forces. Assemblages, she argues, "allow us to be attuned to movements, intensities, emotions, energies, affectivities, and textures."[23] Puar's 2012 article, "I Would Rather Be a Cyborg than a Goddess," elaborates on this view.[24] The article explains how the tension between intersectional and Deleuzian approaches consists, in part, of the tension between "theories that deploy the subject as a primary analytic frame, and those that highlight the forces that make subject formation tenuous, if not impossible or even undesirable."[25] This is a long-standing tension in feminist queer thought, one that was central in debates concerning poststructuralism or postmodernism in feminist theory and especially in the reception of Judith Butler's writing.[26]

I do not mean to suggest that we need recognizable subjects in order to have politics, and Puar's analysis of the limitation of subject-centered approaches is convincing. My intervention, instead, focuses on the ways in which affect and assemblage have been understood. Assemblage theory, Puar insists, looks to "what is prior to and beyond what gets established."[27] And yet Puar draws on Massumi's *Parables for the Virtual* to provide an example of an assemblage, and this example clarifies that assemblages are neither "prior" nor "beyond." Massumi reads an instance of domestic violence on the occasion of a Super Bowl Sunday. This scene portrays an encounter between a TV, living room, and bodies, an encounter that results in an assemblage, the "movement of hand against face."[28] Massumi contends that "the 'game' is rigged by the male's already-constituted propensity to strike."[29] Puar argues that Massumi problematically "presumes sex/gender differentiation as the primary one that locates bodies on the grid."[30] But more could be made of this passage. In this case, the event of "hand against face," an event that emerges through the assemblage of TV-living room-and-bodies, is neither prior to nor beyond what gets established: Massumi writes of an "already-constituted propensity to strike." This suggests that assemblages do not come before positioning. Rather, assemblages engage what already is. But what is, in this case, is not formed once and for all. Structure, position, location are not stable. Rather, these are events of the world being created and recreated. In other words, positionality and affect, identity and affect need not be read in tension. Affect emerges in particular locations such that these very locations cannot be imagined as stable. Location is not a place of gridlock (to use Massumi's phrase, which Puar cites). Rather, it is the place not simply from which we become but that is itself becoming.[31]

In other words, drawing on Deleuze, and Massumi's reading of Deleuze in particular, Puar seems to suggest that assemblage theory allows us to write about the constitution of bodies, events, and things. This allows for the development of nonessentialist theory that neither relies on nor reproduces the disciplinary production of the subject, positionality, or identity. And yet, as Puar builds this argument, the place of the subject or of identity becomes unnecessarily congealed, imagined as unchanging and stable. In addition, it becomes hard to theorize how the location from which affect emerges shapes the affect itself. Instead, could we conceptualize positionality in movement? And could we localize affect?

That said, it is true that Massumi recognizes that affect is contextual. He writes, for instance, that "the body doesn't just absorb pulses or discrete stimulations; it infolds *context*."[32] He continues to explain that while "intensity is asocial" it is certainly not "presocial—it *includes* social elements but mixes them with elements belonging to other levels of functioning."[33] In this view, while Massumi argues that affect is autonomous, he does not mean to suggest that affect is completely autonomous from the contexts within which it emerges. But to insist, as Massumi does, that affect is "asocial" implies that the notion of the social does not come to be transformed by his analysis of affect. Sociality remains imagined as something fixed, unlike affect, which is transformative. Instead, what happens when we see the sensory as partly constitutive of the social? The social then appears as a place of movement, as that which is moving itself.

A similar argument emerges when reading Arun Saldanha's "Politics and Difference." Saldanha builds on the distinction Deleuze draws between molar differences, such as differences of identity or differences that are organized into group formations, and molecular differences, which are "*smaller*, not-yet-structured, even prepersonal intensities."[34] He reads William Foote Whyte's ethnography, *Street Corner Society*, to think about the encounter between white girls and black men on a city street. Saldanha writes, "[A]lthough from the molar perspective we are dealing with a *relational* situation of two distinct groups—white girls and black men—it is on the molecular, precognitive level that the gestures, gaits, excitements first occur."[35] For Saldanha, the molecular or the affective is prior to the molar or the identitarian. And yet is not this molecular located within particular social arrangements? The molecular or the affective is in part patterned through habit and transmitted across generations. It appears within the context of molar relations. In such a reading, can we really conclude that the molecular is "not-yet-structured," as Saldanha posits?

Compare this understanding of affect to Linda Martín Alcoff's "Toward a Phenomenology of Racial Embodiment." Drawing on Merleau-Ponty, Alcoff develops what she calls a "subjectivist approach" to race, focusing on how "race operates pre-consciously on spoken and unspoken interaction, gesture, affect, and stance."[36] Race, she argues, is lived in every day interactions as people visually perceive both themselves and others, and interact. "Greetings, handshakes, proximity, tone of voice," she writes, "all reveal the effects of racial awareness."[37] This awareness, Alcoff argues, is not conscious, but that does not mean it is asocial. Instead, it takes the form of tacit knowledge, "practical consciousness," or common sense that is not "imposed from above, but by the sediment of past historical beliefs and practices of a given society or culture."[38] This common sense shapes perception itself such that we (both white people and people of color) perceive certain differences instead of others. This does not mean, however, that there is a world out there that is covered over by our ideas (however tacit). There is a material reality—but through practical consciousness, we perceive certain differences in particular and make sense of them (cognition is subtractive). Alcoff's approach can better address the emergence of racialized preconscious bodily tendencies, perceptual habits, and affects. She provides a mode of understanding how history and culture inform human responsiveness to the world in ways that we are not necessarily even aware. Following her argument, the realm of affect need not be understood as asocial, even though it is preconscious.

I present one final example—this time, in film criticism. In her essay, "The Immersive Spectator: A Phenomenological Hybrid," Maria Walsh tries to negotiate a place between Merleau-Ponty and Deleuze, so as to theorize a form of "immersive spectatorship" that is attuned to the "absorption of the seer in the image" but remains "considered in terms of embodiment, in terms of location rather than purely mental contemplation."[39] In finding this place, Walsh does not advocate a return to phenomenology, however. She takes Laura Marks's phenomenological *The Skin of the Film* to task, arguing that "the problem in Marks' analysis is that bodies are assumed to have definite owners and are culturally bounded by custom and personal memory."[40] Walsh is invested in Deleuze's understanding of what she terms "the unknown body [...] removed from autobiographical knowledge and ownership, which is why it can offer liberation and transformation rather than habitual repetition."[41]

Walsh's essay both touches on my central argument, and at the same time symptomizes the problem. She too is concerned with the location of perception. And yet she frames "autobiographical knowledge and ownership" as necessarily the realm of "habitual repetition."[42] In her view, it is only with an "unknown body" that "liberation and transformation" are possible. This distinction between the autobiographical as the realm of habit and the anonymous as the realm of transformation is not necessary. Rather than understanding autobiographical, phenomenological approaches as binding bodies to custom and personal memory, we could see these approaches as providing an account of this binding, one that makes visible the contingencies and indeterminacies of such binding, an account that shows how transformation is possible from particular locations, an account, even, that is itself transformative.

Quite simply: the autobiographical or the phenomenological is not necessarily the location of stasis. Instead, these approaches can provide a description of the becoming of social difference or the movement of affect that constitutes, at least in part, social worlds. Distinctions between affect and the social, movement and identity, intersectionality and assemblage then become harder to maintain.

In the section that follows, I illustrate this argument through an autobiographical exploration of swimming. My investigation navigates between first-person prose, historical contextualization, and theoretical commentary. I locate the practice of swimming with which this chapter began, showing how the sensation of swimming is productive of and informed by social difference. This is clear when we consider both the politics that shape the lived body and the creation of the space and places within which bodies move.

Swimming and the Autobiographical

I love to swim, yet the word *swim* is not exactly right. It's not swimming that I love—though I do like to swim—it is not floating either; it is rather being in water, being underwater, moving in water, and not with the goal of getting to a particular place, not with a set of choreographed, repeated strokes, but with the experiment of moving limbs in ways not possible on land: stretching, twirling, falling away from the world, sensing the water around me. It is a feeling of being touched, surrounded, but not held in place. To be embraced while moving. It helps when the temperature is just right, when the water is moving and deep, when there are no clear boundaries to how far I can swim (no walls, no buoys). I imagine that I would like scuba diving, but I don't have the sinuses for it.

To those psychoanalytically inclined, it's cliché, I know, but my love of swimming has to do with my mother. When my mother is near water, or better yet, in water, suddenly and consistently, she is happy and playful. As a child who either took the emotion of others' as her own or who narcissistically saw herself as the cause of all emotion around her, I too came to love being in water. Water was a welcomed respite from feeling that I was a problem or feeling worried that I'd do something wrong. I was a joy. I felt joy. My mother's happiness became my own, or perhaps we both came to exist within a common realm of happiness that would only intensify as the feeling circulated between us.

Years later, when I first came out to my mother, her reaction was fear. "But the world is a nasty, nasty place," she begged me, worried that as a lesbian, I would not make it. My mother often saw the world in this way. She understood venturing off a traditional path as dangerous. It's not that indiscretion or deviance would be punished; it's not simply that I would not be happy; it was that the world was "nasty." I would not simply be sad. I would only find cruelty.[43] This nasty world provides the background for swimming's joy. To be in water, near water, and with my mother all gave me (and still gives me) an immediate sense of relaxation, a lessening of anxiety. The water was a place where, consistently, the world was not terrible, and where we could explore what our bodies could do and what they could sense without fear of reprisal. Underwater, I/my mother/we are capable. My mother is a strong swimmer, a strong athlete in general, and although I do not have her grace, I too am comfortable and capable in water. In other words, swimming consists in an activity not simply where I am not scrutinized and where I do not have to attend to others, but also where I feel the bodily "I can" Merleau-Ponty assumes of motility. Iris Marion Young argues that "the feminine body underuses its real capacity. [...] Feminine bodily existence is an *inhibited intentionality*, which simultaneously reaches toward a projected end with an 'I can' and withholds its full bodily commitment to that end in a self-imposed 'I cannot.' "[44] In water, I do not think my mother experiences such inhibited intentionality. She is not always self-confident, but in water, she can, and so can I, and even better, experiencing this "I can" is pleasurable. In addition, being immersed underwater can feel like a welcome form of covering, especially because such immersion often appears right after a moment of relative undress, when one moves toward the water in a bathing. In its proximity to this moment, the space underwater feels like a place where gender norms relax.

Upon first announcing that I was dating a woman, some of my female friends suffered lesbian panic (poor souls!). The result was a tightening of traditional gender norms: the purchase of bikinis, makeup, and, I kid you not, pink clothing, which had previously been the object of great disdain. Hair grew longer—at least on the head. A few months later, I joined this group of friends at a summer cottage, outside Montreal. We were, I was to find, no longer to swim. Bodies were now to be displayed, laid out by the water, toes carefully painted. We were to look and to be seen (the irony that only women were present did not escape me). In a two-piece Speedo, I was the only one who swam. But I wanted to play. It had only been the year before that we had competed to see who could balance, standing on the greatest number of noodles in the water. I wanted to move. Was it really the same people who were now reading women's magazines, claiming that some behaviors were not feminine and hence had to be banished? In consciously trying to inhabit heterosexual femininity, my friends gave up the water. They wanted to be seen displayed alongside it rather than moving in it. They would choose the moment for me that is most uncomfortable about swimming: being in a bathing suit in public.

I asked my mother about her love of swimming, and she responded in a careful, crafted email. She explained how she learned to swim: her mother taught her, and her parents, she writes, were both excellent swimmers. She was not given formal lessons: "C'est en jouant dans l'eau que j'ai appris," she explains, and "C'était très enjoué, s'amuser était le but."[45] ("It's in playing in water that I learned," and "It was all very playful, and having fun was the goal.") My mother relates swimming to summer vacation and its respite from both winter and work. Her birthday is at the end of June, and she explains that for her birthday, she would receive everything to play in the water: "Palme, tuba, masque, planche, matelas pneumatiques, flotteurs, variétés d'object gonflants petits et énormes, etc., etc."[46] ("Flippers, snorkel, mask, board, air mattress, floatation devices, a variety of inflatable objects, small and enormous, etc., etc.") These are not gendered gifts; they are gifts for active, bodily play.

I leave my mother's writing in the French because the language is significant. I was raised in a bilingual home in Montreal, Québec, and spoke fluent French, especially as a child, and yet my parents sent me to an Anglophone school. I remember being told this was because when I had children, I would be able to choose to which school to send them to. Quebec's 1977 *Charte de la langue française* (Bill 101) only allowed parents to send their children to Anglophone schools if at least one parent had gone to an Anglophone school in the province. I was sent to English school so that the children I was expected to bear could go to the school I chose in the province.

I do not write "Québec," "Quebec" or "Montreal," "Montréal" consistently in this book, because to name this territory in either French or English is to embed it within one nationalist project or another. Ironically, my performance of bilingualism is itself likewise a project of nation building: Pierre Elliott Trudeau's insistence on bilingualism haunts my writing.[47] I am, indeed, the product of such a national imaginary. It is worth noting how I have framed this choice between English and French. This indexes the limitations of multiculturalism and the naturalization of settler colonialism—although arguably, it is not Haudenosaunee territory that I write of here but rather of this land as it has been taken up in the project of Quebec and Québec.

Regardless, that I attended an Anglophone school meant that my friends were Anglophone and the majority of my schooling was in English. This slowly created a divide between my mother's family and me; my father and his family were Anglophone, unlike my mother's. I felt like I did not have the linguistic skills to communicate effectively or to be myself with my mother and her family. I spoke like a six year old, even though I was sixteen, then twenty-six, then thirty-three. I was nervous and ashamed about this insufficiency and remain so. I did not see myself as belonging, either in the family or in the province with its nationalist movement based on linguistic identity. Within this context, the bodily, affective connection I share with my mother around swimming becomes still more significant. The practice and its joy tie me to my mother and her family; they place me within this maternal line apart from linguistic constraint. The corporeal activity that does not center language gives me a sense of belonging both in the family and in the French-speaking nation.

I experience the sensation of swimming as entangled with the emotion of joy. This coupling has to do, in part, with the transmission of affect from my mother to me. This is not an instance of the reproduction of the same. There is a difference between my mother and myself. But it is in our relation, in my body's proximity to my mother's that I develop an orientation toward swimming, one that finds in the practice pleasure, confidence, and belonging. The transmission of affect between my mother and me is, in part, about the production of my gendered identity, one that finds reprieve in the water. In addition, the practice of swimming becomes important to me in the context of linguistic identity. And so it may be that in swimming, I am moved by sensations that are not my own, sensations that index a body-without-organs or a vitality that is not contained by my lived body. But all this is made possible by my knowing how to swim, by a connection I've developed since I was an infant between joy and swimming, and by the histories that contribute to my body finding joy in water.

One might, however, understandably interrupt this analysis. One might want to argue that the sensation of swimming is different from the emotion of joy. Affect is not emotion. In this case, the sensation of swimming might be read as asocial or molecular, while the joy might be viewed as the personal capture of the sensation, its mobilization in molar relations. Likewise, one might want to argue that this autobiographical exploration traps the sensation of swimming in a lived body (my own) such that what is only ever produced is the same, the same structures, the same identity positions. And yet such an analysis is insufficient, since it is in part because of the coupling of joy with the sensation of being in the water that I seek out more of the sensation. This means that the sensation emerges within the context of its connection to joy. The sensation of swimming is not simply molecular or prepersonal. Or more precisely, if prepersonal, it is nonetheless sought within the contexts of molar, social relations. And still more, rather than understand this autobiographical reading as entrapping the sensation of swimming within a lived body, we might read this story I am elaborating as one of emergence: the coming to be of this swimmer's body. While I am placing the sensation of swimming within a specific context, this context itself is not unchanging. For example, swimming is in part about the negotiation of gender rather than about the expression of a female identity. Swimming is about the creation of a connection to family and nation rather than the consolidation of a preexisting sense of belonging.

This autobiographical story emerges within a particular history. In the email my mother sent me, she explains that she learned to swim "dans un lac"[48] ("*in a lake*"). Such a claim can be read in dialogue with the discourse of nature and wilderness that, as many scholars have argued, was instrumental to the development of white identity in Canada and the United States during the nineteenth and twentieth centuries. In the United States, John Muir's writing provides a good example. Founder of the Sierra Club and key to the development of modern environmentalism, Muir argued for the development of national parks as clean, pristine places where elite, urban men could purify and strengthen themselves from the degenerate effects of urban living. The city, in his view, was polluted by non-Europeans; white men needed the space of the national parks to fortify themselves.[49] As Catriona Mortimer-Sandilands argues based on such evidence, "Parks were born *from* a gendered and racialized view of nature, and were also used to impose gendered and racialized relations *on* nature."[50] Still more, national parks become key to the expansion of settler colonialism. As Mortimer-Sandilands writes, "[B]oth Yellowstone and Banff were *inhabited* at the time of their creation: In order to become sufficiently pristine for travelers in search of picturesque wilderness they were physically and legislatively *emptied* of their aboriginal populations."[51]

In the Canadian instance, the space of "nature" is foundational in the imaginary of the nation. As those who study Canada know well, nature is central to hegemonic Canadian nationalism, which has often defined Canadian identity by an attachment to "wilderness." For example, the Group of Seven painters from the 1920s are most well known for their paintings of Algonquin Park and Northern Ontario, which is to say, their paintings of lakes and trees. The Group of Seven was understood in its time as "finally" bringing about a *Canadian* form of modernism. Its portrayal of Canadian, nonurban and nonagricultural space was seen as marking its art as *Canadian*.[52] Canadian literature has been understood similarly. For instance, Northrop Frye, who is often credited with establishing the study of Canadian literature, argued in his 1971 monograph, *The Bush Garden*, that the "Canadian imaginary" is shaped by the vast and sparsely settled Canadian territory.[53] Margaret Atwood, another central figure of Canadian culture, argued similarly. In her 1972 *Survival: A Thematic Guide to Canadian Literature*, she claimed that the Canadian environment poses such a great threat to life that Canadian writing is a tool for survival.[54] "Canadian" music partially follows suit: in 1967, Glenn Gould, one of the most celebrated Canadian classical musicians, launched the first of three parts of his "Solitude Trilogy." This first part, "The Idea of North," aired on the Canadian Broadcast Cooperation's radio, and used music to explore what Gould felt was the solitude and isolation that characterizes the Far North.[55] In short, *Canadian* music, like *Canadian* painting and *Canadian* literature, was framed around Canadian territory. More precisely, Canadian nonurban space has been understood as providing inspiration for the cultural production and identity that becomes marked as *Canadian*.

I read this Canadian cultural production as an expression of dis-ease within the segment of the earth that becomes the territory of Canada. The representation of nonurban space within Canadian culture can be understood as an attempt to claim it as one's own. This is a practice of taking possession that attempts to transform the possessor into the indigenous or to replace the indigenous with a supposedly better form of stewardship or care. In other words, this cultural production displaces indigenous nations while taking possession of the earth. It is in "conquering" the wilderness in part through paint, sound, and language that "the Canadian" emerges. This framing of the territory is about the production of whiteness, which, as Sara Ahmed argues, is often characterized as a feeling of comfort in "one's environment."[56] Ahmed writes, "[W]hiteness allows bodies to move with comfort through space, and to inhabit the world as if it where home. [...] Such bodies are shaped by motility, and maybe even take the shape of that motility."[57]

It is within this context that I understand my mother's and my own love of swimming. My mother learned to swim in a lake during the mid-1950s. In Quebec at this time, lakes were particularly spaces of racial and ethnic segregation.[58] My mother's family would spend the summers by such a lake, away from the "polluted" city, in this case, Shawinigan, Québec. In the 1950s and early 1960s, Shawinigan was largely racially homogenous, inhabited both by French Canadians (or Québecois) and an Anglophone minority. The 1961 Census of Canada lists the population of Shawinigan at 32,169; of these, 30,791 are of French origin and 1,065 from the British Isles. The population of "Negros" is marked at zero, while there are supposedly one Jew, six "Native Indian and Eskimos," and thirteen people "from Asia." In the neighboring Shawinigan-Sud, of the 12,683 inhabitants, 12,017 are of French origin, 488 from the British Isles. There are no Jews, no "Negros," no "Native Indian and Eskimos," but forty-six people "from Asia." These ethnic categories were traced through a person's father, and to be "from" the British Isles or French does not mean being born in these places, so much as being able to trace one's patrilineal line to these countries.[59] These categories are quite different from those commonly used in the United States. For instance, in the 1960 US Census, "color or race" was highlighted (unlike "ethnicity," in the Canadian version), and "white" created a grouping, unlike in the Canadian census, which listed multiple possible countries of origin.[60]

Regardless, Shawinigan was an industrial city, centered around the businesses of pulp and paper, aluminum mining, and hydroelectricity. The resultant air quality was particularly bad, and my mother became seriously asthmatic. To go to the lake was to get away from the city, but resulted practically not only in a departure from the pollution but also from the city's large working-class population, who could not afford a lake house or respite from the pollution. My mother's yearly migration was facilitated by class—my grandfather was a doctor—and consolidated a class-based identity that did not recognize itself as such but rather articulated itself in an attachment to the lake. Swimming in this water also worked to consolidate a sense of belonging in the nation and a sense of white, settler-colonial, national identity with its feeling of possessiveness and belonging. It is significant that it was a Québec lake that the family went to—not the ocean, not south to the United States. Staying near Shawinigan allowed for my grandfather to work during the week and return on weekends. But it also aligned their summers in Canadian national culture, physically inhabiting the space mythologized in art, literature, and music. By going to the lake, my mother physically became Canadian and practiced Canadianness. She developed a settler colonial sense of belonging.

This discussion certainly begs the question of Québecois identity, and yet throughout my mother's email, she clearly identifies herself as Canadian. She writes about how she enjoyed a new pool that was built in the context of celebrating one hundred years of Canadian Confederacy (Canada first became a nation-state in 1867). The swimming pool was built in a moment of nationalism to celebrate Canada. She also insists that her love of swimming emerged within the context of living "in a Nordic country."[61] This links swimming to a Canadian, and not particularly Quebecois, space. The cold runs across the nation. As I explained in the previous chapter, Canadian nationalism often frames itself in relation to the cold, to the fact of being "Nordic." Therefore, implicitly, her email makes clear that she was swimming in Canada, rather than in a Québec that is separate from it.

Following my mother, I too spent many summers swimming in lakes—but also rivers. When I was little, my family vacationed at Portage, a small town on the shores of St. Lawrence River where my mother had previously worked as a lifeguard and swimming instructor. Portage was lovely, but cold, my parents eventually agreed. And so we tried out Cape Cod in Massachusetts, where my father had once vacationed with a friend. The decision to go to Cape Cod certainly had to do with temperature, but not only. As Anglophones, my father's family had spent more time in the United States. They were Jewish, working-class Canadians, less tied to Canada and Québec than my mother with her French Canadian roots. They were less attached to any lake in particular—Jews had been both symbolically and legally excluded from the Canadian lake. My father was an Anglophone, city person—although he had been born in Rouyn-Noranda, in Northern Quebec, which was a source of many jokes. How could a man who so resembled Woody Allen be from the North Country? At times my father played into such jokes; other times, he insisted on his and his parents' belonging.

An oversized American flag greeted my parents, sister, and me as we followed Highway 6 up the Cape to Eastham, MA. And it was (and is) at Eastham's

Coast Guard Beach—part of Cape Cod National Seashore—that my mother and I played in the waves together. We were taken by the currents, undone by them. We returned each summer for three weeks at a time. Ultimately, it was this ocean swimming that I came to prefer. Specifically, the place I love to swim is at the tip of Coast Guard Beach, where the beach gives way to an inlet and marsh. Depending on the tide, the currents here can be particularly strong, and the waves unpredictable. There are many sandbars, meaning that for some time each day, one can venture quite far from shore, swimming from sandbar to sandbar. Few people walk to this point on the beach. There is no parking lot nearby. No bathrooms—certainly no boardwalk. In other words, there are not a lot of people around. Able-bodied, I hike there.

It was in imagining swimming in this location in particular that I wrote about the sensation of swimming in general. But this sensation of swimming is actually quite localized. The sensation can be read as a white settler colonial feeling. As Ahmed argues, "[W]hiteness is an orientation that puts certain things within reach. [. . .] Race becomes, in this model, a question of what is within reach, what is available to perceive and to do 'things' with."[62] In this case, it is not simply the placement of particular "things" or one's sense of bodily motility that is key, but also the production of the spaces and places within which bodies move. To make this argument clear, it is worth revisiting the history of the Cape Cod National Seashore.

John F. Kennedy signed the Cape Cod National Seashore into existence in 1961. In the 1959 proposal for the park, the United States Department of the Interior explained that while the shoreline was "spared the great industrial buildup" of the "eastern coast," "the modern highway" made it vulnerable to the "surging tide of modern progress" that had wiped out "the natural open spaces long cherished as an American birthright."[63] In other words, protection of this land would allow Americans to continue to experience "natural open spaces," which is to say to experience the imaginary terra nullius at the heart of the settler colonial imaginary here framed as a "birthright." The proposal recognizes that "Indians were living on Cape Cod well before the Christian era. Sites excavated by archeologists disclose a continuous Indian occupation down to historic times."[64] Notwithstanding this continuous occupation, indigenous presence is framed as historic, even ancient—something archeologists could identify. However, indigenous nations inhabited the Cape when the park was founded. The Mashpee Wampanoag nation, which existed in Cape Cod in the 1960s and today, could have also testified to a native presence.[65] The land of the park then gets cleared of indigenous presence in order to frame it as a "natural open space."

The park was also framed in relation to heteronormative ideals. The National Park Services' proposal for Cape Cod argues that it is "time to set aside, preserve, and protect the last of the 'old' Cape so that the inspiration of its surpassing beauty can be kept intact and handed down to future generations."[66] In his remarks upon signing the park into existence, Kennedy built on such logic: the park would "acquire and preserve the natural and historic values" of Cape Cod "for the inspiration and enjoyment of people all over the United States."[67] Kennedy elaborates that he is certain "future generations" would "benefit greatly from the wise action" of preservation.[68] Here, the park is established, in part, in the name of future generations. This links the park to what Lee Edelman terms "reproductive futurism," a belief in a redemptive futurity symbolized by the beloved figure of the child. For Edelman, "what is queerest about us, queerest within us, and queerest despite us is [a] willingness to insist intransitively—to insist that the future stop here."[69] In this view, discourse surrounding the park legitimates its creation within a heteronormative framework of generation, which in this case consolidates settler imaginaries and settler identities into the future.

It is not clear whether officials involved in the development of the park were concerned that it bordered Provincetown, and included some of Provincetown's beaches, or whether they saw the park as a way to make Provincetown anew. Provincetown was already known as a popular vacation spot for a transnational group of white, middle-class lesbian and gay tourists, many of who would return to Provincetown year after year, like my parents, sister and me would return to Eastham.[70] Although Provincetown appears over and again in the archive surrounding the park's establishment, there is no explicit mention of its queerness. The Official Report of the Proceedings Before the US Department of the Interior may implicitly refer to Provincetown's reputation, however. In considering the possible effects of the park on nearby inhabitants, the director of the National Park Service, Conrad Wirth, argues that "the establishment of such areas does have a real effect on the communities adjacent to it." He continues, "It does change the habits; it does change the economic balance. It does bring new economic values. It does have an effect on the over-all management of lands and the people living within a radius of the area established."[71] The "habits" that might change as a result of the park are not elaborated on. There was, in addition, an extended conversation over whether the park would unjustly encroach on the expansion of Provincetown. In this debate, the issue of Provincetown's population recurs over and over again, as those who appear at the hearings before the Subcommittee on Public Lands of the Committee on Interior and Insular Affairs argue that Provincetown is not expanding, need not expand, and cannot expand. In 1961, Senator Leverett

Saltonstall put this succinctly: "Provincetown with a steadily falling population does not need additional land."[72] In as much as it was assumed that gays and lesbians would not have children, this might be an implicit recognition of the town's queerness. In contrast, Cape Cod National Seashore was to be "kept intact and handed down to future generations."[73] It was for Americans yet to come.

But which Americans? The ones who could afford a holiday, but not only those. Kennedy insisted that the park was for the "enjoyment of people all over the United States," yet he did so three years before the passing of the Civil Rights Act of 1964, which included the claim that public accommodation, such as hotels and inns, could neither discriminate against potential clients nor segregate clients on the basis of race, color, religion, or national origin.[74] Provincetown clearly needed such legislation and notwithstanding its passing, African American tourists continued to be turned away from restaurants and boarding homes. They were also made to feel unwelcome, as some residents fought to keep blackface minstrel shows well into the 1990s.[75,76]

Finally, the National Park Services imagined the seashore for male bodies in particular. They argued that the health and morality of both men and boys would improve when they visited it. The Services' proposal for the seashore explained that the beach provided a space for "healthful activities, which bring us close to earth and sea."[77] On Cape Cod, "boys can play in ... wild spaciousness" and a "man may stand 'and put all America behind him.' "[78] The language of placing America "behind" the (masculine) self is particularly interesting. The phrase is Henry David Thoreau's, from the last sentences of his 1865 *Cape Cod*: "Here is the spring of springs, the waterfall of waterfalls. A storm in the fall or spring is the time to visit it; a lighthouse or a fisherman's hut the true hotel. A man may stand there and put all America behind him."[79] In such passages, Thoreau frames Cape Cod as the location of natural archetypes, which is to say, as archetypical nature: "the spring of springs, the waterfall of waterfalls." This is a strange formulation because there are no significant waterfalls in Cape Cod. In other words, although Thoreau claims to ground his writing on Cape Cod, and although he wrote this text after the 1850s, which is to say after Thoreau began, according to Lawrence Buell, to take "a more empirical and 'scientific' approach to nature," Thoreau's writing invokes the realm of the mythic or transcendental.[80] Following his teacher, Ralph Waldo Emerson, Thoreau understood "nature" as spiritually meaningful; he defined himself not as a scientist but, in part, as a mystic.[81] In this spiritual rendition, Cape Cod becomes a place of both nature and simplicity. This is why, according to Thoreau, it is best to visit the Cape during a storm, when nature's force is apparent. One should stay in a lighthouse or fisherman's hut, places unadorned with comfort and connected to economies not of tourism but of fishing. This lighthouse or hut, however, is a place to experience, not a place from which to work. And it is in this place, part material, part imaginary, that a "man may ... put all America behind him." A man stands alone. Were others present, human relations would return to complicate the scene: "America" would no longer be left behind, even though, in effect, America is very much present in Thoreau's mythical imagination. It is present in his imaginary of an uninhabited nature, in his insistence that it is a man standing alone (the phallic figure on the beach), and in his claim that it is a lighthouse or fishing hut that ought to be visited, connecting this travel to a particular the local economy.

This analysis of Thoreau's writing is significant within the context of my argument, because my own description of swimming repeats elements of Thoreau's framework. I began this chapter writing a passage where I appear alone in the water. I described how the sensation of swimming felt like the sensation of vitality itself.[82] The ocean later became a place to escape social constraints, especially conventions of gender. But all of this is a familiar trope, a common mode of understanding the experience of "nature" in a settler society. An uninhabited (read: emptied) nature becomes the scene for me to develop a sense of belonging that escapes the social convention of gender. A woman might swim and put America behind her. However, the place where I imagine swimming, the place where, in fact, I actually swim, was informed by and is part of the history of the American settler-colonial state, with its understandings of race, gender, and sexuality. In fact, "America" might be "behind" the man on the beach as in supporting him rather than apart or away from him.[83]

This is not to argue that the park is merely produced by human actors, and it is not to say that writing about the park is simply about human imagination and discursive intratextuality. "Nature" is not simply a human production but involves the more-than-human.[84] The sensation of swimming is shaped by the movement of water, wind, and sand. Cape Cod is a peninsula. Parts of it are, every year, eroding. The rate of erosion increases as the sea level rises, and as storms increase in strength and frequency. Nauset Spit, in particular, is the place where I love to swim. This place is part of the dynamic coast, where sand moves dramatically each year. And with that movement, currents transform and water temperature shifts.[85] This movement is clear when looking at GIS images of the location—even just from the 1990s until the 2000s. These images, taken from planes by the State of Massachusetts, show transformations, even on the small scale of just a few years. From this angle, the view from above, a viewpoint whose development is tied to military history and to sovereignty, change is apparent.[86] But this change is sensed not simply remotely by these cameras. One year, I don't remember exactly when, my mother and I walked out to the point, expecting to find the sandbars, expecting to play in the breaking waves and in the currents around them. There was, however, not a single sandbar. Instead, the water was simply deep—and cold, even though it was low tide. It was not particularly turbulent. And so as a result, I did not feel moved by the water. I remained quite aware of myself. My mother and I did not stay long. Did we walk back in silence?

The water, of course, is also home to multiple species. Over the past three years, large colonies of gray seals have come to live in the waters right off of the spit.[87] The seals are amazing; they are curious and watch the humans watching them by the sand. The seals smell a little; their presence attracts sharks.[88] In other words, the water now feels a little less like mine within which I can lose myself. It is becoming the territory of these others.

In short, the sensation of being in moving water, a sensation in which I can lose myself, in which I reach toward a body-without-organs, and where I am affected molecularly in a prepersonal encounter between my cells and the water—all of this—emerges within this particular context of nature-culture-power, which is shaped by histories of race, nation, gender, sexuality, and class, as well as by changing climates and ecologies. This context gives shape to the place where I swim. It allows for my body to be placed in this location, to feel as though I might belong in this location, and to develop an attachment to the location. Quite simply, the park facilitates the emergence of the sensation of swimming with which I began. Tropes that established the park, especially tropes that invoke nation, race, gender, and sexuality, are present in my description of swimming—most notably the idea that the practice allows me to escape social norms and get in touch with liveliness itself. This feeling is productive of white, settler identities.

This account of the sensation of swimming also makes it difficult to distinguish between the molar and the molecular. In the encounter with the water, my body may be affected on a molecular, precognitive level, but all this happens within the context of molar, social, structural relations. I do not mean to argue that these relations are stable—in effect, my attachment to the sensation of swimming is productive of my particular racialized, gendered, classed, able-bodied identity. But this attachment is transmitted along these lines, in relation to them.

Autobiography, Writing, and the Aesthetic

In turning to autobiography, I am making an implicit argument for the continued potential of feminist autobiographical writing notwithstanding critiques of the genre.[89] Following a long history of feminist writing, I am not ready to let go of this method, a method that moves both authors and readers. Autobiographical writing has been central to the development of feminist scholarship, which has highlighted the importance of "situated knowledges," "positionality," and the "politics of location."[90] In turn, such concepts have been foundational to the development of women's and gender studies as a field, which has highlighted relationships between subjects and objects of knowledge. It is not simply affect and sensation that can bring transformation of social structures. Critical descriptive and explanatory investigation remains important.

Feminist theorists have used autobiographical writing to draw attention to locality. Adrienne Rich's autobiographical "Notes toward a Politics of Location" provides a good example. The text's use of the first person constructs a sense of intimacy between the reader and the authorial voice, but more significantly, its use of the autobiographical is a practice of the very method the essay calls for. "Notes toward a Politics of Location" rallies feminists to bring attention to locality, and to think about the position from which feminist politics emerges. "Locality" here is understood as a corporeal, geographical, and social position. Rich begins "not with a continent or a country or a house, but with the geography closest in—the body."[91] She moves from this body, as it is gendered and racialized, to the nation of which it is a part, and then this nation as it exists in transnational economic and geopolitical relations. She suggests that this method is central to radical feminism, and she posits it as a form of radical materialism, though not necessarily Marxist: "Begin [...] with the material, with matter, mma, madre, mutter, moeder, modder, etc., etc."[92] In Rich's essay, the politics of location grants women authority to know. It provides a safeguard against "lofty and privileged abstraction," and is a method for making visible racialized gendered lives as well as differences between women.[93] To dismiss such writing as a form of navel gazing is to miss the ethical impulse behind close readings of one's life, readings that examine the self while addressing an audience, making oneself vulnerable, showing how the self is articulated in the terms of the other, and experimenting with how these terms can be redeployed to different ends.[94] In other words, to focus on the self is not simply to produce a self, but also to undo it while opening others to becoming remade.

It is in similar terms that bell hooks understanding autobiography. In her view, autobiography is transformative. It does not capture a preexisting self so much as re-creates it. In "Writing Autobiography," for instance, hooks composes, "to me, telling the story of my growing up years was intimately connected with the longing to kill the self I was without really having to die. I wanted to kill that self in writing."[95] Autobiography, for hooks, does not reproduce the structures or the forms of self that always already exist, but rather re-creates the self: "This death in writing was to be liberatory."[96] It is in this vein that I turn to critical autobiography—which is to say, a practice of writing the self that considers the contexts that make that self possible in order, finally, to denaturalize that self and understand its constitution within power relations.

This method is aligned with the practice of phenomenological bracketing that Johanna Oksala outlines. That is, I start from a "naïve, precritical experience of the world," and take the "philosophical, transcendental step that immanent social critique requires, [...] questioning the appearance of things and asking what kinds of conditions or structures make them possible."[97] This process is, potentially, transformative. Alcoff explains how many people have been hesitant to take a phenomenological approach to the analysis of race in the fear that it would naturalize the social structure, treating racial difference as a cause rather than as an effect. However, Alcoff argues that "only when we come to be very clear about how race is lived, in its multiple manifestations, only when we can come to appreciate [...] its power over collective imaginations of public space, can we entertain even the remote possibility of its eventual transformation."[98] Descriptions of the lived experience of race are, potentially, performative. They are forms of articulation that can transform that experience by denaturalizing certain experiences, validating others, and increasing awareness.

Postscript: In the Swimming Pool

A year after I first wrote and researched this chapter, I returned to Nauset Spit. Some of the magic was gone. I was eager to lose myself in the water, to feel the pull of the current, and with it, to lose myself, yet something had changed. Swimming felt less like an escape from the social than its reproduction.

And nonetheless, it is hard for me to let go of my love of swimming—and more specifically, it is hard for me not to want to universalize it. I know that not everyone likes to swim, but I can't help but think this is because they haven't had the opportunity to learn. I want to teach people to swim. I want beaches to be accessible. I want free, public swimming pools in the middle of cities. I want buses that take people to lakes. I want us all to swim. I recognize that this might sound extreme. Or perhaps more specifically, I recognize that this is a dangerous universalism. But my feelings are not unique. Public swimming pools in particular are sites of segregation, violence, and discipline, but they remain powerful imageries of utopian community as well. For example, after Jeff Wiltse examines decades of the American history of municipal pools, he concludes that they have "rarely realized their full promise as public spaces," yet they harbor an inherent potential "to foster community life, level social differences, and empower ordinary Americans."[99]

And so I was horrified when I moved to New Jersey for graduate school. It was hot, and the city of New Brunswick, New Jersey has no public swimming pool.[100] I remember one oppressively hot afternoon in the late 2000s, witnessing a father of two beseech—and then try to bribe—the lifeguard of a private pool to let his children swim. His efforts left him only with sweat. The man would not have had more success twenty miles down the road, in Princeton, NJ. Princeton Borough and Princeton Township share a beautiful swimming complex, complete with a wading pool, a diving area, and luscious green landscaping. In 2012, it added a waterslide. But on a hot summer day in 2008, another man, with his children in tow, was also turned away. The man argued with the pool guard: he worked in Princeton. He should be allowed to use the swimming facilities. But he did not live within the borough or township's boundaries. He was one of the many Latino workers who make the wealthy city of Princeton function, yet he and his children were barred from using its services. Perhaps he would have been hired to clean the facilities.

My sensation of swimming both enfolds and is productive of social contexts, including structures of nation, race, class, gender, and sexuality. But more broadly, the sensation indexes that I have access to "public" space, that there exists a public infrastructure that is accessible to me, that I have leisure time to make use of this infrastructure, and that I have been taught ways of moving my body that feel good.

When I say that I want everyone to swim, what I mean is not that everyone ought to swim but rather that there ought to exist an accessible, public infrastructure that allows for playfulness, for physicality, for a feeling of security and of well-being in one's body. The sensation of swimming enfolds such contexts.

Sensation is not separate from social structures, and social structures are not separate from sensations. These sensations emerge in contexts and in spaces and places that have been coconstituted in human and more-than-human encounters. We feel these structures through our moving bodies; such sensations give form to who we are. And as we feel, we become. Social formations take form and transform.

three   "Being Kissed by Everything"
Race, Sex, and Sense in Bessie Head's
A Question of Power

I have, so far, framed this project primarily as an intervention into feminist theory. Inspired by new feminist materialisms' attempt to develop thought that does not center on humans, yet concerned by the tendency of this scholarship to give unlocated accounts of materiality, I have turned to the analysis of sensation, highlighting the sensation of more-than-human worlds: the sensation of the cold, the feeling of being immersed in the Atlantic Ocean. This intervention into new materialisms is at once a reworking of affect studies, developing the relevance of phenomenology to the field. In this chapter, I continue the discussion of sensation, but I place the analysis more squarely within the context of queer theory.

Implicit in early queer theory was the belief that something related to pleasure, desire, or the erotic exceeds the categories and social formations that try to contain it.[1] Human bodies are capable of inventing new forms of pleasure that give rise to better worlds. Herein lay a form of vital materialism: faith that the body is not closed or determined but rather in a process of becoming and potentially affective of social change. But what place can we give pleasure, desire, or the erotic in the creation of more just worlds? Against early queer theory's tendency to posit desire as a force that "conflict[s] with the present order," Sharon Patricia Holland suggests "the erotic" exists "at the threshold of ideas about quotidian racist practice."[2] Holland's reading aligns with more recent work in queer and queer of color studies about the collusion of LGBT politics with state violence, racism, and exclusion.[3]

The tension between approaches to queer studies that frame pleasure, desire, or the erotic as exceeding or even destroying social formations and approaches where these entities are understood as symptomatic and productive of social structures, relations, and inequalities has given form to a central debate. On the one hand, we have the position that sex is "self-shattering" and as a result, asocial and antirelational.[4] On the other hand, we have the contention that the attempt to

45

separate sex from social relations, to see sex as antisocial and destructive of the self, is in effect characteristic of a particular subject position, notably white masculinity.[5] Between these approaches, we have an attempt to understand sexuality and the erotic as both sites of pleasure and pain—even pleasure in pain and pain in pleasure. In particular, this has been a central approach in contemporary black feminist and queer work on sexuality, which continues to carve out a space of erotic sovereignty, however compromised because of histories of black women's hypersexualization, the racial and sexual violence of slavery and its afterlife, and the culture of dissemblance.[6] Arguably, what all sides of this debate share is an attention to sex, broadly construed. Indeed, "the sexual" may be understood as the field's proper object and as such, pointing this out might at first seem both obvious and trivial.

But what happens when we move the framework of discussion from the sexual to the sensual? There is precedence for such a shift in queer studies and black feminism itself. For instance, in "The Uses of the Erotic: The Erotic as Power," Audre Lorde lays claim to a form of sensuality that she calls "the erotic." This erotic is more diffuse than prevalent understandings of sex and sexuality. Lorde writes, for instance, "[T]here is, for me, no difference between writing a good poem and moving into sunlight against the body of a woman I love."[7] Both are erotic, and neither of these sensations is strictly delimited to a narrow view of sexuality: Lorde includes the sunshine in the feeling of moving toward a woman. She does not argue that these sensations are erotic for all women (being careful to include the qualifier, "for me"); however, in her vision, by laying claim to the erotic, women, especially black women, become "less willing to accept powerlessness . . . resignation, despair, self-effacement, depression, self-denial."[8] The erotic provides self-sustenance. It is a potential source of strength; its relegation to the bedroom is part of women's oppression.

Similarly, though in a different context, Michel Foucault also looks toward sensations that are not necessarily sexual. In "Sex, Power, and the Politics of Identity" he claims, "The idea that bodily pleasure should always come from sexual pleasure as the root of *all* our possible pleasure—I think *that's* something quite wrong."[9] He insists on exploring the human body to find other sources of pleasure. This argument resonates with his conclusion to the first volume of *History of Sexuality*: "The rallying point for the counterattack against the deployment of sexuality ought not to be sex-desire, but bodies and pleasures."[10] And yet the focus in queer studies has often remained on something recognizably sexual or something related to "sexuality."

In comparison to the "sexual," the field of the sensual is a less explored, more inchoate realm of bodily pleasure. It is a field that is not overdetermined, where questions of kinship and identity less immediately come to the surface. The sensual has been less obviously framed, even produced by, sexology in its imbrication with scientific racism. It is present in the texture of everyday life: in the touch of a particular material brushing against the skin, in the sensation of being immersed in warm water, in the pleasure that a surface might provide as one lies on it. What promise can these sensations offer to the re-creation of social relations, forms of selfhood, and modes of being in the world?

To address this question, this chapter explores Bessie Head's 1974 autobiographical novel, *A Question of Power*.[11] The text presents sexuality as entangled with gendered and racialized violence and exclusion. However, it also explores pleasurable sensations of the more-than-human world that are not necessarily sexual. It frames this sensuality as key to the development of a capacious form of belonging apart from the nation-state, gender, and race-based violence and exclusion. It suggests that highlighting these sensations is productive of a form of human self that is ordinary, common, or general, a self that is unmarked by social categories, yet belongs to the places that nourish it.

For readers not familiar with this novel, a brief synopsis would be helpful: *A Question of Power* tells the story of a mixed-race woman, Elizabeth, who leaves South Africa with her young son on a one-way exit visa for Botswana. There, Elizabeth becomes haunted by debilitating and consuming dreamlike presences—Sello, Dan, and Medusa—that are the result, Elizabeth at first suspects, of witchcraft. These dream figures subject Elizabeth to sexual, emotional, and physical violence. They degrade her as a "Coloured" woman.[12] Possessed, Elizabeth loses her work as a teacher and is twice hospitalized, but she eventually finds solace in a vegetable garden. The novel begins with displacement: Elizabeth feels as though she is an "out-and-out outsider."[13] But it ends with "a gesture of belonging" (206). It does not arrive at this belonging through the nation or through sexuality or kinship, but rather through sensations that lead to what Head frames as the ordinary and the common.

Existing scholarship on the novel is divided. Many have argued that Head is disparaging of sex and sexuality. For instance, Lewis Nkosi contends that Head disapproves of both homosexuality and sexuality in general.[14] Huma Ibrahim mostly agrees: the novel, she writes, negates "sexual 'pleasure' both hetero and homosexual."[15] Along this vein, Clare Counihan concludes that the novel's utopian vision requires that Elizabeth "give up *all* attachment to her body," rejecting herself as a "desiring subject."[16] In contrast, other readers have developed a more reparative approach, arguing that the text reaches toward same-sex female pleasures. Anissa Talahite contends that the novel describes the garden "as a space of female creativity and bonding between women . . . [that] remains in the realm of unrealized desire."[17] In turn, Brenna Munro, attending to histories of same-sex eroticism in Southern Africa, concludes that the novel develops a "discourse on female love" that is contrasted to the "very explicitness of Elizabeth's nightmare world."[18]

In contrast to these modes of reading the novel, my approach shows how the text upholds pleasures that are not *sexual* but *sensual*. In other words, I agree that Head's novel is disparaging of sex and sexuality, but I show how it does not give up on embodied pleasure, *tout court*. The novel forges a "gesture of belonging" through sensations that connect the self both to the land and to humans in general. By focusing on these sensations, my reading also departs from those who excavate female-female bonding in the text. It is not that this bonding is not present, but rather, my contention is that to focus on it is to miss the embodied pleasures of the more-than-human world that the book clearly frames as healing. Seeking female love in *A Question of Power* reasserts the importance of something akin to sex and sexuality; it reasserts interhuman relations, but the pleasures that the book offers are more expansive. They involve the feeling of the wind on one's face, the sense of dirt on one's hand, the feeling of "being kissed by everything" (202).

Reading with the grain, this chapter argues that *A Question of Power* finds in the refinement of particular sensory experiences a sense of belonging and a mode of selfhood that is reparative, communal, and sustaining. In addition, the rendering of these sensations in the form of a novel in particular is generative of empathy, one that allows the reader to feel, alongside Elizabeth, the repair of the sensory. But this experience is only made possible by Head's vision of the particular political situation of Botswana. Therefore, reading against the grain, I argue that it is not sensation itself that produces the form of belonging or commonality Head seeks. It is, rather, the sensation of being in place, which means that the politics of the production of space and place is also key.

To make this argument, the chapter's first section analyzes the novel's treatment of sexuality, showing how Head entangles the sexual with forms of racial belonging and spatial exclusion that the novel ultimately seeks to undo. I show how and why scholars have understood the text as against sex. However, Head is not against all forms of sensuality. In the second section, I turn to the analysis of the sensations of the more-than-human world, which the novel posits apart from the sexual. I demonstrate how Head understands this sensuality as productive of a common, general human. I consider the place of the aesthetic and of writing in the communication of these sensations, and I show how this sensuality is made possible by particular manifestations of place and space.

Ultimately, I argue that while a certain version of queer studies has been insistent that something linked to sexuality exceeds current diagrams of power,

A Question of Power explores sensations that are somewhat different, sensations that, according to Head, foster forms of belonging that transcend race and racism, gender, and sexuality, reaching toward a common and general form of the human. And yet these particular forms of sensation are located in place. The political vision Head provides is not simply one that turns to the sensory to get away from inequality and violence and to find a form of commonality. It is rather one that develops places and space wherein these sensations become possible.

One final note before proceeding: in turning to *A Question of Power*, this chapter moves from this book's prior focus on the territory currently named "Canada," to the region of Southern Africa. This raises some crucial questions. What is the relationship between Botswana, where Head writes, and queer theory on which I draw? Am I engaged in a colonial project here, subsuming the novel under the gaze of the West or treating the novel as a resource for the intellectual project of American, European thought? Do I recenter the West in this analysis? In effect, "including" Head's work in the framework of this project "can ressemble a neocolonial annexation," one that, as Ashley Currier and Thérèse Migraine-George argue in an analysis of the possibilities of queer African studies, might partake in the "academic tendency to co-opt, appropriate, and generate 'margins' to bolster canonical fields of studies."[19] Currier and Migraine-George's concern could be used to articulate the beginnings of a valid critique of this chapter. And yet, at the same time, my turn to Head seeks to make clear how her text articulates a "radical skepticism toward Western taxonomies," notably, taxonomies of the sexual.[20] And the text goes further still to explore the potentiality of sensory connections. My goal, in other words, is not to "bolster canonical fields of study," but rather to transform them, engaging with the ideas of the novel (though, indeed, perhaps this is the way that canonical fields of study are bolstered). I neither read Head to develop a "local" understanding of sexuality and the sensual, nor do I subsume her work under a particular theoretical apparatus. Rather, I highlight the theoretical arguments that the book itself makes. Alexander Weheliye explains that "because women-of-color writers articulate their critiques as a result of and in relation to their identities, the knowledge they produce is often relegated to ethnographic locality within mainstream discourse."[21] My treatment of *A Question of Power* does not ignore the location from which Head speaks, but rather treats what she says as not only relevant to that location.

This is to take Head at her word. Head was a reader of world literatures.[22] She "constructed her identity as a writer in a global context."[23] The novel clearly places itself within the parameters of a world literature: *A Question of Power* includes several references to authors in England, the United States, and India. It invokes a transnational vision where people, books and ideas travel across borders to develop communities that are not defined in relation to the borders of a nation-state. Head is also interested in reconceiving the human and with it, the universal. Like Fanon, she does not reject humanism but re-creates it. Her treatment of sensation is central to this project and provides an important intervention in queer studies, one that decenters the field's American referent.

Race, Sex, and Space

Sharon Patricia Holland's contention that there is no "'raceless' course of desire" is everywhere evident in Bessie Head's 1974 autobiographical novel, *A Question of Power*.[24] While Holland focuses on the United States, and Head on Southern Africa, neither treats sexuality as a field independent of race and racism. *A Question of Power* links sexuality to feelings of racial belonging and exclusion, which in turn map onto forms of belonging (or not) in space as well. This first section of the chapter examines Head's treatment of sex and sexuality in the novel, showing both how Head maps homosexuality onto the racial logics of apartheid and how the novel connects heterosexuality to racialized, gendered violence. In both cases, sex and sexuality are connected to exclusion and the feeling of not belonging in space.

The connection Head draws between race, sex, and space is not surprising given South African apartheid. Deriving from the Afrikaans word *aparthood* (the condition of being separate or apart), apartheid manipulated space and regulated sexuality to instantiate a regime of racial supremacy. The 1913 Native Land Act stipulated that only 7 percent of the South African country could be owned by "natives." With the 1949 Immorality Law, the South African government prohibited mixed-race marriages. In 1950, it prohibited adultery between white and nonwhite people. That same year, it passed the Group Areas Act, which created residential areas designated for particular races. 1951 saw the passing of the Bantu Building Workers Act, which prevented black Africans from performing skilled work outside particular designated areas, as well as the Prevention of Illegal Squatting Act, which gave the Minister of Native Affairs the right to displace black South Africans into resettlement camps, and the Bantu Authorities Act, which created "black homelands." Neither the 1949 Immorality Law nor the 1950 law against mixed adultery targeted same-sex sexuality, though South Africa inherited British common law, which criminalized sodomy. But the 1949 Immorality Law was amended in 1957 to allude to homosexual sex acts. It was revised again in 1969 to explicitly target emergent gay subcultures.[25] Finally, in 1970, the Bantu Homelands Citizens Act stripped black South Africans of citizenship, requiring them to become citizens of the homeland reserved for what was considered their ethnic group. Quite simply, apartheid's racial regime was dependent on the regulation of sexuality as well as the striation of space.

In *A Question of Power*, Elizabeth navigates this particular configuration of race, space, and sex. The biological daughter of a white woman and a black man, Elizabeth is born in a psychiatric institution where her mother has been driven following her illicit and illegal affair with Elizabeth's father.[26] From the mental hospital, Elizabeth is sent to a nursing home, but then returned because she does "not look white" (17). From there, she is sent to a Boer family, but returned again because she is said not to belong, racially. She is then taken in by a mixed-race woman, only then to be enrolled in a boarding mission school. Apartheid's racial dynamics mean that Elizabeth spends her childhood moving between places and relations of kin. Elizabeth is displaced physically. She does not clearly belong to a particular family or to a particular place.

In the racialized world of South Africa, Elizabeth is classified as "Coloured," neither white nor African. Head maps this categorization onto male homosexuality and gender nonconformity. For instance, Head writes that Elizabeth "had lived for a time in a part of South Africa where nearly all the Coloured men were homosexuals and openly paraded down the street dressed in women's clothes" (45). In the logic of the novel, to be Coloured is to not belong in state-recognized racialized relations of kin. This is especially true for people in positions like Elizabeth's. While they were categorized as "Coloured," their parents were not. Elizabeth is thus left without relations of kin. These relations, in turn, were reproduced through heterosexuality, hence the novel's linkage between being Coloured and being homosexual: both live outside racialized modes of kinship. The passage that links homosexuality with being Coloured also frames Coloured men as not belonging in space. They "parade" on the street, which is to say that they are highly visible. They stand out or stand apart from the place through which they walk. They are not seen as part of that place, the South African street, but are rather framed as not belonging. In a word, *A Question of Power* describes both "homosexuals" and "Coloured people" as belonging neither in space nor in relations of kin.

The text also features characters who make it appear as though homosexuality is a result of racism; however, it is unclear whether the authorial voice agrees with the characters' opinions. For instance, Head writes that an "African man" gives Elizabeth an explanation for the prominence of homosexuality among Coloured men. The African man, Head narrates, explains Coloured men's supposed proclivity for homosexuality with the following anecdote: "How can a man be a man when he is called a boy? I can barely retain my own manhood. I was walking down the road the other day with my girl, and the Boer policeman said to me: "Hey, boy, where's your pass?" Am I a man to my girl or a boy? Another man addresses me as a boy. How do you think I feel?" (45). The man in this scene negotiates the 1952 Pass Laws that required Africans to carry identification. It was a criminal offence not to provide it to the police when asked. In this passage, the policeman's interpellation threatens the man's heterosexual masculinity. To be a man, this passage implies, one must be recognized as a man both by other men and by one's "girl" (45). The "girl," in turn, only recognizes the man's masculinity when other men see it. This diminutive use of "girl" is part of the production of "manhood" and is not understood as a result of racism, like the diminutive "boy."

What remains particularly curious about this passage, however, is that it is offered as an explanation of *Coloured* men's homosexuality. According to the characters in the novel, it is Coloured men in particular who have a tendency toward homosexuality. But both African and Coloured men could be called a "boy" by a policeman. How does this story explain their supposed different sexual tendencies? Elizabeth, upon hearing this anecdote, judges the explanation "most reasonable" (45). The authorial voice of the text offers no additional comment. It is therefore unclear whether Head agrees with the protagonist or if she is in fact portraying the unreasonableness of apartheid logics.

On the basis of such passages, Rosemary Jolly argues that "Head's stigmatization of the homosexual is clearly one which depends upon the false identification of the evils of *apartheid* with homosexuality itself," and Isabel Balseiro likewise encourages such a reading, interrogating why "feminists and lesbians champion [...] the often homophobic writings of Head."[27] However, the novel does not seek resolution in heterosexuality either. For example, when Dan, one of the figures who haunts Elizabeth, will not stop reminding her of "homosexuality and perversions of all kinds" (137), Elizabeth (and seemingly Head) concludes, "It was one thing to adopt generous attitudes, at a distance, it was another to have a supreme pervert thrust his soul into your living body. It was like taking a walk on slime" (138).[28] This passage, however, is not only disparaging of homosexuality. It goes on: such an experience "was like living in the hot, feverish world of the pissing pervert of the public toilet—the sort of man who, in buses and cinema queues, pressed himself against a woman" (138). Elizabeth may be horrified by Dan's "homosexual record," a "record" that plays in her head, claiming that homosexuality is a "universal phenomenon" (138), yet she is not impressed by aggressive, masculine heterosexuality either.

In fact, Dan uses heterosexuality and his "extreme masculinity" to gain control over her. Upon Dan's arrival in Elizabeth's dream world, he puts "his mouth on her hand" and the "most exquisite sensation passes from him to her" (106). It is "a heightened ecstasy" (106). Although Elizabeth at first thinks, "I ought to find out more about this," she slowly starts to understand that his attention thrusts "her down to the position of one who is being given a supreme gift by one in a station far removed from her" (106). Dan is "satisfied with this arrangement" (106). He says, "'Ah,' as though he had triumphantly acquired Pavlov's dog" (106). And so Dan uses sexuality to gain power over Elizabeth, making her feel indebted to him, desiring, and subordinate.

Dan also links Elizabeth's racial identity to her supposed feminine, heterosexual deficiency. One night, he invites a series of African "girls" (or "Nice-Time girls" [128] as he puts it) into her dream. These women, including "Madame Squelch Squelch," "Miss Sewing-Machine," "Miss Pelican-Beak," "Miss Pink Sugar-Icing," "The Womb," and "Madame Make-Love-on-the-Floor," are eager for Dan's sexual attention. Dan plays a record for Elizabeth, instructing her, "You are supposed to feel jealous. You are inferior as a Coloured. You haven't got what that girl has got" (127). Elizabeth is "not properly African," which in Dan's view makes her insufficient for heterosexual pleasure. Thus, in such passages, heterosexuality is clearly not a site to escape apartheid's racial hierarchies. It is, rather, a place in the novel of the continued exclusions of racism.

Two final scenes are likewise disparaging of heterosexuality. In one of Elizabeth's dreams, Dan travels back along the path of the meteor on which he arrived: "Its journey was flung far out, right to the outmost edge of the universe" (108). In the "heaven" from where he came, he finds "a man and woman ... wrapped in an eternal embrace" (108). This couple is a symbol "of their [own] love" (108). Head describes this love in reproachful terms: "There was nothing else, no people, not sharing. It was shut-in and exclusive" (108). That they are a symbol of their own love only highlights this solipsism. Alongside the couple stand "two grape-trees with the roots entwined" (108). These trees connect to heterosexual love both to belonging in place and to kinship, in the form of roots coming together. The couple's love is "shut-in and exclusive" (108), productive, one might imagine, of the forms of belonging that exclude Elizabeth. Thus, when Tom, a white, American Peace Corps volunteer suggests that Elizabeth find "a husband" (192), she retorts, "It's not a part of my calculations" (192). Heterosexuality, especially in its couple form, reproduces relations of kin and modes of belonging that exclude Elizabeth as a Coloured woman.

In short, while the novel is disapproving of homosexuality, it does not espouse heterosexuality either. It is deeply suspicious of heterosexuality and ultimately rejects it. It frames both heterosexuality and homosexuality as entangled with forms of belonging and exclusion—forms of belonging both in place and in racialized networks of kin—that ultimately lead to the rejection of Elizabeth.

Sensation and the Land

However, while the novel rejects sexuality, it does not turn away from the body and its pleasures altogether. It would therefore be mistaken to conclude, with Eleni Coundouriotis, that Head exemplifies the "argument that missionary education inculcated Victorian values in colonial subjects to such an extent that much African writing displays a Victorian sensibility."[29] Likewise, we would miss important features of the text were we to settle on the view that Head responds to a pernicious form of racism that frames black sexuality as excessive and rampant by rejecting embodied pleasure.[30] Head is not suggesting that it is only with the "suppression of the erotic" that "women" can "be truly strong."[31] Instead, sensuality—something akin to Lorde's erotic—is central to the novel's resolution.

It is striking how scholarship on the novel has paid little attention to the sensations that the text valorizes. Munro's reading, for instance, focuses on desires between women that do not easily map onto the category "lesbian," but she still highlights interhuman relations. Talahite analyzes the scene of the garden, arguing that the garden provides a mode of communal belonging apart from "cultural or ethnic modes of identification."[32] Yet she does not highlight the embodied feelings that are integral to the practice of gardening. *A Question of Power*, I argue, forges a "gesture of belonging" through sensations that connect the self both to the land and to humans in general. These sensations are not concerned with bonding among women. They exceed any discourse on "female love." And they do not involve relations of desire between particular people; they are not relations that are satisfied in the form of a couple. Rather, they are whole-bodied, immersive relations that connect the self to that which is around it. They are sensual, not sexual.

I realize that my framing of this argument posits an unnecessary distinction between the "sexual" and the "sensual." Clearly, "sexual" relations include "sensuality"—even in *A Question of Power*. For instance, Elizabeth does experience sensual pleasure when Dan touches her sexually (106). Likewise, the novel does use language that is related to sexuality to describe the sensual relations through which it finds resolution: "embrace" (206) and "kiss" (202). However, while there is overlap between the sexual and the sensual, the novel reaches toward some distinctions. In the text, the sexual, unlike what I am terming "the sensual," highlights genital relations, and as such, the sexual could be understood as entangled in a particular erotic organization of the body that favors some zone as potentially productive of pleasure. There is, indeed, a lot of language in the novel that clearly references vaginas and penises. In addition, the novel relates the sexual to a form of selfhood where the "I" stands in relation to the other in a position of desiring or wanting. This "I" turns in on itself: it seeks pleasure through contact with the objects it desires. It reaches out to the world only to turn back onto the self in pleasure. In contrast, the sensual relations upheld in the novel do not produce interiorizing worlds. Rather, the self expands or even dissolves into an exteriority through touch. It does not treat the world as that through which it can satisfy itself, but rather it expands into the world.

The distinction that I am drawing in the novel between the "sexual" and the "sensual" overlaps in some ways with the distinction Audre Lorde makes between "the erotic" and "the pornographic," though not perfectly. For Lorde, the pornographic "emphasizes sensation without feeling."[33] It is a "plasticized sensation."[34] The erotic, in contrast, is "an internal sense of satisfaction."[35] It is an internal sense that provides direction, brings joy, connects us to others, and gives us a sense of "fullness and completion."[36] It is a "life-force."[37] While the erotic certainly includes sexuality, it need not be "relegated to the bedroom alone."[38] Rather, erotic pleasure can emerge "dancing, building a bookcase, writing a poem, examining an idea."[39]

The category of the sexual in *A Question of Power* could be linked to Lorde's "pornographic," and indeed, as Munro and Margaret Tucker argue, Elizabeth's nightmares resemble a filmic world where women appear as "'nice-time girls' available for male viewing."[40] Here, Elizabeth becomes a passive viewer, a witness, and her dreams resemble a pornographic theater. In contrast, the sensual overlaps with Lorde's "erotic" in that it references a feeling of pleasure beyond, though also including sexual pleasure. But Head's vision departs from Lorde's in that the sensual pleasures the novel depicts are less about an internal sense of direction and particular activities one undertakes in the world. The self, in other words, that appears in Head's novel is different to Lorde's. The sensual relations Head explores consist in an expansion of the self where the self becomes long or lays itself down to belong.

These sensory experiences appear in several important passages of the text, scenes that provide Elizabeth with a sense of relief from her violent, painful dreams. The novel is divided into two parts, each named for one of the male figures who haunts Elizabeth: Sello and Dan. The first section ends with Elizabeth awaking after a particularly horrific night where Sello revealed a hole into which an "endless procession of dead bodies" was "pitched in" (97). As Elizabeth contemplates this dream of mass burial, dawn arises, and with it, the conclusion of the section: "The soft shifts and changes of light stirred with a slow wonder over the vast expanse of the African sky. A small bird in a tree outside awoke and trilled loudly. The soft, cool air, so fresh and full of the perfume of the bush, swirled around her face and form as she stood watching the sun thrust one powerful, majestic, golden arm above the horizon" (100). Sensing this, Elizabeth, whispers, "softly," "'May I never contribute to creating dead worlds, only new world'" (100). This scene of the rising dawn is a scene of life, a familiar trope of rebirth that comes with the beginning of the new day. It offers Elizabeth a place apart from the horrors of her nightmares, which enact one of the worst consequences of power relations between humans: mass killing. In other words, the scene is not simply about a form of rebirth; it also conjures a vast place apart from the "death worlds" of apartheid.[41]

The passage repeats the word *soft* several times. There are the "soft shifts . . . of light" as well as "the soft, cool air." Elizabeth herself speaks, "softly" (100). Head even highlights this adverb by using a comma to separate it from the verb it qualifies. She writes: "'Oh God,' she said, softly. 'May I never contribute to creating dead worlds, only new worlds'" (100). In all this softness, a sensuousness appears. The natural scene is not something to contemplate from afar. Instead, it is something to touch and be touched by, something to be immersed in and to contribute to, softly in speech.

Softness emerges when the boundaries between two entities come into contact gently. Rather than a sense of two absolutes pushing against one another, scratching, grazing each other, in softness the space of contact is a space of blending or lying together—in other words, of being long together, of belonging. The association between softness and belonging is especially clear in Head's use of the word *soft* to describe the shifts of light. These shifts are "soft" in that only small gradations of light exist between them; they run together and have no clear distinct identity. But such an understanding of softness is also present when Elizabeth speaks "softly." She joins into the space she senses, projecting herself into the scene by making a sound that reverberates through it. But she does not take over the space, either. She speaks softly. This is neither a form of appropriation nor self-abnegation. It is, instead, a living with, a joining, a being-long with. "Belonging" here is not to be longing, as in wanting something. Rather it is touching alongside, being long. This form of belonging is not forged through the sexual or through kinship. It is not about enclosing and possessing so much as extending and touching.

For the reader of the novel, whom Jacqueline Rose claims cannot help but feel as though she is "going a little bit mad" while reading the text, this scene is a welcomed site of respite.[42] *A Question of Power* is a philosophical novel in that it explores relations between good and evil, lucidity and irrationality, and life and death within the context of apartheid racism. Head could have chosen to write this exploration in the form of an essay or treatise as opposed to a novel, but the form of fiction does important work in itself. By encountering Elizabeth's ruminations on these topics in the context of her own (fictional) life, the reader is able not simply to consider but also to partially experience how these thoughts feel. The pain caused by Elizabeth's visions comes to be shared with the reader. The novel is hard to read given its violent imagery and its long, descriptive passages where Elizabeth battles with Sello, Dan, and Medusa in debates and physical altercations that sometimes make sense and sometimes are hard to follow. The reader becomes, at times, lost in these pages—just like Elizabeth herself. In this context, when one reaches a passage of clarity, a description of the external, physical world, one cannot but feel some relief. The reader might not actually sense the softness of the pastoral scene, but she is incited to feel something akin to it: a world out there, apart from the tortured mind, a world in which one might rest.

A second scene figures the pastoral quite similarly: it offers particular sensations that give rise to a feeling of repose. After the first time she is hospitalized, Elizabeth goes to the Motabeng Secondary School to meet Eugene, the Afrikaner director of the school. Motabeng Secondary School is situated at the edge of the bush, "a wild, expansive landscape dotted with wind-bent, umbrella shaped thorn trees" (55). Before Elizabeth enters the school, she looks "down a long brown road" (55). She wants to hold onto this image and this moment. She has not yet had "enough of her own peace" (55). As she stands there, a bird sings "in a tree nearby; a long, deep trilling melody, heightened to an intense sweetness by the silence" (56). "A grey-brown wild rabbit" scampers "across the road," while "some insects" commune "in plaintive, brooding soliloquies with their own selves" (56). Elizabeth thinks that someday she will live in this place—and indeed, this place becomes the site of her first home three months later. The birds, rabbit, and insects give her a sense of a possible home. In other words, she can belong in the space with them; she can live there among them. Their presence—as opposed to the presence of other humans, this place—as opposed to the urban space in which she lived in South Africa, gives her a sense that she could belong. The feeling of standing by the road, listening to the insects, bird, and rabbit, produces in her a sense of belonging. These sounds index the existence of multiple species inhabiting a place together, with no reference to the nation-state. The novel does not consider what would happen if a bird ate an insect. Rather, this is a scene of peaceful coexistence.

In fact, *A Question of Power* posits a form of universal love that extends beyond the human to include animals, plants, and insects. Particular sensations appear here, too. Whereas doctors, nurses, and friends instruct Elizabeth to forget Sello, the novel finds resolution as she engages with him. In a key concluding dialogue, Sello apologizes "for all that's happened" (198). He claims that his friendship with Elizabeth will never end. Elizabeth asks if he would like to be her brother, and he agrees. She replies, "I'll look around for suitable parents" (201). Elizabeth wants to develop kinship with Sello. This is a queer form of kin, where children choose parents, and brothers and sisters decide to be related. In this model, parents do not grant the identity of the child, but rather children find parents with whom they can identify. This is also a form of kin where children are not the primary objects of love. Elizabeth goes on to explain that she wants parents who love "birds, insects, vegetable gardens and people" (201). She wants parents, then, whose love transcends the human, reaching out toward birds, insects, and vegetables; she wants parents whose love transgresses boundaries.

Such an expansive form of love is one that Elizabeth and Sello share. Thinking about her relation with Sello, Elizabeth considers how together, they have "been lovers of mankind" (202). Head writes, "To rediscover that love was like suddenly being transported to a super-state of life. It was the point at which all personal love had died in them. It was the point at which there were no private hungers to be kissed, loved, adored. And yet there was the feeling of being kissed by everything; by the air, the soft flow of life, people's smiles and friendships" (202). This love is a love in general. It does not fulfill a "private hunger" for one person in particular. It is not about one's own particular desires. It is generalized, but not disembodied. Elizabeth develops a "feeling of being kissed by everything" (202). This "vast and universal love" includes, in Elizabeth and Head's vision, "all mankind" (202). And while many "things could be said about it ... the most important" is that it equalizes "all things and all men" (202). The love endorsed at the end of the novel, one encapsulated by the feeling of being kissed by everything, does not organize itself around categories—although Head does use the word *men* to describe it. Head writes that it "equalizes" things and men, which is to say both that it does not posit a racial hierarchy and that it does not posit a hierarchy between entities in the world more generally. But Head does not fall into an easy form of posthumanism either, one that fails to recognize the violence involved in dehumanization.[43] Head writes of how Africans in South Africa "were the living victims of the greed inspired by I and mine and to hell with you, dog" (134). This "dog" returns throughout. Dan, for instance, torments Elizabeth, calling her a "dog" (47). The "record" he plays, with its refrain, "Dog, filth, the Africans will eat you to death" (47) is dependent on a double form of dehumanization, one that frames Elizabeth as a dog but then also posits "the Africans" as animal-like, eating her to death. While aware of how transgressing the borders between the human and the nonhuman can be dehumanizing and linked to racism, at the same time, the novel imagines a form of love that goes beyond the human. And with this love comes the sensation of the more-than-human world. The novel posits a feeling of being kissed by everything. This feeling consists in a sense of belonging forged in a somatic connection between humans and place, a relation that Head understands as standing apart from racialized, heterosexual relations of kin. It is a feeling of boundaries falling away to highlight coexistence, rather than differentiation.

This sense of belonging is especially clear in the final section of the novel. *A Question of Power* ends with Elizabeth falling asleep. While in the past Elizabeth's sleep was tortuous, filled with Sello, Medusa, and Dan's violence, this time Elizabeth embraces "the solitude of the night with joy" (206). Head repeats the word *embrace* twice in this final section. She writes that Elizabeth "embraced the solitude of the night with joy" and she explains that Elizabeth "had fallen from the very beginning into the warm embrace of the brotherhood of man" (206). Embracing and being embraced, Elizabeth is both held and holding. But she is also falling—both falling into the embrace and falling asleep. She falls. And as she is held and holds, she places "one soft hand over her land" (206). The novel ends, "It was a gesture of belonging" (206).

It is improbable that this gesture is actual. While lying in bed, how is she to place her "soft hand over her land?" Such a vision of "land" is certainly expansive. But where is she placing her hand? And how does the land become hers? Is this a scene of autoeroticism? Her hand is described as "soft," which places it in a potential relation of being touched by another sentient surface since the quality of softness highlights touch. Elizabeth places her hand in a "gesture" (206). She does not "put" her hand "over her land" but she rather "places" it. In other words, she puts her hand in place, and this action is not a simply an act, not simply a doing, but rather an action that means something, a gesture. The gesture is performed as its performer falls asleep.

The moment between sleep and waking, the moment where Elizabeth places "her soft hand over her land" is a moment of possible reprieve from power. To be asleep is to be in a position of vulnerability. Sleep can be understood as a falling away from selfhood, as a letting go of violent sovereign personhood or of the self, figured as an active agent.[44] Falling asleep is not a matter of will. Rather, "there is a moment when sleep 'comes,' [. . .] and I succeed in becoming what I was trying to be."[45] In this reading, the land becomes Elizabeth's not as she "finds herself," not as she becomes sovereign, but rather when sleep comes to her, as her hand feels soft, and as she herself embraces and is embraced.

Thus, alongside its aversion toward sexuality, *A Question of Power* upholds a second form of sensual relation that has largely been neglected in scholarship on the novel. *A Question of Power* forges a sense of belonging not through traditional notions of kinship as these intersect with race and sexuality, not through human-human relations, but rather through the fine-tuning of particular sensations: the touch of wind, the sense of softness and letting go in sleep, the "feeling of being kissed by everything" (202). Embodied sensations of the more-than-human world are valued throughout the text.

We can, however, remain skeptical. What happens to racial belonging in these sensations? Most critically, what happens to those forms of racial belonging fostered for the purposes of antiracism or decolonization? The idea of "moving beyond race" has been much criticized, especially in the United States, where "racial blindness" has been used as an argument to dismiss movements that address structural racism, such as affirmative action.[46] In effect, the novel includes a scene where Elizabeth dismisses black power: "I've got my concentration elsewhere," Elizabeth says. "It's on mankind in general, and black people fit in there, not as special freaks and oddities outside the scheme of things, with labels like Black Power or any other rubbish of that kind" (133). Elizabeth rejects American-based identity politics. The authorial voice of the novel seems to agree with its protagonist because it offers no alternative.

In addition, we can also remain skeptical of Head's treatment of gender. This love equalizes all "men." Is Elizabeth included here? Can Elizabeth only be included to the extent that she is "masculine," as Head describes Elizabeth's relationship with Sello (24)? Head never considered herself a "feminist," and rejected the label: "I do not have to be feminist," she wrote, "The world of the intellect is impersonal, sexless."[47] Within the field of women's and gender studies, as well as more broadly in the humanities, especially as practiced in the United States and Canada, we have become skeptical of universalisms, skeptical of any attempt to posit a common humanity beyond gender and race. Such universals have been understood as false, complicit with the move to reject antiracist and feminist organizing, thought, and creation.

Head, however, is not writing from the position of rejecting concerns having to do with racism and gender inequality. Her book directly addresses gendered and racialized forms of inequality and violence. Because of this, rather than dismissing Head for false universalism and a quick rejection of identity politics, it is more powerful to read her text in line with how Alexander Weheliye has recently articulated the project of black studies. Weheliye recognizes how black people remain and ought to remain at the center of the project of black studies. And yet, he contends that the object of analysis for the field ought not to be delimited to blackness. Rather, Weheliye asks us to understand black studies as a disciplinary site that re-creates and reimagines new genres of the human. Weheliye draws on Sylvia Wynter to make this argument. "Wynter," he writes, "disentangles Man from the human in order to use the space of subjects placed beyond the grasp of this domain [of human as Man] as a vital point from which to invent hitherto unavailable genres of the human."[48] He remarks how "Wynter is interested in human trouble rather than 'merely' woman-of-color trouble, even while she deploys the liminal perspective of women of color to imagine humanity otherwise."[49] Weheliye's reading departs from common interpretation of women of color scholarship. Skeptical of antihumanism as it developed in late twentieth-century French thought, he considers how Wynter posits a form of universalism from a different location.

Drawing on Weheliye, we might read Head similarly. *A Question of Power* asks the question: how might we reimagine and assert selfhood and belonging without reproducing structures of inequality? Head's response is by reimagining the human self. The self that emerges in the text is not an object of knowledge. It does not have sovereignty over the more-than-human world. It does not find belonging through appropriation or through exclusion. Rather, this self senses the more-than-human world. The novel suggests that it is through the recognition of this common sensory responsiveness that we can belong alongside one another, together. We might say that Head replaces the body as something to be seen and sorted within categories of race and gender with the body as a site through which we sense.

However, and this is critical, the sensations Head is interested in are not unlocated. While it is tempting to say that the refinement of particular sensations offers new forms of selfhood as well as a common model of the human, this form of commonality does not emerge anywhere. Head locates her novel in Botswana, and not in South Africa. One could imagine the feeling of being kissed by everything in Johannesburg, but this sense would not have the same meaning there.

Like her character Elizabeth, Head left South Africa when many South African authors fled, exiled by apartheid. Unlike these other authors, however, Head does not set the majority of her prose in South Africa, but rather in her contemporary location: Botswana.[50] Her writing is grounded in the place where she is. Head understood this place, Botswana, and the village of Serowe, the town where she settled, as a land that had "largely escaped the ravishments of colonialism."[51] She saw "Botswana as a place of imaginative possibility, a country in which she could 'look.'"[52] Head sets *A Question of Power* in Motabeng, an invented place that is nonetheless located in geography: "It was a village remotely inland, perched on the edge of the Kalahari desert. Seemingly, the only reason for people's settlement there was a good supply of underground water" (19). The place is rural, which, in contrast to the urban, more obviously features more-than-human lives and forces. But what is important here is that the village has no particular interest to those seeking to extract natural resources from it in order to gain profit. At the time Head wrote *A Question of Power*, she thought that Botswana's "hostile landscape offered colonists neither gold nor diamonds."[53] In this way, Head framed the land itself as a form of resistance to colonization, and the novel upholds the sensory connections that Elizabeth develops to this land in particular.

A Question of Power does not explicitly reference Seretse Khama and Ruth Williams's marriage, but it too seems relevant to the novel's plot. Head considered Khama a hero.[54] In 1948, Khama, heir to the Ngwato chieftaincy, one of the Tswana political units, and Williams, a British white woman, married in England, while Khama was reading law in London. Responding to the recent election of the National Party in South Africa, the British government banned Khama from the Bechuanaland Protectorate for six years. In 1956, Khama returned as head of the Botswana Democratic Party to become Prime Minister during the phase of Responsible Self-Government, and then the first President following independence. Botswanan independence was spearheaded by a man whose mixed-raced children would belong in the territory. This history could function as a background to Elizabeth's finding belonging in the country, but the novel does not directly reference this history, perhaps because of its entanglement with the life of the nation. Instead, the text separates its treatment of land from the question of independence even though, for Head, Botswana, in comparison to South Africa, provided an important feeling of respite.

This analysis of the place of Botswana in *A Question of Power* suggests that sensation alone cannot circumvent the forms of exclusion that constitute apartheid. It cannot undo histories of expropriation and deprivation. Thus, while the novel offers the sensory as key to developing a feeling of belonging, a feeling that is not exclusionary and that is common, this sensation depends on a prior access to spatiality. In the context of South Africa apartheid, Head implicitly contends, this sensation was not possible.

Sovereignty of the Senses

Head models a form of belonging in space that is neither possessive nor self-denying. Her work can be understood in line with a central question that reappears in postcolonial, critical race, feminist, and queer theory: how we can imagine modes of selfhood and belonging that do not reproduce structures of inequality? While it is understandable given colonialism's history of dispossession that appropriation and the assertion of the nation-state provide a model for decolonization, at the same time, this model is in danger of reasserting exclusions and inequalities itself.⁵⁵ The text points toward a mode of occupying space that does not take possession or exclude, but that nonetheless finds a sense of belonging. The land might become Elizabeth's when Sello, Dan, and Medusa no longer occupy her, but her own form of occupation, ultimately, does not take, does not mark as one's own. Instead, it consists in a particular form of appropriation that does not mark the world with signs of the self, but rather falls into it, touching and being touched by it. Elizabeth belongs when she senses that she is being kissed by everything surrounding her. Using Ann Cvetkovich's language, Elizabeth develops "radical self-possession" or "a sovereignty of the sensory of embodied self" that takes the form of "emotional, somatic, or sensory connections to place rather than nationalist or essentialist claims."⁵⁶ Yet this sense is not enough: the novel ultimately shows that sensation itself cannot forge this radical self-possession. Instead, sensation emerges in particular places and spaces. The power relations involved in the production of these spaces shapes the sensory possibilities within them.

In short, *A Question of Power* does not negate all passion in women. It is not against bodily sensations. It explores sensations that we might term *queer*, sensations not linked to the couple, to heterosexuality or to homosexuality, but sensations that develop forms of belonging apart from apartheid's regulation of race, space, and kin. And while we might remain skeptical of both Elizabeth's and Head's desire to transcend gender and race, the novel's analysis challenges us to think about the place of sensation in imagining new forms of belonging, suggesting that sensation itself is not enough for the production of something new: the appropriation of land and the striation of space remain formative.

four   Psychic Territory, Appropriation, and "Geopower"

Rereading Fanon, Foucault, and Butler

"It is not the soil that is occupied," Frantz Fanon concludes in his discussion of the role of women in the Algerian Revolution. "It is not the ports or the airdromes. French colonialism has settled itself in the very center of the Algerian individual."[1] Fanon's assertion is overstated to make its point—the soil, he argues elsewhere, is occupied.[2] But this statement develops a key theme in Fanon's writing: spatial occupation takes psychic form. Through violence and law, engineering, architecture, surveying, geology, agriculture, and planning, colonial power transforms and appropriates the surface of the earth. This transformation occupies not only the land, however, but also the psyches of the colonized. Fanon, by contributing to antiracist, materialist, psychoanalytic, and phenomenological traditions, thus exposes the psychic life of occupation.

Building on the previous chapter's conclusion about the appropriation of land, this chapter investigates the traffic between territorial and psychic occupation. I consider the relation between psychic life and the material transformation and appropriation of the earth; I question how one's material inhabitation of space shapes one's sense of self; and I probe the relationship between exteriority and interiority, conceptualizing this exterior not simply as the place of social and cultural norms that take discursive form, but also as the locus of more-than-human forces as well as legal, political, and economic relations that shape space and place. I turn to Fanon's writing for this study because Fanon was keenly attuned to relationships between place and the embodied self, territory, and the psyche. He traces these relationships in part by building on drawing on existential phenomenology.

For Fanon, appropriation is at the heart of psychic life. In addition, Fanon shows how the psychic life of territory overlaps directly with the psychic life of

65

race and racism. For instance, Fanon explains how settler colonialism in Algeria striated space to create racialized zones of inhabitation. It also granted residents different levels of access to appropriation based on their racial categorization. As a result, in Fanon's writing, it is very clear that the psychic life of territory is part of the psychic life of race. Fanon thus contributes to psychoanalytic thought not simply by bringing a discussion of race and racism to the field (as is widely acknowledged), but also by bringing a materialist perspective to the psyche, one that considers space, place, land, and appropriation in part through phenomenological inquiry.

Such an approach is uncommon in psychoanalytic discourse, which is not to say that spatial arguments never appear in the field. For instance, in *Studies on Hysteria*, Freud contends that the unconscious is "organised in strata." He uses metaphors such as "anterooms" and "frontiers" to imagine the borders between the unconscious, conscious, and preconscious.[3] In turn, Jacques Lacan's mirror stage bears important spatial significance: he writes of the "lure of spatial identification" and of the way the "*I* is symbolized in dreams by a fortress, or a stadium."[4] And finally Donald Winnicott stresses the place for analysis: "work was to be done in a room, not a passage, a room that was quiet and not liable to sudden unpredictable sounds, yet not dead quiet and not free from ordinary house noises."[5] Notwithstanding this attention to space, psychoanalysis rarely attends to the more-than-human world, and the space more closely tied to psychoanalysis is the bourgeois, Western European home, the site of domesticity.[6] This is the place of the Oedipus complex. And if the more-than-human appears, its force is often understood as "mere unconscious displacements of the inner dialogue with ... parents."[7] Fanon's writing does not partake in this trend. In his work, the material world has psychic effects of its own, even if this world is inseparable from the interhuman power relations that shape it.

This chapter begins with a brief detour, making the case for the existence of geopower, the force relations that transform the surface of the earth. I then make two arguments: first, I show how Fanon posits the existence of a form of vitality whose expression requires access to space and to land. When this space is not available, the psyche, Fanon contends, retracts, and is reformed into musculature. And second, I explain how Fanon develops a territorial understanding of subjectivity wherein the subject emerges as it partakes in geopower, giving shape to the earth and partaking in the process of appropriation. In the final section of the chapter, I consider whether this is a model of subjectivity that we might wish to adopt, and whether we can imagine forms of life without appropriation. Ultimately, I argue that human relations to the earth, to appropriation, land and space, are central to subjectivity and the psyche. Fanon's work makes this clear.

Geopower: The Force Relations that Transform the Surface of the Earth

I begin this analysis with a brief foray into Butler's *The Psychic Life of Power*, considered alongside Fanon and Michel Foucault to show how Fanon's writing highlights a relevant form of power relation that Foucault's work merely points toward, geopower. This recognition raises the problem of how then to rethink subjectivity, subject formation, and even the psyche while acknowledging the existence of this form of power.

A central part of Butler's project is to fill in what she sees as a significant gap in Foucault's writing. Foucault provides an account of the disciplinary production of the subject. Yet his powerful project, as Butler notes, leaves the "entire domain of the psyche . . . largely unremarked."[8] We might then, following Butler, explore the psychic life of power. But what if, rather than starting with Butler's and Foucault's understanding of power, we push Foucault to his limits, taking his argument about power to its radical conclusion? According to Foucault, power relations are constituted by the encounter of forces: when one force meets another, when one force resists another, a power relation is formed. Implicitly, this suggests that power does not only involve interhuman relations, yet Foucault's writing does not explicitly address this point. Karen Barad argues that Foucault and Butler, though at times critical of humanism and concerned with the force relations through which bodies are materialized, fail to consider the body's materiality, including its anatomy and physiology as well as other material, nonhuman forces. Barad writes, "Crucial to understanding the workings of power is an understanding of the nature of power in the fullness of its materiality. To restrict power productivity to the limited domain of the social, for example, or to figure matter as merely an end product rather than an active factor in further materializations is to cheat matter out of the fullness of its capacity."[9] In Barad's argument, "power" involves all material forces—forces traditionally understood as social, cultural, and natural. If we understand power broadly in these terms, how might we then revisit its psychic life?[10]

Fanon's work helps to address this question because, unlike Foucault, Fanon highlights the force relations that give shape to the surface of the earth. When Foucault analyzes the spatiality of power relations, he often subsumes the manipulation of space under another form of power whose target is not the earth itself. For example, in *Discipline and Punish*, Foucault's analysis of space, or more specifically of architecture, traces a movement from sovereign power to disciplinary power. Foucault famously uses Jeremy Bentham's design for the panopticon, an ideal prison, to encapsulate disciplinary power. This architecture inculcates a feeling among prisoners that a singular gaze constantly surveys them. Inmates then internalize this gaze, regulating their own conduct accordingly. With this example,

Foucault argues that a different form of punishment, and hence a new form of power, disciplinary power, emerged in eighteenth-century Europe. Whereas illegalities were once punished in a spectacle that made visible the strength of the sovereign, in this case prisoners are made visible, and watched in minute detail. A self-regulating, self-surveying population is formed. This regulation constitutes the necessary underside to liberty and freedom.[11]

However, Foucault is not interested in the transformation of the earth, the actual construction of the panopticon, the displacement of the matter that could be used to build it. He does not ask what was in the location of the panopticon before it might have been built. He does not write about the appropriation of the place where the panopticon can be constructed or about the physical geography that might make it possible to build the panopticon there. It is true that Bentham's panopticon was but a plan, yet Foucault's book includes pictures of actual prisons, towers, and halls that were built in line with Bentham's design. The power relations Foucault focuses on begin, however, after the panopticon is constructed. They do not involve its construction; they do not involve the appropriation of the place where it is built.

Fanon's approach is different. The practice of physically transforming the earth and appropriating land are central to his writing. His work sheds light on a form of power relation that is not explicit in Foucault's writing: geopower, the force relations that transform the surface of the earth. Geopower physically transforms the earth through techniques such as urban planning, architecture, engineering, agriculture, and surveying—but also through digging, logging, and marking territory. Whereas biopower makes the population it seeks to manage visible, and sovereign power makes the sovereign visible, geopower brings attention to the earth. But it does not necessarily make the earth visible. To prioritize vision would misleadingly develop an understanding of geopower around humans' transformation of the earth. Instead, geopower develops knowledge of the earth, but also through scent, touch, sound, and sight. The analysis of geopower shows that power relations are not only operative between humans. Geopower therefore puts pressure on Foucauldian understandings of power themselves.

Geopower is central to Fanon's description of colonization and decolonization. Colonization, as Fanon describes it, involves the physical transformation of the land. It involves "cutting railroads through the bush, draining swamps."[12] This manipulation of the earth fosters the life of the colonizers, not the colonized. Decolonization, in Fanon's vision, reappropriates land and transforms it. Fanon explains that the new nation must conduct a "reliable survey" in order to ascertain the best way the land could be put to use.[13] In addition, he insists that there is work to be done: "[T]here are houses to be built, schools to be opened, roads to be laid out, slums to be torn down, cities to be made to spring from the earth."[14] The earth does not figure tradition, stasis, or purity in his work. It is, rather, that which is transformed both in the process of colonization and decolonization.

It is important to recognize that these relations that Fanon indexes certainly overlap with sovereign power according to Foucault's formulation, but they are somewhat different in that they do not only involve questions of the law and violence. In other words, although the question of who, legally, owns land is important, the actual labor performed in physically transforming the earth remains key in Fanon's writing as well. To be clear, Foucault's discussion of the panopticon also references the built environment, but it is not the construction of the panopticon that interests him; it is not the appropriation of the place where the panopticon comes to be built, either. It is, rather, how, once built, the architecture affects those interned.

I purposefully use the term *geopower* as opposed to *geopolitics*. By doing so, I am following Foucault who, through his analysis of power puts pressure on traditional understandings of "politics," opening the field of political discussion to the microrelations between bodies, discourses, and architectures. Foucault's project of expanding the political overlaps with the feminist insistence that the personal is political, and this overlap is certainly one reason feminist scholars have drawn so much on his writing. *Geopolitics* often refers to the relations between nation-states. It consists in politics at a global scale. By *geopower*, however, I mean something quite different: the force relations involved in the physical transformation of the earth, especially its surface. These force relations churn soil, build towers, damn rivers, dig burrows, erode dunes, and blast rock.

Acknowledging this gap in Foucault's writing, a series of questions then emerge. Foucault argues that "the real, corporal disciplines constituted the foundation of the formal, juridical liberties."[15] His *Discipline and Punish* might be read as a radicalization of Marx in that he brings attention to the disciplining of the body required in the production of the worker, and therefore to a series of power relations that are not strictly economic. Yet what is the place of appropriation in the relation he draws between discipline and "liberty"? The training of the body that concerns Foucault is dependent on a prior appropriation and physical transformation of the earth. What is the relation between the disciplinary subject and this appropriation or physical transformation? What form of subject is produced through appropriation? Bringing these questions back to Butler's *The Psychic Life of Power*: what is the psychic life of geopower? And how does taking geopower into account transform modes of understanding the psyche?

From *Black Skin, White Masks* to *The Wretched of the Earth*

Fanon's oeuvre can help to address these questions. His early writing, notably *Black Skin, White Masks*, treats psychic life in relation to cultural forms: texts, films, and images. His later work departs from this approach, not, however, to displace his attention to psychoanalysis and psychic life, as Henry Louis Gates has argued, but rather to develop these in a more materialist fashion.[16] It is here that we can begin to consider how territory and appropriation shape the psyche and subject formation.

Fanon's initial revisiting of psychoanalysis comes in *Black Skin, White Masks*. The text examines the experience of growing up and being educated in the Antilles as a French, colonial subject and then migrating to France (an experience that mirrored Fanon's own life). Through this exposition, Fanon reworks psychoanalysis both for Antillean men and white men and white women. Fanon's description of the effects of colonial subjugation does not consider the place of the Antillean woman and girl; indeed, he writes, "I know nothing about her."[17] Fanon argues that, into contrast to the white child, "a normal Negro child, having grown up within a normal family, will become abnormal on the slightest contact with the white world."[18] The Antillean boy comes in contact with the white world through film and books, magazines and radio. Exposed to this media, the boy identifies with its white heroes. He places blackness onto the Senegalese.[19] When he arrives in France, however, the Antillean man is no longer able to identify in the same way. He is viewed by white men and women as the already vilified Negro. Since this racial drama is played out in the open, the man has no time to "make it [the drama] unconscious."[20] Neurosis, in this model, does not follow from family relations that are especially formative during infancy and that, through a child's development, become unconscious. The racial drama is different: it is not located during infancy, but rather repeated in the everyday. As a result, Fanon contends that for the Antillean man, there is no Oedipal complex. Rather, Fanon writes, "[E]very neurosis, every abnormal manifestation, every affective erethism in an Antillean is the product of his cultural situation."[21]

Throughout this discussion, Fanon presents colonialism's psychic life as taking shape through ideological means: "[T]here is a constellation of postulates, a series of propositions that slowly and subtly—with the help of books, newspapers, schools and their texts, advertisements, films, radio—work their way into one's mind and shape one's view of the world of the group to which one belongs."[22] In this framework, the traffic between territorial and psychic occupation seems to take place primarily through the colonial occupation not of the physical earth, land, space or territory, but rather of culture. Psychic life is construed in relation to culture. Psychic occupation develops *alongside* the colonial appropriation and transformation of land. The implication is that the appropriation of land does not itself affect psychic life.

The same is true in Fanon's treatment of white psyches in *Black Skin, White Masks*. Fanon studies Negrophobia, arguing that this fear emerges with the fear of the biological and the loss of sexual potency that, Fanon claims, necessarily accompanies intellectual gain.[23] The white man projects his own sexual desires "onto the Negro," behaving "'as if' the Negro really had them."[24] He develops a conscious white guilt that is symptomatic of his unconscious aggression toward the Negro, an aggression mired with desire, intimidation, and awe of the Negro-figured-as-phallus. In turn, the Negrophobic woman fears and yet also desires the black man. More precisely, fear is the conscious form taken by the prohibited, unconscious desire. Fanon insist that this unconscious is not genetic or congenital. Rather, there exists a collective unconscious that is "purely and simply the sum of prejudices, myths, collective attitudes of a given group."[25] In short, in Fanon's early writing, the psychic life of Negrophobia is symptomatic of cultural forms: prejudices, myths, and attitudes. It is superstructural, ideological, and psychic. The appropriation and transformation of land do not seem particularly relevant to Fanon's analysis of this unconscious, either.

However, as Fanon moves from France to Algeria, from *Black Skin, White Masks* to *The Wretched of the Earth*, his writing develops a more materialist approach to the psyche and to phenomenology. Reading his work suggests that racial logics concern not simply relations between people within a nation but also differential relations to land, territory, and appropriation. "Race" involves biopower, geopower, and sovereignty.[26]

In a key passage from *The Wretched of the Earth* Fanon writes, "in the colonial world ... the psyche retracts, is obliterated, and finds an outlet through muscular spasms."[27] It is here that we can start to analyze the traffic between territorial and psychic occupation in Fanon's work. Fanon describes a "world divided in two": the indigenous colonized sector that is cramped, "famished, ... hungry for bread, meat, shoes, cola, and light";[28] and the white colonist's sector, "where the streets are clean and smooth" and the "belly is permanently full of good things."[29] The border between these sectors is patrolled by "barracks and the police station."[30] The colonized are "contained by rifle butts and napalm."[31] Violence frames the colonial subject. He becomes a "man penned in."[32] Learning to "remain in his place," he develops muscular tension. His dreams are filled with "aggressive vitality ... jumping, swimming, running, and climbing."[33] He remains permanently tense, on guard, ready "to do the right thing."[34] At first, this muscular tension is released in dancing or in spiritual possession. Sometimes, the tension becomes violence, turned toward the self or other colonized people. But eventually, this tension turns outward, starting the process of decolonization. This muscular tension is the form the psyche takes in its obliteration.

In Fanon's original French, "to obliterate" does not appear in the passive voice, but rather as reflexive: "le psychisme se rétracte, s'oblitère, se décharge dans des démonstrations musculaires."[35] It is not then that the psyche is obliterated by something but rather that it self-destructs. Fanon writes that the colonized psyche obliterates itself. This obliteration is not exactly a disappearance. While obliterated, the psyche takes on a new form. It "finds an outlet" in muscular spasms. In Fanon's model, the behavior of muscles is not symptomatic of psychic repression. Rather, the violent containment and starvation of the body leads to a transformation of the psyche—not a repression of particular drives or desires. The psyche retracts, is obliterated, and finally reformed into muscles and nerves. This model revises Freudian understandings of symptoms, which often focus on the conflict between a desire, wish, or thought and an internalized voice of repression. In this case, a superego does not regulate the id, and a form of double-consciousness does not arise.[36] Rather, the psyche is obliterated as the body is violently contained and the psychic is transformed into musculature.

At first, this psychic obliteration might appear less as a description or exposition of the effects of colonization than as uncannily complicit with colonial discourse. Fanon cites Erich Stern, a German-born, Jewish psychiatrist who published studies that investigated how psychic conflict can create physical ailments. Stern argues that the Algerian Muslim "has no inner life or introspection."[37] Does Fanon's argument here repeat Stern's claim? Fanon's contention appears to flatten colonial subjectivities, framing—even containing—colonized men in the biological. This repeats the "Negro myth" Fanon analyzes in *Black Skin, White Masks*, where "the Negro symbolizes the biological."[38] But Fanon's argument is not that the colonized "lack" a psyche because of an inherent biology or limit. This condition is, instead, the result of the violence and containment of colonization. It is sociogenic. An intriguing passage of *Black Skin, White Masks* can also help in this context. Fanon writes,

> A close study should be divided into two parts:
>
> 1. A psychoanalytic interpretation of the life experience of the black man;
>
> 2. A psychoanalytic interpretation of the Negro myth.
>
> But reality, which is our only recourse, prevents such procedures. The facts are much more complicated.[39]

In this passage, Fanon implies that reality makes it impossible to separate the analysis of a black man's life experience from the Negro myth. The myth has so saturated the man's life experience that it is impossible to get to any experience apart from it. Similarly, in the context of Algeria, the colonized man's psyche, according to Fanon, is flattened into musculature. Fanon makes this argument notwithstanding its overlap with colonial discourse.

Darieck Scott argues that Fanon frames muscular tension as a psychiatric diagnosis and a reservoir of political power, which is to say that it is symptomatic of an embodied psychic response to the violence of colonization, but that it also harbors political potential.[40] Scott reads muscular tension in *The Wretched of the Earth* as both metaphoric ("an umbrella term encompassing all those reactions that are 'like' the flinches of an open wound") and literal.[41] In particular, he focuses on how muscular tension is a response to the lived experience of terror. Terrorized, the psyche retreats while muscles tense, which is to say that the native, to use the language of *The Wretched of the Earth*, responds to terror at the level of the body. This terror is "disorienting," and recognizing this disorientation, Scott links the experience of being a native as described in *The Wretched of the Earth* to the experience of having been blackened in *Black Skin, White Masks* (the chapter "The Lived Experience of the Black," in particular). Under colonial domination, the native (like the black man) is incited to "despise his own skin and abjure his own body."[42] This experience produces a feeling of "double-bodiedness."[43] Fanon writes of a "body which is no longer altogether a body or rather which is doubly a body since it is beside itself with terror."[44] The resultant muscular tension, Scott argues, is "located on the side of that which is unconscious or that which does not rely on the 'I' narratives of an intact ego."[45] However, this muscular tension also trembles with incipient political potential. Flexed muscles quaver toward a future and are a source, in Scott's reading, of black power. For example, muscular tension appears as immobility and manifests itself as a rejection of punctuality. This might produce the belief that the natives are lazy, but in effect, this immobility can function as a form of "sabotage of the colonial machine."[46] Next, Fanon argues that muscular tension is released in dance, and this movement, in Fanon's reading, invokes "the past of conquest and enslavement [...] to make it present, to reenact its defeat and the possibility of its overthrow."[47] Dance mimes the past in order to make a space for a potential future. Finally, muscular tension, Scott argues, functions as a metaphor for the native's atavistic embrace of precolonial culture. Although Fanon ultimately dismisses this return because he understands precolonial culture as "dead," he nonetheless interprets this moment as an incipient recognition of national culture and hence, as a step toward decolonization.[48]

Scott argues that muscular tension "draws its vitality, its existence even, from the anonymous life that, while it could never have meaning or know itself without its social production, illustrates a property or quality that is not limited to blackness itself."[49] Torture and death strip away the ego and reveal an "irreducible *something*," an anonymous existence, to use Merleau-Ponty's phrase, that is indeterminate and a source of freedom.[50] The violence of colonization and the epidermalization of racism brings attention to the body, which, however, is not an inert object but rather a source of freedom, openness, and indeterminacy. Thus, while Fanon generally brings his attention to sociogenic and political arguments as opposed to ontological, essential, or universal ones, Scott argues that Fanon's work also makes at least an implicit ontological argument.

Yet we need to consider why terror takes the form of tense muscles. Why would terror lead to the self-obliteration of the psyche? Even if Fanon uses muscular tension as metaphor, how is it that this metaphor makes sense? To address these questions, I suggest that we read Fanon as more phenomenological than psychoanalytic, which is certainly not to say that he is not making contributions to psychiatry, psychology, and psychoanalysis. As Scott explains, in Merleau-Ponty's writing, human spatiality and human embodiment (which is itself the locus of selfhood) are fundamentally intertwined.

Scott mentions in passing that "the narrow space of the colonial world ... is the concomitant, and also the result and reflection, of that nonintegrated double-body in which the native/black is entombed and which *exists* as the foundation for his life."[51] Ultimately, however, Scott favors a more temporal reading of Fanon, focusing on the relationship between the past, present, and future and the disruption of linear time.

But a spatial reading also leads to important insights. Although it is not his focus, in *The Wretched of the Earth*, Fanon reworks Merleau-Ponty's phenomenology in a colonial context, showing how, for the colonized, the projection of the self through space, the "I can" that Merleau-Ponty assumes of embodied experience is cut off because of the experience of violence, hunger, and occupation. It is not simply that human embodiment and human spatiality are fundamentally linked in both Fanon's and Merleau-Ponty's writing. It is also, as I will show, that Fanon posits the existence of a distributed form of vitality that exists between the lived body and the more-than-human earthly spaces on which life depends. This distributed vitality explains why, when human beings face dispossession (which Fanon explicitly links to hunger), they come to experience a lack of mobility, a form of death-in-life, in a word: muscular tension.

And this argument has psychoanalytic implications, as well. Although Fanon and Foucault imagine psychic life quite differently, a peculiar consensus emerges between them. In Foucault's writing, the disciplinary subject may be imprisoned, but at the same time, the body is trained to be productive. Energy is directed toward transforming the world. There exists a spatiality in which to move—even when the disciplinary society is modeled on the prison. Unlike disciplinary power, which attempts to make the body economically productive and politically docile, colonial power, which is exercised on the bodies of the colonized, works through violence and deprivation. In this context, power takes form on the surface of the body. Power, then, is not primarily internalized, which, at least in Butler's reading, suggests that the distinction between interior and exterior is not formed. No distinction between inside and outside is possible because there is no space: colonial man is "penned in." Or rather: we might say that a distinction between inside and outside emerges, but in this case, the inside does not take the form of an interior voice of consciousness, the unconscious, and preconscious. Instead, this interiority becomes the muscular body itself. In other words, a distinction between self and other emerges, but both come to exist on the same plane of externality.

From this discussion, we can draw several conclusions. First, it is not simply that colonization takes psychic form through ideological means, through the dissemination of "prejudices, myths, collective attitudes."[52] Rather, the colony's physical infrastructure affects psychic life as well. Next, Fanon's understanding of psychic form highlights embodiment. He suggests that there exists a vitality, a force within the body, and that when that force is stifled through violence, containment, dispossession, and deprivation, the psyche obliterates. In other words, the internality of the psyche, or the psyche itself, seems to require a spatiality—a space within which to move—through which one is nourished, and that one can call one's own. When this space is cut off through violence and dispossession, the psyche retracts and is obliterated. And, finally, my reading suggests that the internalization Butler writes about—the internalization of norms that is productive of the distinction between inside and outside—depends on, though does not recognize, a prior inhabitation of spatiality that allows for mobility, appropriation, safety, and nourishment.

Decolonization, Appropriation, and the Psyche

The process of appropriation is key to understanding Fanon's psychic materialism as well as his understanding of life. In a critical, underread passage of *The Wretched of the Earth*, Fanon writes, "for a colonized people, the most essential value, because it is the most meaningful, is first and foremost the land."[53] This value given to land replaces Western values that, Fanon explains, are violently hailed by colonists during decolonization as part of a "rearguard campaign."[54]

The colonized reject these Western values (such as rational discourse and truth). They "thumb their noses at these very values, shower them with insults and vomit them up."[55]

A first approach to this passage could read the valorization of land as a particular moment in the process of decolonization. This reading would draw on Ato Sekyi-Otu's approach to Fanon's text as a "dramatic dialectical narrative."[56] It would insist that, much like Hegel's *Phenomenology of Spirit* describes the development of self-consciousness, in this case, *The Wretched of the Earth* describes the process of decolonization. In Sekyi-Otu's terms, this implies that "rhetorics of the human situation evoked at determinate moments of Fanon's text" do not always "commit him to a conclusive and unambiguous endorsement of such pictures and rhetorics."[57] Thus, when Fanon writes that "for a colonized people, the most essential value [. . .] is land," we could argue that this is not Fanon's own valuation, but rather his description of what the colonized, during the process of decolonization, value. In other words, land is not a universal, ahistorical value for Fanon, but rather valuable in this particular moment.

And yet Fanon does not only describe and critique what is, he also makes a case for what he believes ought to be. While the valuation of land comes at a particular moment in the process of decolonization, Fanon does not leave it there. Fanon links land to life itself through the production of food in the figure of bread. Land, he writes, is the "most essential value," because it "must provide bread and, naturally, dignity."[58] A later passage in *The Wretched of the Earth* elaborates.

> Under a colonial regime, man's relationship with the physical world and history is connected to food. In the context of oppression like that of Algeria, for the colonized, living does not mean embodying a set of values, does not mean integrating oneself into the coherent, constructive development of a world. To live simply means not to die. To exist means staying alive. Every date grown is a victory. Not the result of hard work, but a victory celebrating a triumph over life.[59]

Fruit is not the product of work but rather that which, through its consumption, fosters life. The date is a triumph because it allows for the continued simple fact of staying alive. Dignity is not about "embodying a set of values." It has "nothing to do with 'human' dignity."[60] The colonized, Fanon argues, have "never heard of such an ideal. All he has ever seen on his land is that he can be arrested, beaten, and starved with impunity."[61] The "dignity" of land, then, is the dignity of not being "arrested, beaten and starved with impunity."[62] It is the dignity, we may write, of living, but also of something more: of appropriation.

Fanon's writing partakes in, though it also departs from, a Marxist tradition that gives importance to the appropriation of one's own work. In *The Grundrisse* Marx contends that "all production is appropriation of nature on the part of an individual within and through a specific form of society."[63] To produce something is to "appropriate (create, shape) the products of nature in accord with human needs."[64] In this view, human's physical transformation of the earth (assuming it is in accordance with human needs) consists by definition in a form of appropriation. It involves taking something in the world and transforming it according to one's own purpose. For Marx, this appropriation produces a form of property, but that property need not be private: "History rather shows common property ... to be the more original form."[65] That is, communal appropriation can create communal property. The problem, as Marx explains in the "Economic and Philosophic Manuscripts of 1844," emerges when one labors on that which is not one's own: "the worker puts his life into the object; but now his life no longer belongs to him."[66] This produces alienation and self-estrangement. Workers are robbed of the satisfaction of recognizing themselves in their work.

When Fanon writes about the colonized relation to the physical world through food, he highlights how food is key not because it provides a mode of self-recognition, but simply because it allows for life. The point, in other words, is not that the appropriation of the external world allows for self-development, but rather that consumption fosters the continuation of life itself. And yet in his writing on decolonization, Fanon goes onto espouse a Marxian understanding of work, as well. Appropriation can be collective, and the process of appropriation is central to becoming human—even conscious. For instance, one passage provides an example of building a bridge. He writes,

> If the building of a bridge does not enrich the consciousness of those working on it, then don't build the bridge, and let the citizens continue to swim across the river or use a ferry. The bridge must not be pitchforked or foisted upon the social landscape ... but, on the contrary, must be the product of the citizens' brains and muscles. [...] The bridge in its entirety and in every detail can be integrated, redesigned, and reappropriated. The citizen must appropriate the bridge.[67]

Here, Fanon highlights the work of physically transforming the earth. This work consists in a collective mode of appropriation, one that highlights the "brains and muscles" of those building. Such construction requires and makes use of a particular spatiality within which living bodies move and leave signs of themselves.

The citizens transform the earth so that it refers back to those who have marked it. This transformation in turn supports the lives of those who built the bridge. Fanon has great hope for this process: "then, and only then, is everything possible."[68]

A second passage, likewise, gives value to appropriation. Fanon insists that the new Algerian people emerge through appropriation.

> The Algerian people now know they are the sole proprietor of their country's soil and subsoil. And if some cannot understand the FLN's relentless refusal to tolerate any infringement of this ownership and its fierce determination not to accept any compromise on principles, then everyone should remember that the Algerian people are now adult, responsible and conscious. In short, the Algerian people are proprietors.[69]

This passage quite clearly connects being an "adult, responsible and conscious" to being a proprietor; it recounts Marx's valuation of appropriation as well as his contention that property need not be private. It shows how for Fanon, appropriation and consciousness are linked.

A form of vitalism subtends both Fanon's and Marx's assessment of appropriation and suggests that Fanon, revising Freud, posits an instinct for life that need not be reduced to sexuality. Marx understands man as a "corporeal, living real, sensuous, objective being full of natural vigour."[70] This implies, according to Marx, that man "can only *express* his life in real sensuous objects."[71] These objects are external to him: "the worker can create nothing without *nature*, without the *sensuous external world*."[72] This argument, Marx points out, is an important departure from Hegel's understanding of labor, where self-consciousness *posits* a thing of abstraction that has no real independence. For Marx, the life of human beings depends on an external world in which they are caught up, and partaking in this externality is key to developing "natural vigour."[73]

Similarly, Fanon posits something that resembles this "natural vigor." As Matthieu Renault argues, Fanon describes the life of the colonized as a form of death in life, where death comes to penetrate everything that is living.[74] Take, for instance, Fanon's piece, "The 'North African Syndrome,'" which examines how North African immigrants to France encountered the medical profession. Fanon explains how many immigrants found themselves in doctors' offices complaining of ailments that appeared asymptomatic. Rather than rooting the problem in the organic, Fanon suggests a psycho-social-biology reading. He concludes that the North African feels "himself emptied, without life, in a bodily struggle with death, a death on this side of death, a death in life."[75] The story of his life is a "history of his death," a death that he endures daily.

A death in the tram,
a death in the doctor's office,
a death with the prostitute,
a death on the job site,
a death at the movies,
a multiple death in the newspapers,
a death in the fear of all decent folk of going out after midnight
a death,
yes A DEATH.[76]

Uprooted and socially excluded, the North African in France becomes inhabited by death. And yet in Fanon's writing, it is in life itself—even when framed and contained by colonization, even when inhabited by death, even when not psychic but rather muscular—that the source of decolonization is found; life harbors energy, an unfulfilled desire to act that finally explodes. Life ultimately overcomes death's stagnation. This life is expressed as it takes action in the world, as it transforms the world, and as it recognizes itself in these transformations—which is to say, as it appropriates the world. This appropriation is not a "return to the quiescence of the inorganic world," as Freud describes the death drive.[77] Nor is it a practice of Eros, the "life instinct" that Freud links to sexuality.[78] It is, instead, an engagement with the organic and inorganic world that leaves traces of life even when life is no longer there. Similar to Freud's life instinct, the drive to appropriate is entangled with a form of perpetuity: as life appropriates parts of the earth, it transforms this earth so that it exists in reference to this life form, even when the living creature is no longer present. Appropriation creates a territory that exists in the absence of the living in the signs the living has left of itself and in the meaning attributed to those signs. Thus, the collective appropriation that Fanon describes is the expression of an instinct for longevity and life that need not be reduced to sexuality.

This discussion can help explain why *A Dying Colonialism* contends that colonization occupies both a territory and a population itself: "There is not occupation of territory, on the one hand, and independence of persons on the other. It is the country as a whole, its history, its daily pulsation that are contested, disfigured, in the hope of a final destruction."[79] It is not that there exist two forms of occupation: the occupation of land and the occupation of persons. These are one and the same in that to be a person, in Fanon's view, to be conscious, to have a psychic life, to be living, one must appropriate parts of the earth, creating the places and spaces wherein one lives. Colonial occupation of territory is at the same time a colonial occupation of people, and decolonization reappropriates land while expressing life's vigor and asserting conscious human adulthood. In short, rather than understand Fanon's writing about decolonization as a movement away from psychoanalytic concerns, this writing makes particular psychoanalytic contributions. The psyche, figured as an internal space, depends on a prior spatiality that nourishes this body and through which this body moves. An important part of human development is the appropriation of at least parts of this spatiality, and appropriation involves both the work of physically transforming the earth and of having that transformation recognized as one's own. In addition, Fanon's insistence on the surface of the body, or at least his eschewal of the unconscious in the colonial context links to his valorization of the transformation of the surface of the earth. Both psychoanalysis and archaeology have framed that which is seen as deep or buried as existing in the past, and colonial discourse has often figured cultural difference as temporal: it legitimized colonization in part by arguing that colonized people are atavistic. Fanon's insistence on the surface is a rejection of this temporal logic. The transformation of the earth is a practice of the present for the future.[80]

This argument concerning appropriation, the psyche, and life, however, is valid only in Fanon's description of *men's* experience of colonization and decolonization. The argument does not hold in Fanon's discussion of women because Fanon explains the effects of colonization's containment on women and men in very different terms. In "Algeria Unveiled," he argues that under colonization, the withdrawal of "the Algerian woman" to the home allows the woman to deepen "her consciousness of struggle" and prepare "for combat." Such a "withdrawal" consists in a "falling back upon the fertile kernel."[81] Although the woman too is contained, the female colonized subject does not dream of running or jumping. Nor does she suffer muscular tension. Instead, she prepares the home.

Fanon's more clinical writing also highlights this difference. In an essay he wrote with Jacques Azoulay, Fanon outlines the challenges they faced in treating Muslim men at the Blida-Joinville Psychiatric Hospital, in Blida, Algeria. These challenges arose, according to Fanon and Azoulay, because the doctors had not considered the cultural specificity of the activities they organized for patients, such as film and choral festivals, games nights (featuring cards and dominoes), and sessions where patients were to weave raffia placemats. The text describes changes the hospital has and will make to address these problems. It concludes that ergotherapy, which is the use of physical activity and exercise to treat disease, ought to reflect what Fanon and Azoulay understand as traditional North African gender roles. Women might enjoy "raffia, pottery and sewing workshops," but for the men, "it will suffice to give them a pick and a shovel which they will use to break the earth."[82] The authors explain that prior to colonization, "land was owned communally and the notion of wealth was tied to the notion of useful, workable, land (and consequently the possession of a yoke or a plow.)"[83] In providing these tools to psychiatric patients, Fanon and Azoulay would therefore create a feeling of wealth—for their male patients, that is.

In other words, it seems as though the transformation of parts of the earth that is key to decolonization in Fanon's writing is important, in his view, for men, but not for women. The form of psychic healing he envisages from such work is necessary for the transformation of muscular tension into conscious development, but women do not suffer from such tension—they do not seem to require such externality. Rather, they provide a home, which is to say, they provide a form of externality that nurtures man and from which man might act.

In brief, Fanon's contribution to psychoanalytic discourse not only brings race and racism to the field, but also human relations to the earth, to land, to territory, and to property. His writing develops a materialist account of the psyche, one that posits a form of vitality that requires access to land, earth, and space not simply to move through but also to sustain life, particularly through access to food. His writing develops an account of human subjectivity where the subject emerges in part through appropriation, giving shape to part of the earth and recognizing that shape as one's own. When access to appropriation is cut off, Fanon contends the psychic life is also hindered, transformed into the musculature of the body. This model, however, is only true to his vision for men's psyches and bodies, and not for women.

Sexual Difference, beyond Appropriation?

This discussion raises an important question. Is the relation that Fanon draws between life, land, and the psyche one that we want to endorse? More specifically, do we want to develop forms of self-making through proprietorship, even when, as is the case in Fanon, property appears in the collective? Do we agree that central to "man's" existence is the marking of the earth so that the earth comes to refer to "man"? Critical scholarship on Fanon has been troubled by his writings on gender and on violence; it has questioned the exclusions that may be necessary to the establishment of the new nation.[84] Part of these struggles involves the value of proprietorship in Fanon's writing—and yet given colonization's expropriation, we can certainly understand why this valuation is so present in his texts. Notwithstanding, we may also wish to imagine modes of inhabitation, modes of contact with the earth beyond proprietorship that produce a different world, and with it a different form of human. Such a mode of inhabitation goes beyond recognizing the connection between life and the earth and beyond developing forms of contact between life and earth through proprietorship—even when collective. It explores how we might develop alternate relations beyond the human that are not organized around appropriation.

This is, at least partially, a theme that has concerned Luce Irigaray since her 1974 publication, *Speculum: Of the Other Woman*. In this text, Irigaray slides between considering the objectification of woman and the earth. Theories of the subject, she writes, have "always been appropriated by the 'masculine.'"[85] And this masculine subject emerges as it stands apart, elevated above, and in control of the earth. Irigaray writes,

> If there is no more "earth" to press down/repress, to work, to represent, but also and always to desire (for one's own), ... then what pedestal remains for the ex-sistence of the "subject"? If the earth turned and more especially turned upon herself, the erection of the subject might thereby be disconcerted and risk losing its elevation and penetration. For what would there be to rise up from and exercise his power over? And in?[86]

In this passage, phallic pleasure overlaps with both physical construction and linguistic representation. The earth is feminized, and the "subject" is seen as emerging as he both penetrates her and stands above her. The earth is that on which the subject will "plant his foot in order to spring farther, leap higher."[87] Irigaray questions what would happen to this formulation of the subject if we recognized that the earth turns "upon herself."[88] The implication is that the Copernican revolution has not yet been realized.

Fanon partakes in the structure of thought that Irigaray critiques. His valuation of property and of the physical transformation of the earth is a decolonial attempt to create a new man who nonetheless does not appear significantly different from the masculine subject Irigaray describes: in his writing, man's life might depend on land, and yet he becomes fully conscious and alive as he takes proprietorship over it. On the other hand, reading Irigaray with Fanon, we might wonder whether implicit in Irigaray's philosophy is an unacknowledged appropriation of the earth that allows for human life. Does the form of subjectivity that Irigaray calls for still require a form of appropriation so as to live? In its most basic form, this question becomes the following: does human life require appropriation? If so, this would suggest that Irigaray's framework takes at least one form of appropriation for granted, a form of appropriation that is not available to (or at least that is curtailed for) the colonized in Algeria, but one that fosters life. If life does not require appropriation, the implication is that Fanon's valuation of appropriation, though significant in the context of decolonization, is ultimately limited because it is both implicitly and explicitly masculine; the feminist goal in this context should not be to lay claim to appropriation for feminist ends.

To address these issues, it is first helpful to review the definition of appropriation. As it has appeared in this chapter, appropriation involves two steps: a physical transformation of the earth and the shared recognition or the interpretation of this marking as one's own. In Marx's vision, the physical transformation shapes the material world in accordance with human need, which is to say it transforms elements of the earth so as to foster (at least some people's) life. Implicitly, this suggests that human life requires one aspect of appropriation: the physical transformation of the material world. To live, humans transform the material world, whether creating shelter or at the most basic level, picking plants to eat. These actions need not be colossal; no matter how small, these acts leave traces of human presence, though they need not necessarily be read as such. While the human does give shape, however minimally, to the materiality around him or her, it is not necessary that this shaping be read in any particular way. This means that the second aspect of appropriation, the interpretative moment, is not necessary to human life. We might shape parts of the earth without seeing these as our own.

As a result, we can argue that nonappropriative forms of human life are possible. These forms give shape to the material world and recognize that the forces that transform the surface of the earth are not only human, but a concert of human and nonhuman forces. The environment is not a product of our own making, but rather a shared assemblage. The earth turns around her own axis. This framework interrupts the mode of subject formation that Irigaray critiques. And yet, crucially, it does not attend to inequality between humans. Posthumanism might appear as a form of escape from a position of proprietorship, but not from the place of deprivation. A second point is also necessary: one that envisages shared commons between humans. A feminist, more-than-human, decolonial vision must attend to both these positions, not to resolve them, but to develop politics and thought (praxis) that makes room for the more-than-human while attending to inequality between humans as well. In this case, one can imagine human life beyond appropriation while at the same time recognizing how reappropriation can address inequality.

Foucault concludes *The Order of Things*, famously, with the ocean. He imagines the end of "man" whom he deems an "invention of recent date."[89] He speculates, "If those arrangements were to disappear as they appeared, if some event ... were to cause them to crumble, as the ground of Classical thought did ... then one can certainly wager that man would be erased, like a face drawn in sand at the edge of the sea."[90] The sea's edge remains unenclosed by regimes of property. It is that which is moving, that place on the earth that is not quite solid, where traces left of the self are quickly displaced. And it is here that "man's" face disappears. Foucault's simile harbors more than poetic resemblance. It opens the imaginary to the place where wind, water, and sand meet. It opens to a place beyond property. Foucault himself explores genealogy and sadomasochism as modes of self-transformation. Yet his reference to the sea here suggests other modes through which proprietors might make themselves anew by developing relations with objects and the earth beyond proprietorship.

five   Location, Sensation, and
        the Anthropocene

According to many earth scientists, we have entered a new geological epoch: the Anthropocene.[1] This epoch marks the end of the Holocene, the period that is often dated to about 11,000 years before present and is characterized by relatively stable global temperatures and sea levels. Scientists debate over when to date the beginning of the Anthropocene, but overall, many agree that "humankind has become a global geological force" affecting changes at "the scale of the Earth as a single, evolving planetary system."[2] These changes include: marked increase in atmospheric carbon dioxide levels leading to higher global temperatures; extinction of several animal and plant species; alteration of the earth's surface and water cycle due to agriculture, construction, and the damming of rivers; and finally, significant oceanic change, including ice melt, rising sea-levels, and acidification. These transformations point to the existence of a new geological era (or at least of a geological boundary event). They threaten human and other forms of life as we have come to know them, and call for a response across disciplines and milieus.

In 2015, I received an email asking me to sign a petition addressed to the leadership of the International Union of Geological Sciences. The petition, which was circulated through *MoveOn*'s online platform, beseeched the Union to reject the Anthropocene thesis. It explained: "We do not accept the idea that the Holocene is over, or that some essential 'human' quality has caused the severe destruction of nuclear war, strip mining, ocean acidification and species extinction. The term 'Anthropocene' masks the work of capitalism, colonialism and other systems of domination in creating climate change and current global ecological hardships. It therefore misidentifies the problem, and misdirects attempts to address it."[3] To be clear, the author of the petition does not question whether or not the earth has undergone change. Rather, she believes that the term *Anthropocene* obfuscates the agent of transformation and on that basis should be rejected. It is not humans in general who have given shape to the earth, but rather global capitalism in its imbrication with colonialism and other practices of domination.

Especially since we live at a time when many in power deny the existence of climate change, I find the petition's insistence that the Holocene is not over to be a counterproductive starting point for addressing questions concerning inequality and the environment or environmental justice. That said, it is certainly worth pointing out that much of feminist theory has always been critical of the belief that there exists a "nature" out there, something external to us that provides some sort of ethical touch-point (such as, for instance, the Holocene).[4] The petition introduces a central and important debate. On the one hand, scholars such as Dipesh Chakrabarty have argued that the geological era calls for postcolonial critics to move away from critiques of "humanity" as an "effect of power" toward the universal category: the human species.[5] While the effects of climate change are differentially experienced along lines of social, political, and economic difference, Chakrabarty argues that it is as a collective human species that "we" have become a geological force, and it is as a collective human species that "our" existence is threatened. Species-thinking, he claims, is key to understanding the Anthropocene because this concept places the human within the temporality of the deep history of life. We need to think at the level of the species in order to understand how human lives are, albeit differentially, imbricated in biological, ecological, and geological time-scapes that exceed the scale of human history, the story of capitalism, colonialism, the slave trade.[6] At the very least, reading Chakrabarty, one might respond to the petition arguing that both capitalist *and* communist economies frame the earth and nonhumans as resources for (some) human's consumption without concern for ecology, without attention to the entanglement of human life with other beings.

On the other hand, other thinkers, such as Andreas Malm, Alf Hornborg, Jason Moore, Rob Nixon, and Donna Haraway have insisted on the continued centrality of difference and inequality when thinking about global change.[7] "What does it mean to speak of 'the human,'" Nixon asks, "when what it means to be human is being wrenched apart by the forces of inequity"?[8] Malm and Hornborg argue that it is only from the perspective of polar bears, amphibians, and birds that it makes sense to think of global changes as anthropogenic.[9] From the perspective of a human being, the discourse of the "Anthropocene" erroneously renders invisible the forms of domination and inequality that are inextricable from the actions that gave rise to it. These scholars argue that climate change along with the other changes encapsulated by the term *Anthropocene* are not the effect of "natural" "human" activities, but rather sociogenic—which is to say, not universal but uneven, both with regards to responsibility and vulnerability. In the place of the Anthropocene, they offer the term *Capitalocene*. And the story of the Capitalocene, Haraway insists, need not only consider the development of British industrialization (as is sometimes the case in the literature, which often cites the English invention of the steam engine as the starting point). It must also look to the "networks of sugar, precious metals, plantations, indigenous genocides, and slavery; ... the relocation of peoples, plants, and animals; the leveling of vast forests; and the violent mining of metals [which] preceded the steam engine."[10]

Haraway's discussion of the Anthropocene goes still further. She argues that if we are to use biological discourse to understand planetary change, it does not make sense to insist on "species-thinking," in as much as the concept of species misleadingly disentangles critters (humans, in this case) from their worlds and from their interdependence with other living beings. "Neither biology nor philosophy any longer supports the notion of independent organisms in environments, that is, interacting units plus contexts/rules."[11] In the place of both the *Anthropocene* and *Capitalocene*, Haraway offers the term *Chthulucene* to index the ongoing world making practices of multispecies "becoming-with."[12] "Human beings are not the only important actors in the Chthulucene," Haraway insists. Instead, "human beings are with and of the earth, and the biotic and abiotic powers of this earth are the main matter."[13] Haraway's approach addresses a central irony in Anthropocene discourse: on the one hand, the epoch is framed as decentering humans, as pointing to our vulnerability and interdependence on that which is beyond us. On the other hand, "the Anthropocene" recenters humans, positing the species as engineers of our own world.[14] In contrast, as Neel Ahuja argues, environmental politics or planetarity "suggests a politics that starts from the presumption of transspecies assemblage; it thus requires not simply an appeal to bring animals into representation, but rather to recognize the fundamental ways in which transspecies embodiments constitute [...] object-worlds."[15] In other words, we can say that a problem with both the *Anthropocene* and *Capitalocene* is that they tend to prioritize the agency of humans—and a particular subset of humans, in particular. In doing so, they reproduce hegemonic attributions of agency. Instead, how can we imagine planetary change in a way that recognizes the vibrancy or "animacy," to draw on Mel Chen's concept, of "matter that is considered insensate, immobile, deathly, or otherwise 'wrong'"?[16]

This chapter both extends the critique of conceptualizations of the Anthropocene and also contributes to its figuration. That is to say, while I recognize that the discourse surrounding the "Anthropocene" tends to hide questions of inequality, domination, and uneven responsibility, at the same time, the term has gained some prominence and recognition that can be used to doing important work, so I do not jettison the word altogether.[17] I nonetheless expand the existing analysis of the discourse's false universalization to focus on a second universal that has not yet been widely subject to debate. In addition to "man," "humans," or "humanity," another universal is central to scientific writing on the Anthropocene—that is, the idea of the Earth as a single, global system. In fact, as I will show, these two universals—the earth and the human—are thoroughly entangled with one another.

The Anthropocene's representation of the earth rests in stark contrast to this book's central line of argumentation. I have argued that the analysis of sensation provides a lens to consider the more-than-human world without either reducing this world to discourse or creating universal representations that cover over the politics of their illocution; I have also explained that alongside the forms of power Foucault described at length exists another form of power, geopower, the force relations that transform the surface of the earth. To think of the Anthropocene is to think of geopower. The Anthropocene draws attention to the force relations that transform the earth. However, in contrast to discussions of the Anthropocene, my analysis of geopower did not make a claim about the transformation of the "Earth as a single ... planetary system." Drawing especially on Fanon, I focused on local transformations of places and spaces. I tried to bracket, as much as possible, the question of what the earth *is*, focusing instead on particular examples of physical change. This strategy is consonant with the book's argument concerning sensation. I turned to the analysis of sensation as a lens that avoids totalizing, universal accounts of materiality or the more-than-human world.

But does the Anthropocene require thinking of the earth as a single system or as a whole? In this final chapter, I examine the figure of the earth that is embedded within discourse on the Anthropocene. I argue that alongside this representation of the earth, a second set of place-based imaginaries is also necessary—both in scholarship and in politics—for it is here that global change is lived and will be lived as a crisis. In other words, while I allow that the Anthropocene's representation of the earth as global, universal, and whole is strategic, it is not sufficient even as a strategy. Attention to location or particularity to place remains necessary, and to the extent that these are transcended, the narrative of the Anthropocene becomes, in the words of Stacy Alaimo, "enlisted in all too familiar formulations, epistemologies, and defensive maneuvers—modes of knowing and being that are utterly incapable of adequately responding to the complexities of the Anthropocene itself."[18] As Alaimo argues, many representations of the Anthropocene reproduce the " 'God's-eye view' that Donna Haraway critiques in 'Situated Knowledges.' "[19]

This chapter builds on Alaimo's work by showing how addressing this problem requires a different spatial imaginary.

My argument concerning the spaces and places of the Anthropocene also has repercussions concerning the place of sensation, perception, and phenomenology in humanities-based scholarship on the topic. Chakrabarty and Timothy Clark argue that the Anthropocene is beyond human perceptual experience, and therefore that a phenomenological approach to it is impossible. This claim, I will show, is tied to the Anthropocene's spatial imaginary. However, while the Anthropocene thesis requires the image of an entire planet, we do not live on such a planet. From the perspective of life, we live in differentiated, multiple places. It is in such locations that planetary change is effected, and if this change is a danger for living beings, it will necessarily be sensed, though perhaps indirectly. Neither phenomenology nor experience are therefore irrelevant. I explore this argument in a discussion of *AIR (Auto Immune Response),*" a multimedia exhibit by the Will Wilson (Diné).

The chapter begins with a brief overview of literature on the Anthropocene, introducing the figure of the earth that emerges therein. I then explain how this figure can be understood as a form of universalism, and I identify two problems embedded in this figure in order, finally, to offer an alternative. The chapter ends with the analysis of experience, sensation, and the Anthropocene, as well as the reading of Wilson's work. Overall, this chapter defends my approach to earthly, sensory encounters.

Introducing "Earth System Science"

The notion that the earth is a single entity appears over and again in high-profile articles that make a case for the existence of the Anthropocene. In effect, the Anthropocene thesis requires such an understanding of the earth as singular: it is easy to argue that humans have transformed particular places. What is specific to the theory of the Anthropocene is that humans have transformed the earth as a whole.

Representations of the earth that appear within the literature on the Anthropocene are largely similar. Paul J. Crutzen and Eugene Stoermer's "The 'Anthropocene'" (a text that is often cited as coining the term, *Anthropocene*) argues that human activities have affected "earth and atmosphere, ... at all, including global, scales."[20] This means that no matter from how close or from how far we view the earth, we will always see that it is marked by human activity. A fundamental sameness comes to characterize the planet: a human signature. And this signature, Crutzen and Stoermer claim, comes into view at every scale, including "the global." The Anthropocene thesis is not an argument about a particularity but about a global condition, one that appears at every scale. Will Steffen, Jacques Grinevald, Paul Crutzen, and John McNeill's 2011 article, "The Anthropocene: Conceptual and Historical Perspectives," makes a similar argument. The authors begin: "Climate change has brought into sharp focus the capability of contemporary human civilization to influence the environment at the scale of the Earth as a single, evolving planetary system."[21] In this opening phrase, it is not simply "contemporary human civilization" that emerges as a whole, but the earth as well, this time as a "single ... planetary system." The earth, in this view, is "a system," a term that Crutzen and Stoermer did not first use, but that has become pervasive, including in Crutzen's writing. The latter article highlights the "planetary" scale, unlike the first text, which insists that the Anthropocene is evident at all scales, but stresses the global in particular. In either case, however, this largest scale is crucial. And at this scale, the earth appears as a singular whole. In fact, the appearance of the earth as a whole defines the scale of the Anthropocene.

Arguments for climate change that predate the Anthropocene thesis posit the earth similarly as a single system. H. J. Schellnhuber's 1999 "'Earth System' Analysis and the Second Copernican Revolution" provides a good example. While making a case for climate change, Schellnhuber argues that we have entered a "new revolution" that enables us to "look back on our planet to perceive one single, complex, dissipative, dynamic entity, far from thermodynamic equilibrium—the 'Earth system.'"[22] Later he defines this "Earth system" by an equation:

$E = (N, H)$

where $N = (a, b, c, \ldots)$; $H = (A, S)$.

E represents the "Earth system," which is constituted by N, the ecosphere (itself made up by "sub-spheres a [atmosphere], b [biosphere], c [cryosphere], etc.") and H, the "human factor" (itself made up of A, "the aggregate of all individual human lives, actions and products" and S, which Schellnhuber describes as a "global subject," a subject, he claims, that has emerged with the internet, and that he sees as both global and singular).[23] In this representation, the earth figures as an inclusive set of the planet and a singled-out life form, humans (who are curiously not included in the biosphere). The Earth system is not made up of one thing but it comes together as a "system"—one system—in that all the elements that constitute its set affect one another.

This representation of the earth as a singular system does not only appear in scientific writing, but also in policy documents. For instance, an overlapping notion of the "Earth system" is at the heart of the Amsterdam Declaration, the 2001 result of a three-day conference on climate change. The conference included members of the media and of the scientific, policy, and resource management publics. The Declaration begins by stating, "The Earth System behaves as a single, self-regulating system comprised of physical, chemical, biological and human components."[24] It continues: "the interactions and feedbacks between the component parts are complex and exhibit multi-scale temporal and spatial variability."[25] There is a place for difference here—there is variability—but nonetheless, critically, these differences come to constitute a larger, singular system.

The representation of the earth as a system is at once a representation of the earth as a whole. This language of "systems" recalls "systems theory," which came into vogue in the 1950s and 1960s in mathematics and the physical and social sciences.[26] Michael Chisholm's 1967 article, "General System Theory and Geography," explains the basic premise of systems theory: "all things (as objects primarily but also as ideas) have connections with many other things and the significance of any one depends on its relationships with others. Hence the unit of study should be not on a single thing but a system of interrelated objects or ideas."[27] Citing Ludwig von Bertalanffy, a theoretical biologist, Chisholm shows how this understanding of a system is related to a notion of wholeness. In "biology, psychology, sociology and other sciences," "wholeness" has taken different forms, from an organism to gestalt, but these concepts, von Bertalanffy claims, have been vague. In contrast "General System Theory" provides "a new scientific doctrine of 'wholeness.'"[28] In other words, although system theory recognizes parts, these parts only have meaning in reference to a whole, and it is this whole that becomes the object of study.[29]

Understanding the earth as a singular system, which is to say as a whole, is tied to the emergence of a particular field of study, Earth System Science (ESS). The field emerged in the late 1980s when NASA began using the term to describe its research program.[30] ESS, as John Lawton argues, takes "the main components of planet Earth—the atmosphere, oceans, freshwater, rocks, soils, and biosphere—and seeks to understand major patterns and processes in their dynamics."[31] It is not simply each of these components, however, that are important, but rather the "intersections *between*" them. Lawton continues, "It is the need to study and understand these between-component interactions that defines ESS as a discipline in its own right."[32]

Since its definition, ESS has been widely funded. It has given shape to university hiring practices, and it has become institutionalized in government research programs.[33] Particular methods characterize the field. Schellnhuber explains that there are two feasible ways to "achieve 'holistic' perception of the planetary inventory": "the bird's-eye principle" or a view from above; and "the digital-mimicry principle" that makes use of "remote sensing and a worldwide net of *in situ* measurement devices" to build complex computer models of the earth's system.[34] This modeling remains especially critical, though difficult because of the complexity and as well as the chaotic features of some elements of the earth system (such as the weather) and the varied spatial and time scales of both the data and the models.[35] Nonetheless, for the most part, discourse surrounding the field remains optimistic.[36] A. J. Pitman writes, "The expectation is that Earth System Science will provide solutions to major world problems because it moves away from reductionist approaches and does not recognize disciplinary boundaries ... bar[ring] the first photographs from space, [it] will have the greatest consequences on Human development since the Industrial Revolution."[37] Such grandiose expectations frame ESS as redemptive. They highlight a continued faith in science, even though the Anthropocene is widely understood in this literature as caused by industrialization, and thus is attributable to science.

Comparisons between ESS and medicine are not uncommon. Both fields, authors write, are interdisciplinary, and both seek a form of reparation; the earth, like the human body, will be healed by the work of the expert.[38] Schellnhuber's version of this story is especially ironic. He writes of "'Earth-system' diagnostics" and includes an illustration.[39] Someone dressed as a surgeon floats in outer space while holding what appears to be a scalpel and flashlight. The scalpel cuts into a surface (presumably the earth) revealing a vaginal-shaped hole through which light shines. The surgeon remains at a distance, adorned in protective gear. He or she (the gender of the surgeon is not clear in the image) will heal by cutting and by looking from afar, aided by technologies. Faded arrows and squiggly lines subtend the earth's surface; the earth, indeed, is a system constituted by interrelated processes.[40] The surgeon appears almost as large as the earth; the earth does not act upon the surgeon, but the surgeon upon the earth. And yet what defines the Anthropocene as a crisis is, at least in part, the threat it brings to life. The objectifying distance of the surgeon's view-from-nowhere misses the point. Quite simply, the earth as a whole system comes into view from this distant gaze, yet this distance misses both our implication in the Anthropocene and our uneven vulnerability within it.

Universalisms at Play

The notion that the earth constitutes a singular system is a form of universalism. Most commonly in philosophy, the "problem of universals" goes, roughly, like this: "Why do we group a collection of particulars under a general term (like chair, house, tree)"?[41] Some argue that actual, particular chairs share a common feature. It is this shared nature that defines the universal term and justifies the grouping. Others contend that the only thing chairs have in common is what we call them, "chair." In political theory, "universals" often signify something slightly different. Frequently associated with the Enlightenment, "universalism" generally connects to the belief that "rational human nature" is "a universal impervious to cultural and historical differences."[42] On the basis of this shared nature, humans (or, rather, some humans) come to bear rights. The philosophical problem of universals is at play in this political story: one might ask what connects various particulars (individual people) under this general term, *human* (or *man*). But a universal in this context is a concept that is supposedly untouched by space and time in that it is applicable across temporal and cultural difference, and on the basis of the recognition of this applicability, the belief is that some form of good is meant to follow. We can, finally, add that in both the philosophical and political cases, the universal—whether it be "chair" or "human"—is *one* entity, no matter how it is conceived. That is to say, the universal, "chair" or "human," joins multiple instantiations (chairs, humans) into one whole, "chair" or "humanity." The first definition the *Oxford English Dictionary* (*OED*) provides of "universal" highlights this connection between universality and wholeness: "Extending over or including the whole of something specified or implied, esp. the whole of a particular group or the whole world; comprehensive, complete; widely occurring or existing, prevalent over all."

The understanding of the earth embedded in discourse surrounding the Anthropocene consists in a universal in several ways; however, a certain circularity of thought emerges here because imaginaries of the earth are implicated in the notion of universality itself, and vice versa. In the *OED*'s definition, for instance, that which is universal is that which extends over the "whole of a particular group or the whole world." It is not much of a leap to extrapolate that the universal extends across the earth—"the whole world." Similarly, when a "transcultural, transhistorical human nature was posited as identical, beyond particularisms," the argument, at least ideally, was that this human nature did not exist in a particular place. It existed across the earth. French universalism provides another example. During the seventeenth century, French became understood as the language no longer of nobility and polite society, but of humanity at large.[43] This French language was distinguished from other languages, but also from regional dialects.[44] In other words, this form of French was seen as unmarked by place or region; it was universal in that it could travel across the earth—and yet it referred to a particular center of power. For the moment, it is not this contradiction of universalism on which I focus. The point is that the Anthropocene appears at the same scale as the universal, and the universal itself has been conceived often, at least implicitly, as that which exists across the earth. That is to say, the earth as a whole, as a planet, the place of the Anthropocene, has stood for universality. It is not simply that this representation of the earth functions as a universal in a similar way that humanity functions. Instead, the notion of humanity as a whole is connected to an imaginary of the earth as a whole and both these forms of wholeness have been critical to conceptualizing the universal—even though, in fact, we are only talking about one planet, and not the universe.[45]

Two important implications follow from this analysis. First, we should expect that feminist, queer, and postcolonial critiques of universality are relevant to the Anthropocene's representation of the earth. And second, the Anthropocene/Capitalocene/Chthulucene itself, in as much as it transforms understandings of the earth, could at the same time and in a related fashion also transform understandings of universalism.

But the Anthropocene's representation of the earth is a form of universalism in other ways as well. For instance, in this discourse, the earth is posited as a whole singular system across a large expanse of space and time. The "earth" is not figured as a singular system within a particular context. So long as it exists, the earth is understood as a singular system no matter when or where we consider it. The representation of the earth in discourse on the Anthropocene consists, in other words, of a view-from-nowhere. We might also understand this figure of the earth as a universal in that this singular wholeness consists in an inclusive generality (such as humanity) that ties together multiple particularities (such as humans). In this case, the earth as a singular system joins together in a whole all the other "earthly" systems or materialities. It is a universal much like "humanity" or even "chairs."

Figuring the earth as a singular whole is a problem, like many universals, because the representation fallaciously posits itself as a view-from-nowhere or as unmarked by location, whereas in fact, this representation is situated. More specifically, the understanding of the earth as a single system emerges from a particular tradition of knowing that is entangled with particular power relations. This false universal excludes other modes of knowing, modes that are connected to other distributions of power. Indeed, the modes of knowing embedded in ESS have histories deeply intertwined with military history and imperialism—they are entangled in particular workings of power.[46] The earth sciences received massive military patronage in the United States during the Cold War. Just as geological exploration was critical to the emerging nineteenth-century America (and its railroad), during the 1950s and 1960s, because of national security concerns and foreign policy planning, the earth sciences received similar support.[47] The Cold War incited the production of a worldwide network of *in situ* planetary monitoring, a network that has become critical to scholarship on the Anthropocene. In the late 1950s, for instance, the US Army created "Camp Century," a research station in Greenland; in 1961 this was renamed the Army's "Cold Regions Research and Engineering Laboratory," the largest American polar laboratory.[48] During the 1980s and 1990s, it was this military infrastructure that was used to reveal climate change.[49] In addition, satellite images taken by the US during the Cold War were eventually semi-declassified in the 1990s, providing scientists visual evidence for climate change.[50] This science depends on this military history.[51]

ESS is also linked to NASA's Apollo space program. In 1968 and 1972, still in the context of the Cold War, this program produced the first photographs of the earth as a whole. Image AS17-22727 revealed a "whole, unshadowed globe in the blackness of space."[52] This became a vision of universalism that places the United States as leader. This is clear in investigating the context of the image. For instance, John F. Kennedy's 1962 speech at Rice University marshaled support for the space program. This speech heralded human universalism yet centered the United States in this universal. Kennedy said, "the eyes of the world now look into space, to the moon and to the planets beyond, and we have vowed that we shall not see it governed by a hostile flag of conquest, but by a banner of freedom and peace." Here, it appeared as though the space program is not about asserting world dominance but rather about following the direction of the "eyes of the world" so as to manifest peace. This is a global vision that transcends the nation state. And yet this sentence is predicated by Kennedy's insistence that the United States will not only be part of the space age, but rather will "lead it." And it is not just the race to space that the United States will lead: "No nation which expects to be the leader of other nations can expect to stay behind in the race for space," he clarifies.[53] Thus, within this vision of universal peace, the United States becomes the leader of other nations. It is this vision that promoted NASA and that produced these photographs of the earth. Although NASA's image is not exactly new (as David Cosgrove argues) such images produce a "divine and mastering view from a single perspective."[54] They bring together diverse elements, creating a "vision of unity."[55] And yet at the same time, they reference a particular center of power.

Indeed, many scholars have argued that such images of the earth as a whole are connected to imperialism and to war.[56] Kelly Oliver adds that while it is common to understand this image of the earth as an image of the earth as a whole, in fact, only one part of the earth is visible in NASA's image. Even in moving the point of view far away from the earth still produces a view from somewhere that is necessarily limited.[57]

But before coming to the conclusion that the understanding of earth which appears in ESS is a false universal, we might want to argue that just because this vision of the earth developed as part of this military history, it is not inextricable from it. This is certainly plausible, and yet scientific and policy documents on the Anthropocene and climate change reveal this not to be the case. Over and again, positing the earth as a whole and finding a problem that exists at this scale seems to bleed seamlessly into calls not simply for the creation of international research institutions, but also for global forms of governance that implicitly or explicitly recenter existing economic and political powers. For instance, the International Geosphere-Biosphere Programme (IGBP) was founded in 1987, and has become an important platform for the promulgation of ESS and research on the Anthropocene. Its newsletter first published Crutzen and Stoermer's article that coined the term, Anthropocene. The IGBP's website is adorned with images that it credits to NASA. In its 2010 Vision statement, it recognizes that it must "encourage greater participation from developing World researchers." It claims that it will use "the latest technological networking tools to achieve this."[58] In 2014, however, this aim does not appear to be going well. The IGBP announced its ten-year research initiative, which spanned three continents and centered five "global hubs": Montreal, Paris, Tokyo, Stockholm, and Boulder, Colorado. The website explains, "Discussions to develop an African hub are underway, with plans in other regions also under consideration."[59] For the moment, however, the global south is not represented in this manifestation of globality. IGBP is certainly not alone in positing a globe that is not a globe, but given that the IGBP terms itself a platform for global research, given that its object of study is the earth itself, given that it is the case that the global south will bear the most challenging consequence of climate change, this global vision appears limited.

Other texts also show signs of this tension. Schellnhuber provides an extreme example. He figures the earth as "Gaia" and he imagines something he calls "earth power" as Prometheus. Here, he is referencing Greek mythology. But then, he posits the force of "destruction" as Shiva. Hinduism enters only as destructive. We might be willing to overlook this, until, that is, we reach the end of his article: "A global redesign could aim at establishing a more 'organic' distribution of labour," he writes, "where the temperate countries are the main producers of global food supplies, the sub-tropical zones produce renewable energies and high technology, and the tropical zones preserve biodiversity and offer recreation."[60] Such an international division of labor recalls imperialist notions of climatic determinism. Schellnhuber also speaks of a "global subject" who has emerged with telecommunications. This global subject, he writes, has "conquered our planet." This subject's "teledemocracy" will "reign over centuries to come."[61] Yet of course the internet is not "universally" accessible, and even if it were, we would still have serious problems that would make it difficult to institute "teledemocracy." The global subject thus appears far from global and yet, in Schellnhuber's gleeful account, this subject will reign. As Haraway argues, "Anthropocene is a term most easily meaningful and usable by intellectuals in wealthy classes and regions; it is not an idiomatic term for climate, weather, land, care of country, or much else in great swathes of the world, especially but not only among indigenous people."[62]

It seems therefore that while discourse surrounding the Anthropocene posits the earth as one whole, global system, at the same time, this representation bares a particular history that implicitly recenters if not the West, then at least existing economic and political powers. A certain doubling of thought appears while making this argument. It is not simply that the image of the earth as a united globe is, in effect, a view-from-somewhere that centers particular political and economic powers. It is also that in recognizing this to be the case, we move away from a global vision of the earth toward considering particular places. We consider the United States, for instance, and its relation to the USSR. The critique of universality is at once the production of a different spatial imaginary.

Multinaturalisms, Sensation, and Amazonian Cosmology

The problem, framed in these terms, is one of representation. If the Anthropocene provides a representation of the earth, we must then ask, whose representation is it? And how is this representation embedded within and productive of existing networks of power-knowledge? Posing these questions, we might then compare the understanding of the earth central in discourse on the Anthropocene to alternate understandings. How might the earth be imagined differently within, for example, Amazonian indigenous cosmologies? And how are these cosmologies entangled with indigenous survivance and self-governance?[63] This latter question highlights the relation between knowledge and power. In this next section, I turn to Amazonian indigenous cosmologies both to provide an alternative understanding of the earth and to draw on the theoretical arguments posited therein. I show how, drawing on these cosmologies within this context reintroduces the importance of the sensory and offers an additional location for imagining the Anthropocene.

In his ethnographic work on the Candoshi people of the High Amazon, Alexandre Surrallés describes how space in Candoshi cosmology is organized around the home. Concentric spaces extend from this center.[64] Surrallés explains that, in this view, space is not abstract but rather related to inhabitation and the place of the body. Comparing Candoshi and Euclidean geometry, he writes, for example, that "whereas the later describes a set of rules that govern the unfolding of an abstract space understood as an infinitely extensive area, 'Candoshi geometry' makes do with offering the walker the elements that allow him to initiate the dialectics between perception and action, necessary to advance in his environment."[65]

While my goal here is certainly not to reproduce colonialist discourse, I recognize that drawing on this anthropological text in the way that I do here is troubling. For instance, I provide Surrallés's proper name but treat the "Candoshi people" as a unified, ahistorical whole. This is a limit of the literature I am working with, and I have therefore been hesitant to cite it. However, I nonetheless do so in order to consider a different way of figuring the "Earth." Crucially, I do not leave the discussion here. The chapter ends with an analysis of Wilson's photography in a way that more productively engages with indigenous studies and more clearly contributes to a decolonial project.

But for the moment, building on Surrallés's analysis, we might surmise that rather than figure the earth as a whole system, Candoshi cosmology would imagine it as the places that radiate out from the home, places through which one might move. In this view, the earth would become most centrally the location of inhabitation, perception, and action.

Although the representation of the earth found in discourse on the Anthropocene does not figure space as empty, the earth that appears therein is not, foremost, a place of inhabitation, perception, or action. No one walks through the earth system. In addition, and in contradiction to the vision of the earth as a singular system, in day-to-day life, humans (and other species) do not perceive the earth as a whole or as a singular entity. For the living, there is extension and difference rather than singular wholeness.

However, instead of figuring the tension between ESS's representation of the earth and Candoshi representations as a form of cultural difference, I suggest drawing on Amazonian cosmology to interrupt the ontology usually associated with multiculturalism. Doing so addresses both the limitation of universalism I have already addressed and a second problematic, as well. There are two ways to understand the problem of universalism embedded in the scientific and policy discourse surrounding the Anthropocene. The first is that, far from a view-from-nowhere, this representation is situated. The second argument is that this conceptualization of the earth covers over difference by treating multiple places or entities as one. This is a false universal not because the concept is locatable (are not all concepts locatable?), but rather because the concept misses difference. It prioritizes a system or wholeness over multiplicity. Thus, rather than focus on how different people (or different "cultures") have different understandings of the earth, we could argue that the earth is not singular or whole.

Amazonian cosmology, in effect, develops this argument both by articulating a theory of "multinaturalism" and by prioritizing sensation. In his research with the Araweté, a Tupi-Guarani people of Eastern Amazonia, Eduardo Viveiros de Castro details what he calls "Amerindian perspectivism." De Castro contrasts Amerindian perspectivism with the cosmology embedded in Western multiculturalism. Whereas multiculturalism posits the existence of a unified, given "nature," it allows for a multitude of different cultures. "Nature," in this view, is objectively knowable, guaranteed by the "universality of body and substance."[66] In contrast, culture is subjective, having to do with spirit and meaning and created by humans. A similar argument could be made in the context of this analysis: there exists one, singular whole earth and different, subjective, cultural understandings of it. However, Viveiros de Castro argues that rather than understand Araweté cosmology as a different culture, which produces different representations of nature, in fact, this cosmology puts pressure on multiculturalism's very mode of understanding unified nature and particular cultures. "Amerindian thought," Viveiros de Castro writes, posits "one single 'culture,' multiple 'natures.'"[67] It presupposes a "spiritual unity and a corporeal diversity."[68] This is because it has a "perspectival quality."[69] For instance, many animals "see themselves as persons."[70] Viveiros de Castro writes,

> They experience their own habits and characteristics in the form of culture—they see their food as human food (jaguars see blood as manioc beer, vultures see the maggots in rotting meat as grilled fish, etc.), they see their bodily attributes (fur, feathers, claws, beaks, etc.) as body decorations or cultural instruments, they see their social system as organized in the same way as human institutions are (with chiefs, shamans, ceremonies, exogamous moieties, etc.). This "to see as" refers literally to percepts and not analogically to concepts.[71]

In this view, that which is positioned as subject takes on different forms or different natures. There is a multitude of bodies, multiple "natures," and yet one culture, one mode of relating from the perspective of the subject. Viveiros de Castro argues that this is not a form of relativism because it is not about perceiving things differently but rather similarly. He also insists that this is not about competing representations either. The issue is not about how one represents entities, but rather about how they are perceived.

In fact, both Viveiros de Castro's and Surrallés's ethnographies draw attention to sensation. Surrallés explicitly draws on Merleau-Ponty and finds overlap between his phenomenology and Candoshi cosmology. Viveiros the Castro is more Deleuzian and cites Deleuze's understanding of "percepts," but arguably Merleau-Ponty would be more in keeping with Araweté cosmology. As I have explained, Deleuze, writing with Guattari, separates sensation from the sensory subject. They define sensation as a "compound of percepts and affects," and frame both of these as "independent of a state of those who experience them." As a result, "sensations, percepts, and affects are *beings* whose validity lies in themselves and exceeds any lived."[72] Using the example of sensing a work of art, they claim that this work is "a being of sensation and nothing else: it exists in itself."[73] In this view, it does not matter who is perceiving a work of art or who is affected by it. In any case, the artwork's sensation exists in itself. But this is a form of mononaturalism in that it posits the work of art as a singular being that does not change depending on the subject sensing it. In contrast, in Viveiros de Castro's account of Araweté cosmology, there is not one nature (or one work of art). Rather its sensation emerges as it is engaged from different perspectives. Things are perceived differently depending on who is looking: "jaguars see blood as manioc beer, vultures see the maggots in rotting meat as grilled fish, etc."[74] In other words, Deleuze's account of sensation is quite different from the cosmology Viveiros de Castro analyzes. But nonetheless, what remains significant to my argument is the important place of sensation in both the Candoshi and Araweté cosmology.

The Anthropocene's model of the earth as a singular wholeness is a form of mononaturalism: it assumes a unity of "nature" in the form of a singular earth system.[75] It also does not bring out the place of sensation. Drawing instead on Candoshi and Araweté cosmology, a very different understanding of the earth appears. The earth becomes a place of inhabitation, and as such a place, it is multiple for there exists many perspectives from which it is perceived, many places in which it is inhabited. In this view, the earth becomes, rather than a singular, whole system, a diverse world within which we live.

This understanding of the earth is critical to any ethical, just, and effective response to the Anthropocene.[76] It is not as a singular, whole system that the earth under the Anthropocene endangers life; rather, this danger is apparent in particular inhabited places. Still more, focusing on places highlights questions of political agency and power dynamics. Responding to the Anthropocene requires that we not simply think of the earth as a whole, singular system, but also as a multiplicity of inhabited places. For it is here that the Anthropocene poses a danger for life, for it is here that "we" make decisions, for it is here that we, all of us, live.

I am not suggesting, however, that this alternative vision of the earth replace the one that appears in ESS. Instead, the two can coincide in a productive tension. My argument both draws on Chakrabarty's writing while, at the same time, highlighting a limitation in his vision. Before he published on the Anthropocene, Chakrabarty's earlier writing was concerned with postcolonial historiography. In *Provincializing Europe*, he developed a reading of Marx that posits the existence of two forms of history: History 1 and History 2. The first "forms the backbone of the usual narratives of transition to the capitalist mode of production."[77] This history consists in "capital's antecedent 'posited by itself.'"[78] It is a "universal and necessary history."[79] History 1 is the past in as much as this past was transformed into capitalist life worlds. It is the history of capital. History 2, on the other hand, might also function as an antecedent of capital, but "'not as antecedents established by itself, not as forms of its own life-process.'"[80] History 2 is the past that is not capitalism's per se. It "beckons us to more *affective* narratives of human belonging" that interrupt "the totalizing thrust of History 1."[81] History 2 makes room "for the politics of human belonging and diversity."[82] History 2 is significant to postcolonial scholarship because it allows for a conceptual space to write about history that makes room for differences, differences that are not teleologically oriented toward capitalism's development, differences that do not posit the world as the waiting ground for capitalist expansion. According to Chakrabarty, the relation between History 1 and History 2 also figures a relation between the universal and the particular. History 2 interrupts History 1's universal, teleological narrative. As a result, Chakrabarty contends that "no historical form of capital, however global its reach, can ever be a universal." History 1 is always "modified by somebody's History 2s."

Chakrabarty does not use the language of History 1 and History 2 in his later work. However, it is worth noting that the "universal" Chakrabarty calls for in "The Climate of History" is strategic.[83] He writes that the "new universal history of humans … flashes up" in a "moment of … danger."[84] Chakrabarty's language, as Ian Baucom points out, draws on Walter Benjamin's "On the Concept of History." Benjamin develops an understanding of the historical materialist who attempts to "blast open the continuum of history," to bring about a new epoch all while feeling despair "of appropriating the genuine historical image as it briefly flashes up."[85] It is in this sense that Chakrabarty's universal is strategic. It is not meant to master the "genuine historical picture" so much as to explode its continuum. The universal appears in order to disrupt the present.

Likewise, the figure of the earth embedded in discourse on the Anthropocene is a condition for the Anthropocene's recognition. Understanding the earth as a global, singular system is necessary for diagnosing climate change. This understanding is an attempt to bring about a different future. But this universal appears as a flash; it remains interrupted. Just as in Chakrabarty's writing, History 1 and History 2 work together as History 2 interrupts History 1, the two imaginaries of the earth that I offer can coincide, interrupting one another in a productive tension. History 2 interrupts History 1's universal narrative. Similarly, place-based imaginaries of the earth can interrupt those models that posit the earth as a whole, singular system without replacing this model altogether. The productive tension Chakrabarty posits between History 1 and History 2 figures a way to write about global forces without forgoing difference. In effect, while Chakrabarty's *Provincializing Europe* focuses on history (and hence temporality), his treatment of universality unsurprisingly also calls for a different representation of the planet. The location of History 2, those histories that "beckons us to more *affective* narratives of human belonging,"[86] is not the planet writ large. History 2 makes room for difference. It is not the space of globalization, not the space of the planet as a singular system. It is the earth as a multiplicity of inhabited places.

Chakrabarty asks: "How do we relate to a universal history of life—to universal thought, that is—while retaining what is of obvious value in our postcolonial suspicion of the universal?"[87] One answer is to think of the earth differently: not only as a singular, whole system, but also a multiplicity of inhabited, connected locations. It is, in other words, to continue to think about History 1 and 2.

Sensation and the Anthropocene

This argument has repercussions for conceptualizing the place of experience and phenomenology in the Anthropocene/Capitalocene/Chthutocene. A repeated claim in humanities-based scholarship on the Anthropocene is that this planetary transformation is beyond human perceptual experience. Chakrabarty, for instance, contends that "we" cannot experience ourselves as a species; we cannot experience ourselves as agents of the Anthropocene. He therefore concludes that "there could be no phenomenology of us as a species."[88] In a subsequent essay, he reiterates this point: "[W]e cannot ever experience ourselves as a geophysical force—though we now *know* that this is one of the modes of our collective existence."[89]

Timothy Clark builds on this argument. Ecocritics, he explains, have often turned to perceptual experience to interrupt both "the fantasies of techno-science" and "the capitalist commodification of nature."⁹⁰ But the Anthropocene, according to Clark, requires a different approach. This is because conceptualizing the Anthropocene requires a larger spatial and temporal scale than the scale of the human body, and there exists, Clark argues, a fundamental disjuncture between "the personal scale of the human body," and the temporal and spatial scale of the Anthropocene.⁹¹ Clark goes so far as to argue that the scale of the human body obfuscates the necessary vision. It projects an "illusory ground," he writes. It is "latently ecophobic and even sometimes a form of denial."⁹²

Finally, Tobias Boes drawing on Chakrabarty and overlapping with Clark insists that the Anthropocene cannot be experienced. He writes: "We can at best hope for partial mediation by the victims of local manifestations of such a planetary force—by hurricane survivors, farmers whose livelihood has been taken away by droughts or rising temperatures, or families displaced by flooding, for instance. The gap between this merely local knowledge and comprehensive understanding of the planetary condition [...] is vast."⁹³ It is telling that, while making this argument, Boes glosses the connection between Cold War science, militarism, and the image of the whole earth, but he ultimately dismisses this connection's significance, focusing instead on how still photography of the earth cannot capture temporality, and hence, change. Along the way, Boes does not consider debates over the term *Anthropocene*, debates over the category "human," debates that are arguably prominent in the field.

Boes's essay, like Clark's and Chakrabarty's, is symptomatic of how the understanding of the human (as an undifferentiated totality) and the earth (as a whole) in discourse surrounding the Anthropocene are interconnected, and how, in turn, these understandings are integrally linked to the argument that the Anthropocene cannot be experienced. It is especially striking that Boes and Clark value knowledge of the whole over the lived experience of particular manifestations. Boes writes of "merely local knowledge" in comparison to "comprehensive understanding."⁹⁴ Clark, in turn, insists that to understand the Anthropocene, we need "mediation on the whole Earth image," and it is for this reason in particular that he argues "that the familiar 'life-world' now becomes epiphenomenal, even a 'phantasm.'"⁹⁵ The disjuncture the authors posit between the Anthropocene and experience is, in part, the result of the representation of the earth that is embedded in discourse on the Anthropocene. The Anthropocene refers to the earth as a singular, whole system. And yet, "we," as differentiated multiple beings do not live on such a planet. The planet of the lives of differentiated, various beings is the place of phenomenological encounters with differentiated multiple places.

While Boes and Clark argue that it is the Anthropocene in particular that challenges the validity and relevance of local, experiential knowledge, prioritizing "comprehensive knowledge" over the "merely local" is not exactly new. This trend follows an epistemic tradition that dismisses "local" forms of knowing over the universal, a tradition that dismisses the perspective of marked, embodied subjects (such as those harmed by climate change) over the perspective of those who can inhabit the place of the unmarked (false) universal, a tradition that dismisses views-from-somewhere over the view-from-nowhere. That said, in the history of ecocriticism, a history that Boes and Clark are clearly engaged with, scholars have tended to prioritize place and valorize experiential, embodied knowledge of local ecologies. As Ursula Heise traces, American environmentalism has "invested much of its utopian capital into a return to the local and a celebration of a 'sense of place.'"[96] She argues that such an approach is not necessary to environmentalism per se, but rather to an American cultural context that imagines Americans as "particularly nomadic and mobile."[97] It is, Heise writes, "only in this context" that "authentic rootedness in place [...] comes to seem as a particularly desirable goal to achieve, or as a means of resistance to mainstream culture."[98] Heise argues, however, that such an approach is a dead-end for environmentalism and ecocriticism: for starters, multiple political formations, including national socialism, emerge from "encouraging people to develop a sense of place."[99] Even more, places are connected to one another; local identities are often hybrid, created through the mobility of people, things, ideas and places, as well as through exclusion. Instead of fetishizing the local, Heise calls for the development of an "eco-cosmopolitanism," one that fosters "a sense of planet—a sense of how political, economic, technological, social, cultural, and ecological networks shape daily routines."[100] Boes and Clark, and to some extent, Chakrabarty, can be read in line with Heise's scholarship. These scholars are, in other words, pushing American ecocriticism and environmentalism beyond its prior valorization of the local and of embodied experience. This is an important and welcome development in the field.

The problem, however, is that from the perspective of feminist and postcolonial (and postcolonial feminist) science studies, the situatedness of knowledge about the planet still remains key.[101] In other words, it is not only in the context of an American culture that sees Americans as particularly mobile or nomadic that situatedness is resistant, as Heise argues. It is, rather, also in a context where only privileged social positions are able to claim the view-from-nowhere imagined as necessary for objectivity and where knowledge is imagined as disembodied and hence also not responsible. Heise argues that "besides the valuation of physical experience and sensory perception, [...] an eco-cosmopolitan approach should also value the abstract and highly mediated kinds of knowledge and experience that lend equal or greater support to a grasp of biospheric connectedness."[102]

Without disagreeing with this claim, I highlight that such mediated and abstract forms of knowledge and experience are still physically experienced or perceived through the senses. Mediation does not sublate sensory perception, as Haraway's "Situated Knowledges" argues. It rather produces new and different entities to be perceived. It is telling that while Heise uses the phrase "situated knowledge" throughout her work on eco-cosmopolitanism, she does not cite Haraway or locate the term within the history of feminist science studies. Drawing on this history, in contrast, it becomes clear how even when developing a sense of the planet, a sense of connections through mediated, abstract forms of knowledge, perception is still at play. Bodies remain located, which is not to say fixed but is to say only partially seeing.[103]

In fact, while Clark and Chakrabarty argue that the Anthropocene requires moving beyond phenomenology because the Anthropocene itself cannot be perceived, it is worth remembering that phenomenology has never claimed that everything can be perceived. As David Abram explains, "[F]rom the perspective of my bodily senses, there is no thing that appears as a complete determinate or finished object. Each thing, each entity that my body sees, presents some face or facet of itself to my gaze while withholding other aspects from view."[104] In the context of the Anthropocene, rather than give up on phenomenology, rather than give up on the sensible, we might explore the incompleteness of perception, the resistance of all entities (including the earth) to be perceived in their entirety because of the limited horizon of our own position. Quite simply, when we begin from the perspective of feminist science studies (where knowledge is always imagined as situated) and from phenomenology, the distinction between that which is "merely local" and that which is comprehensive changes. All forms of knowing become local; it is just that only some are identified as such.

It is true that conceptualizing the Anthropocene requires a longer time scale than that of the human and depends on global averages; however, this does not mean that experience needs to be dismissed. In *Animate Planet*, Kath Weston traces how some people who deny climate change mobilize anecdotal experience. "But it's so cold out," they say. This turn to embodied experience, Weston argues, is not "necessarily antagonistic to science."[105] It is, instead, a form of "embodied empiricism," albeit impressionistic and imprecise. Weston argues that we ought to "systematically organize those individual embodied observations. [...] Date them, record them, place the narrative passages in context, expand the number of observers, and see what happens."[106] Weston calls for a form of citizen science that "complements rather than competes with existing lines of research."[107] The benefit of such an approach, Weston argues, is that it could convince those climate change deniers who cite personal experience as evidence.

106   earthly encounters

Weston's refusal to dismiss located, sensory experience, experience of being in a particular place has important implications that Weston herself does not consider. Such an approach is imperative to thinking about the Anthropocene in a way that also addresses inequality and power. To make this especially clear, I briefly turn to *AIR (Auto-Immune Response)*, a multimedia installation by the contemporary artist Will Wilson (Diné). This installation has recently been featured at several museums and galleries in the United States. I turn to Wilson's work not "as a simple orientalization or primitivization of the indigene who is romantically incorporated into an environmental ethic," as Neel Ahuja puts it in his reading of Amitav Ghosh's *The Hungry Tide*.[108] I do not interpret Wilson's art to find an authentic indigenous vision of the earth, but rather to demonstrate how attention to the scale of habitation crucially raises questions having to do with both ecology and interhuman politics.

AIR (Auto-Immune Response)

AIR portrays an uncomfortable place of inhabitation and a largely deserted landscape. At the center of the exhibit, Wilson constructs a metal circular structure, which he designates as a hogan greenhouse. The hogan is a traditional Diné (Navajo) structure. On the hogan, a few plants grow, and in its center, Wilson places a metal cot. In other words, at the heart of the exhibit, one finds a place of inhabitation—though not exactly a comfortable one. The cot has no cushioning; it is just a metal bed. On the walls surrounding the hogan, Wilson displays large photographs (see, for instance, figs. 1, 2, and 3). These photographs feature, as Wilson himself describes, "a post-apocalyptic Navajo man's journey through an uninhabited landscape."[109] The man is actually Wilson himself. He is on Diné land, but the land also does not seem particularly hospitable. In several of the images, Wilson dons a gas mask and in another, goggles (see fig. 2). The mask suggests that the air is poisonous, though also necessary for survival. Invoking a similar double-bind, the exhibit's title, *AIR*, stands for autoimmune response: the immune system supports health, yet here, just like with inhaled air, it also brings the opposite.

We can read this uncomfortable place of inhabitation as a portrayal of the Anthropocene, though the exhibit is clearly not an attempt to display a global condition. A different understanding of the Anthropocene is needed if we are to understand this artwork in this context. Departing from those accounts that prioritize the planetary whole, Anna Tsing reframes the Anthropocene as a period during which there exist few places of refuge "for people and other critters."[110] In contrast, during the Holocene, "places of refuge still existed, even abounded, to sustain reworlding in rich cultural and biological diversity."[111] This understanding of the period brings attention to location and inhabitation; it also resonates with Wilson's exhibit, which focuses on habitability. Although many of the photographs could be understood as landscapes, they never figure the viewer as "outside or separate from the territory."[112] Therefore, similarly to how Leslie Marmon Silko writes of Pueblo imaginaries of the land, the term "*landscape*, as it has entered the English language, is misleading."[113] The viewer in *AIR* is not separate from what is being rendered, but rather, because she or he enters a space with a cot and is surrounded by photographs, she is given a sense of living or dwelling. The images do not evoke a view-from-nowhere or an all-seeing vision, but rather raise questions about habitability, which implies questions concerning connection and mutual affectability.

The land portrayed in *AIR* includes refuges, but not comfortable ones. The images also do not show many creatures thriving, either. The images' theme references a particularly difficult and enduring history: during the 1930s, the Navajo Reservation was the site of a disastrous conservation program. Soil conservationists and federal policy makers with the Bureau of Indian Affairs insisted that the Navajo had overgrazed the land, causing desiccation and soil erosion. Many Diné people, on the other hand, agreed that the land was dry, but argued that the problem was not overgrazing but rather draught. Notwithstanding, the Bureau of

FIGURE 1. Will Wilson, "AIR (*Auto-Immune Response*) #4," inkjet print on archival paper, 44 x 80 inches

108   earthly encounters

FIGURE 2. Will Wilson, "AIR (*Auto-Immune Response*) #5," inkjet print on archival paper, 44 x 110 inches

FIGURE 3. Will Wilson, "AIR: Confluence of Three Generations," inkjet print on archival paper, 44 x 86 inches

Indian Affairs, led by John Collier, ordered a massive livestock reduction program, purchasing and killing sheep and goats and attempting to limit the number of horses, as well. This program, as Marsha Weisiger explains in her environmental history of this period, "took a self-sufficient people, who had supported themselves for at least two centuries with pastoralism and agriculture, and turned them into dependents, who came to rely largely on welfare and what little wage labor they could find."[114] The result has been a "collective memory of trauma."[115]

AIR grapples with the aftermaths of this story. There is no livestock or agriculture in view. In text surrounding the exhibit, Wilson explains that he remembers walking with his grandfather through tall fields of corn just south of Tuba City, Arizona (which is on Diné land). Wilson explains: "My grandfather's cornfields, fruit trees, melons and squash, along with my grandmother Martha's large herd of sheep, had sustained our extended family for generations.... In their lifetime... a way of life attuned to the production of Navajo crops and livestock gave way to the consolidation of a wage-based market economy."[116] This story of change is a story of the Anthropocene, one that is at once about climatic change, colonization, and capitalism, even though it is not about a global condition. Looking at the tree-ring record, Weisiger concludes that at the time of the livestock reduction program, the land indeed was dry—especially in comparison to the prolonged period of wetness from 1905 to 1920. She explains: "[W]hat made it seem so dry to Diné and other locals was the marked contrast with the extreme wetness of previous decades. . . . Beginning in 1925, a shift in atmospheric wind patterns brought a steep decline in the availability of moisture, a rate of decline unprecedented since the last millennium."[117] This dryness was experienced in a context of settler colonialism: it was less easy to move and federal policy failed to attend both to the cultural and economic importance of livestock. The draught and subsequent culling of livestock was experienced as hunger, thirst, pain. It was, in other words, sensed.

Wilson's images evoke this history. They do not focus on planetary change as a whole, but bring attention to a particular place, and with that place, particular embodied experiences (such as breathing with a gas mask or lying on a metal cot). *AIR* also insists on indigenous sovereignty and native survival. Wilson does not, indeed, cannot, disarticulate indigenous politics from climate change. His attention to a particular location makes this possible. Crucially, his photographs are suggestive of response and resilience not death or disappearance. While photography, as Veronica Passalacqua explains, has been used as a "tool of colonization, . . . the very same medium . . . is now used as a tool for Indigenous empowerment and sovereignty by exerting an authority over how, when, and why Indigenous peoples choose to be imaged."[118] Along this vein, several photographs include Wilson himself with a clenched fist in the air, the Marxist, black-and-red power sign of solidarity and resistance. The images also project native becoming into the future: they portray a man responding and adapting to the environment. One of the photographs has him working in what appears to be a lab—he is studying the landscape, figuring things out. Another has him working on a computer by a forest. He appears to be taking notes. In one image of the Hogan, we see a computer and wires (see fig. 1). A final photograph clearly portrays futurity and continuity: *AIR: Confluence of Three Generations* includes Wilson, an older woman, and a young girl on the top of what appears to be Tsékooh Hatsoh, the Grand Canyon (see fig. 3). The elderly woman looks at the girl, and Wilson himself looks over the canyon, but the girl, wearing a gas mask, looks off into the distance, toward a landscape that the viewer of the photograph cannot herself see. This child is headed, we can surmise, into the future. This is not photography of a dying or "vanishing race," as Edward Curtis framed his ubiquitous photographs of native peoples during the nineteenth century.[119] This is about survival, ingenuity, and continuity.

The photography is also not realist. In several images, Wilson himself appears in two places at once. Other images are clearly the collage of several shots, and the borders between these shots do not precisely match up. In still others, the edge of each image does not align so that the border of the work is jagged. Kathleen Ash-Milby argues that Wilson's works "create panoramic views that develop a feeling of multiplicity—physically through digital collage, and contextually by reflecting the multidimensionality of Navajo life today through a thoughtful inquiry of the future."[120] Indeed, Wilson's use of collage evokes futurity because the images suggest a way of being in space (in more than one place at once!) that does not yet exist. It points, in other words, to technological innovation—at the very least, to the innovation of digital photography and collage.

In addition to evoking futurity, this aesthetic also calls attention to how photography is fabricated. This is not an attempt at realism; *AIR* is not an attempt to hide that the images are indeed produced and taken from a particular point of view. Instead, Wilson shows us that they have been made. This departs from the aesthetic that is central to colonial, ethnographic photography of the "Indian."[121] As Gerald Vizenor argues, starting in the nineteenth century, the camera became a "common choice" for simulating the real. Ethnographic photography presented itself as objective truth, hiding its fabrication. For instance, Vizenor explains how Curtis, in preparing his shots, "removed umbrellas, suspenders, the many tracks of civilization, and any traces of written languages."[122] The result was the creation of an Indian other, an image that reduced "native presence to an aesthetic silence and dominance."[123]

Wilson, in contrast, does not present his work as reflections of the world. Instead, he not only features himself as subject matter but also as subject, as artist. Wilson appears as witness, scientist, and political protagonist. He takes the shots, manipulates and presents them as manipulated, thus making his artistry clear.[124] As Wilson explains, "for Indians," he wants to "produce experiences that bring us close to home, while unsettling us with the evidences of colonization." He aims for his "work to strengthen Indians with examples of resistance, and the possibilities of controlling one's own representation."[125] In contrast, for non-Indians, he aims to present an "experience that articulates a history of life constantly remembered, strengthened, and continued in the face of colonization."[126] This is the work of decolonizing photography.

In short, it is true that this exhibit does not portray the Anthropocene in as much as the period refers to a global condition. My argument does not attempt to cover this over. I am, rather, suggesting that when we think about the

Anthropocene, we cannot simply attend to the global because doing so covers over questions of power, politics, sense, and inhabitation. These come to the foreground when we consider how planetary change affects lives, and this requires attention to particular places; it has to do with experience, and it is felt. Boes argues that the Anthropocene challenges the "spatio-temporal parameters in which claims for representation and justice are ordinarily expressed."[127] In contrast, I argue that these parameters continue to be central in addressing the Anthropocene. The scale of lives can continue to interrupt and inform how we understand the universal. This is not to say, following Abram, that "it is only at the scale of our direct, sensory interactions with the land around us that we can appropriately notice and respond to the immediate needs of the living world."[128] It is rather to insist that the two scales coexist in a productive tension without collapsing into one another. *AIR* begs viewers to see how the Anthropocene is experienced and how that experience cannot be disentangled from interhuman politics and history.

Concerning Angels

In "On the Concept of History," Benjamin describes an "Angel of History." This angel faces the past, perceiving it as "one single catastrophe": a heap of rubble. The angel cannot help it; he is flying. A storm blows from paradise. The wind forces his wings open; it "irresistibly propels him into the future, to which his back is turned, while the pile of debris before him grows skyward. This storm is what we call progress."[129]

Although according to Benjamin the materialist historian seizes the past as an image that flashes by, this angel perceives a pile of debris. There is but one pile in Benjamin's evocative writing, and it is an angel, blown by an otherworldly wind, who perceives it. The angel's heap resembles the Anthropocene's effects; it is the material heap of human history. It is the earth affected by Anthropogenic change. It is Chakrabarty's universal human history. It is "progress."

And yet we are not angels.

From the places we live, we do not see one single rubble heap, one single catastrophe. From the many places where we stand, sit, lie, or breathe, the pile before us is and appears different. Benjamin's angel might be positioned to view the universal history Chakrabarty calls for, but this history is interrupted by another plural version, a story that is not otherworldly but tied to the multiple places wherein we live: the earth.

Although the Anthropocene characterizes the earth as a singular, whole system, at the same time, this universal is interrupted by the multiple natures, locations, places, and materialities that constitute the planet as it is lived. It is here that the Anthropocene poses a danger; it is here that the Anthropocene was constituted; and it is here that the Anthropocene can be addressed. Understanding the earth as a singular, whole system is not sufficient even as a strategy. Multiple, place-based imaginaries of climate change are also called for.

Notes

Acknowledgments

1. Beauvoir, *Mémoires*, 481.
2. Beauvoir, *Mémoires*, 481.
3. Qtd. in Le Doeuff, *Hipparchia's Choice*, 136.

Introduction

1. Coates, *Between the World and Me*, 152.
2. I use the term *Anthropocene*, although, as will become clear, I do not treat the "anthropos" or humans as an undifferentiated totality. Nonetheless, echoing Anna Tsing, Heather Swanson, Elaine Gan, and Nils Bubandt, I consider the term useful for entering a conversation. See Tsing et al., "Introduction: Ghosts of the Anthropocene," G3. Similarly, I am aware that while the concept "more-than-human" is helpful, at the same time, to the extent that it draws a distinction between "humans" and "more-than-humans" and to the extent that it relies on the category "human," the concept might be read as relying on and therefore reproducing the exclusionary, racist history of the category, "human." Some humans have been treated as less-than-human, more-than-human, and not human. As much as possible, while considering the "more-than-human," I keep the differentiated position of humans in the framework. It is true, however, that Afro-pessimists such as Frank Wilderson III and Jared Sexton would argue that blackness cannot and should not be redeemed in the category. See Wilderson, *Red, White & Black*, 11, 20–21; Sexton, "The Social Life of Social Death."
3. Tuana, "Material Locations," 238. David Abram also uses the term in *The Spell of the Sensuous*, though he does not elaborate on why he finds it helpful.
4. See, for instance, Allan, "Climate Change" and "Hot Storms Bring Big Rainfall Swings," 130–31.
5. Coates, *Between the World and Me*, 150.
6. Coates, *Between the World and Me*, 151.

7. Malm and Hornborg, "The Geology of Mankind?," 64.

8. Buell, *The Environmental Imagination*, 103.

9. See, especially Buell, *The Environmental Imagination*; Gifford, *Green Voices*, Scigaj, *Sustainable Poetry*, and Coupe, *The Green Studies Readers*. It is worth recognizing that even Nixon, *Slow Violence and the Environmentalism of the Poor* brings attention to nonfiction.

10. Clark, *The Cambridge Introduction to Literature and the Environment*, 47.

11. For more on this approach, see Oppermann, "Theorizing Ecocriticism," 111–12. For other critiques of the turn towards referentiality or outer mimesis in ecocriticism, see Bergthaller, "'Trees Are What Everyone Needs,'" and Phillips, "Ecocriticism, Literary Theory, and the Truth of Ecology."

12. As will become clear, I am drawing here on Merleau-Ponty's *Phenomenology of Perception*. Merleau-Ponty argues that speech is rooted in bodily gestures and expression. "The meaning of words," he writes, "must be formed by a kind of deduction from a *gestural meaning*, which is immanent in speech" (Merleau-Ponty 208). This argument has been taken up both in feminist phenomenology and ecocritical phenomenology, such as Abram's *The Spell of the Sensuous*. Abram argues that to trace the sensory underpinnings (and effects) of language is "to acknowledge the life of the body, and to affirm our solidarity with this physical form," and therefore to "acknowledge our existence as one of the earth's animals" (47). See also Alcoff, "Merleau-Ponty and Feminist Theory on Experience." I draw more explicitly on Alcoff's writing in the pages that follow.

13. Coates, *Between the World and Me*, 107.

14. Citing this section of Coates's text might dangerously fall into the trap of a damage-centered approach, one that "invites oppressed peoples to speak but to 'only speak from that space in the margin that is a sign of deprivation, a wound, an unfulfilled longing'" (413), as Eve Tuck, drawing on bell hooks, explains. Some readers of Coates, most prominently Cornel West, have argued that Coates's memoir gives too much power to whiteness and does not sufficiently account for the real effects of black radicalism and activism. My sense, however, is that while Coates focuses on "historical exploitation, domination, and colonization," his is not a "pathologizing approach in which the oppression singularly defines a community" (Tuck 413). It is in the process of writing in particular that Coates locates a form of struggle that offers a practice that is more than oppression (though it might indeed be more clearly related to activism). Writing, in Coates's vision, consists in a practice of self-sovereignty, and reading and writing might become productive of politicized identities. See West, "Ta-Nehisi Coates Is the Neoliberal Face of the Black Freedom Struggle" and Tuck, "Suspending Damage." For more on the

production of politicized identities through life writing, see Mohanty, *Feminism without Borders*, 78.

15. Morris, *The Origins of the Civil Rights Movement*, 94.

16. In writing that the self is not necessarily singular, I am thinking of work in Latina philosophy, such as Ortega's *In-Between*. Ortega draws on the writing of Gloria Anzaldúa and María Lugones to develop a theory of the self as multiplicitous, which is to say that the self emerges in-between worlds. She "occupies various social locations and is immersed in various cultures" (59). She is therefore more reflective in her every day encounters, and different aspects of her identity can come to the foreground depending on the particular social contexts. Although this self is multiplicitous, it is also unified; Ortega argues that oneness emerges through the sense of existential continuity.

17. Haile, "Ta-Nehisi Coates's Phenomenology of the Body," 498.

18. Spivak, "World Systems & the Creole," 107.

19. Spivak, "World Systems & the Creole," 107.

20. Spivak, *Death of a Discipline*, 72.

21. Spivak, "Imperative to Re-imagine the Planet," 338.

22. Spivak, "Imperative to Re-imagine the Planet," 338.

23. Spivak, "Imperative to Re-imagine the Planet," 338.

24. Spivak, *Death of a Discipline*, 93.

25. Spivak, "Imperative to Re-imagine the Planet," 338.

26. Spivak, *Death of a Discipline*, 72.

27. Spivak, "Imperative to Re-imagine the Planet," 339.

28. Spivak, "Imperative to Re-imagine the Planet," 338.

29. Spivak, "Imperative to Re-imagine the Planet," 341.

30. Spivak, "Imperative to Re-imagine the Planet," 340.

31. Spivak, "World Systems & the Creole," 108.

32. Spivak, *Death of a Discipline*, 78.

33. I use the term *critical theory* to refer to scholarship in the overlapping fields of feminist and queer theory, queer of color critique, postcolonial theory, and cultural and social theory more generally. In other words, by "critical theory" I do not mean to highlight the work of the Frankfurt School but rather an interdisciplinary discussion in the humanities and humanistic social sciences that is generally committed to some form of social justice and that is concerned with how such justice requires conceptual innovation.

34. See Alaimo and Hekman, *Material Feminisms*; Barad, *Meeting the Universe Halfway*; Bennett, *Vibrant Matter*; Braun and Whatmore, *Political Matter*; Brown, "Thing Theory"; Clough, *The Affective Turn*; Coole and Frost, *New Materialisms*;

Grosz, *Becoming Undone*; Grosz, *Chaos, Territory, Art*; Grosz, *Time Travels*; Kirby, *Quantum Anthropologies*; Malabou, *What Should We Do with Our Brains?*; Massumi, *Parables for the Virtual*; Saldanha, "Reontologising Race," Thrift, *Non-Representational Theory*; Whatmore, *Hybrid Geographies*; Wilson, *Psychosomatic*.

35. This is part of Jane Bennett's argument in *Vibrant Matter* and Karen Barad's *Meeting the Universe Halfway*.

36. This argument is clear in Diana Coole and Samantha Frost's introduction to *New Materialisms* as well as Elizabeth Grosz's *Becoming Undone*.

37. This is Brian Massumi's argument in *Parables for the Virtual*.

38. Haraway, "Situated Knowledges." The question that I pose here is also central to Willey's *Undoing Monogamy*. Rather than championing science or returning to science to find useful concepts for queer feminism, Willey seeks an approach that integrates "the politics of science and the possibilities of biology" (3). Toward this end, she reads Audre Lorde's "The Uses of the Erotic," arguing that science is not the only method for approaching matter. Although Willey does not use these terms, one might read her turn to Lorde as, implicitly, an argument for thinking about the lived experience of sensation (such as the erotic) as a way to reframe new materialism as a form of situated knowledge. In this way, my work builds on Willey's.

39. This challenge to the nature/culture distinction is certainly not unique to new materialisms; it is, at the very least, predated by work in feminist science studies, by authors such as Donna Haraway. See Ahmed, "Some Preliminary Remarks," on the founding gestures of new feminist materialism, which, Ahmed argues, posits itself as "new" only by simplifying prior scholarship.

40. For work on the biological materialization of the social construct "race," see, for instance, Kaplan, "When Socially Determined Categories Make Biological Realities," Guthman, "The Implications of Environmental Epigenetics," and Kuzawa and Sweet, "Epigenetics and the Embodiment of Race."

41. *Delgamuukw v. B.C.* provides a concrete example of this. In this legal case, which proceeded from 1984 to 1997, the Gitksan and Wet'suwet'en Nations sought legal recognition for Aboriginal title and self-government over approximately 58,000 square kilometers of land. The case was first heard by the Supreme Court of British Columbia (BC); the decision was appealed and eventually brought to the Supreme Court of Canada. In the BC court hearing, Gitksan and Wet'suwet'en hereditary chiefs used oral tradition as evidence of continued occupancy and social organization prior to and following contact. The BC court, however, under Justice Allan McEachern, decided that this was not valid evidence, unlike the written documents of Hudson Bay traders. The Justice did not simply insist on the superiority of written over oral traditions. He also insisted on an understanding of land

as something that exists out there, apart from us, and he assumed that representation ought to capture this external truth. This was, as Julie Cruikshank points out, particularly ironic because "the Gitksan and Wet'suwet'en preface their Statement of Claim by stressing that their tradition must not be understood exclusively in a literal sense" (Cruikshank, "Invention" 37). Oral tradition consists in "performances to be seen, heard, and witnessed," traditionally at feasts (Cruikschank, "Invention" 40). These performances enact relationships, and these enactments are dependent on the performative force of their repetition. This case demonstrates not simply how the stories we tell about particular places and lands have real effects on how land is appropriated and used. It also shows how competing understandings of representation themselves have legal significance. Such analyses, however, fall by the wayside in most versions of new materialisms that often bracket the question of representation. See Borrows, "Sovereignty's Alchemy" and Daly, *Our Box Was Full*.

42. There exists another related way to understand the problem this book addresses: how can we account for the earth while understanding that this earth can only be accessed as a particular world? As Kelly Oliver summarizes, the "world" is always a world of particular beings. The concept of the world allows for the existence of "multiple worlds constituted by cultural and historical differences (among others)" (31). The "globe," on the other hand, is tied to "fantasies of planetary wholeness" associated with the desire for mastery (31). The question therefore becomes how we can think of the earth while neither reducing that earth to our conception of it nor reproducing a fantasy of wholeness and its related sense of mastery by figuring the earth as a globe. Navigating this problem, this book avoids defining the "earth," but rather focuses on particular, located, sensory, and embodied encounters. These encounters, I argue, give one account of subjectivity as earthly without falling into idealism and without reproducing problematic representations of the globe. Oliver navigates this problem by insisting that the "earth is constituted by a nearly infinite multitude of worlds, all partial, limited, and ultimately determined by their singular bond to the earth" (41). One potential limitation with this formation, however, is how we might understand this "singular bond to the earth" without at the same time positing a singular globe, a planet, which is to say "the earth," to which we are bound. In response to this question, Oliver highlights the earth's "unearthly strangeness," which is to say, the fact that we cannot know it or experience it as it truly is (43). See Oliver, *Earth and World*.

43. Coole and Frost, Introduction, in *New Materialisms: Ontology, Agency, and Politics*, 9.

44. I am certainly not alone in turning to the study of sensation as a way to move beyond the linguistic turn. In her review of feminism and phenomenology, for instance, Helen Fielding argues that phenomenology's focus on embodied

perception allows for a "more robust accounts of the material world without reverting to essentialism" (519). See Fielding, "Feminism." David Howes also contends that the analysis of the senses allows for cultural studies scholars to move beyond the paradigm of the linguistic turn, considering phenomena that cannot be reduced to language. His understanding of sensory analysis, like my own, however, remains attuned to social and cultural significance. "Perception is a shared social phenomenon," he writes, "and as a social phenomenon it has a history and a politics that can only be comprehended within its cultural setting" (5). See Howes, "Introduction: Empires of the Senses."

45. Musser, *Sensational Flesh*, 1.

46. See Willey, *Undoing Monogamy;* Chen, *Animacies*; Ahuja, *Bioinsecurities*; Roy and Subramanian, "Matter in the Shadows; Subramaniam, *Ghost Stories for Darwin*.

47. Roy and Subramanian, "Matter in the Shadows," 28.

48. Roy and Subramanian, "Matter in the Shadows," 37.

49. Merleau-Ponty, *Phenomenology of Perception*, 277.

50. In making this argument, I am joining other feminist theorists and scholars interested in the philosophy of race who have returned to phenomenology (including Emily S. Lee, George Yancy, Mariana Ortega, Iris Marion Young, Sonia Kruks, Diana Coole, Sara Ahmed, Sara Heinämaa, Gayle Salamon, Gail Weiss, Linda Martín Alcoff, Helen A. Fielding, Silvia Stoller, Alia Al-Saji, and Joanna Oksala). These scholars certainly do not develop or read phenomenology similarly. My recovery builds on this research by arguing that the study of the lived experience of embodied sentience is a useful lens for understanding subjectivity in a more-than-human world.

51. Merleau-Ponty, *Phenomenology of Perception*, 66.

52. Merleau-Ponty, *Phenomenology of Perception*, ix.

53. Merleau-Ponty, *Phenomenology of Perception*, ix.

54. More precisely, as Lawrence Hass argues, *Phenomenology of Perception* intervenes in two primary ways that sensation has been conceived, although the text itself does not provide this taxonomy. First is the notion that sensation consists in sense-data, such as "Yellow, White, Heat, Cold, Soft, Hard, Bitter, Sweet" (28). In this view, the external world stimulates our sense organs, producing any given sensation. Perception emerges as a higher-order form of cognition, as we put sensations together in our brains or minds, creating representations of the material world. Merleau-Ponty shows that this understanding of sensation (and perception) is faulty. Central to his argument, which he borrows from Gestalt psychology, is the argument that sense-data is always perceived in a field. That is, I only notice

something as it stands out in the foreground against a background. Because of this, one cannot say that I sense, say, the cold, in itself; rather, I sense the cold as it stands out in relation to something else. Lawrence Hass puts it this way: "[T]here is no sensory 'element' that doesn't presuppose a differentiating, conditioning, field" (30). For Merleau-Ponty, this means that we cannot understand sensations as the primary building blocks from which the mind or brain then builds perception. Instead, perception is prior in that sensations only emerge as we perceive them, as a figure, that is, comes to stand out against a background. This argument also suggests that perception is contextual. What we come to sense emerges in contexts that cannot be separated from sensations but rather give form to them. A relation between elements and a perceiving body-subject together condition what will stand out in the foreground, against a background. The second way in which Merleau-Ponty intervenes in understandings of sensation is that his work makes a case for an understanding of sensation that does not reduce it to neural functioning. As Hass argues, it is not that Merleau-Ponty's work invalidates such physicalist explanation; it is rather that his work shows that such explanations do not exhaustively describe lived experience. See Hass, *Merleau-Ponty's Philosophy*

55. Merleau-Ponty, *Phenomenology of Perception*, 277.

56. de Beauvoir, "A Review of *The Phenomenology of Perception*," 162.

57. As Hass aptly summarizes, "perception is our opening onto things that are *not oneself*" (33), or, as Carol Cantrell explains: "What Merleau-Ponty does that much ecological thought does not do is to put the human perceiver in the picture; indeed, for phenomenology, the experience of the human observer is the starting point, not an irrelevance or nuisance. At the same time, Merleau-Ponty rejects the notion that the human is all that there is, or all that we can know" (27). See Hass, *Merleau-Ponty's Philosophy* and Cantrell, "'The Locus of Compossibility.'"

58. Merleau-Ponty, *Phenomenology of Perception*, xviii.

59. Merleau-Ponty, *Phenomenology of Perception*, xviii.

60. Merleau-Ponty, *Phenomenology of Perception*, xviii–xix.

61. Merleau-Ponty, *Phenomenology of Perception*, 249.

62. Abrams, *The Spell of the Sensuous*, 55.

63. Abrams, *The Spell of the Sensuous*, 89.

64. Abrams, *The Spell of the Sensuous*, 90.

65. Abrams, *The Spell of the Sensuous*, 130.

66. Spivak, "Can the Subaltern Speak?," 294.

67. Butler, *Bodies that Matter*, 8.

68. Braun, *The Intemperate Rainforest*, x.

69. Jameson, *The Prison-House of Language*.

70. See, for instance, Alaimo and Hekman, "Introduction," 1–6.

71. Karen Barad makes a similar argument in *Meeting the Universe Halfway,* 145–46. She focuses her discussion on Judith Butler's and Michel Foucault's writing in particular.

72. See, for instance, the discussion of gender melancholia in Butler, *Bodies that Matter,* 233–36, or Butler's analysis of identity in "Imitation and Gender Insubordination," 26–29.

73. Sedgwick, *Touching Feeling,* 138–41.

74. See, for example, Smith, "American Studies without America" and Guerrero, "Civil Rights versus Sovereignty."

75. Jackson, "Skill and Critique," 73. Jackson considers Merleau-Ponty's example of walking along a beach and encountering some wood: "As I approached, I did not perceive resemblances or proximities which finally came together to form a continuous picture of the upper part of the ship. I merely felt that the look of the object was on the point of altering, that something was imminent in this tension ... Suddenly the sight before me was recast in a manner satisfying my vague expectation" (Jackson 73). The wood contains within it the vision of something that is, at first, indeterminate. Merleau-Ponty's body responds, in tension, as he approaches. He replies, in other words, to "the object's demand" (Jackson 74). The ship then comes into view. This meaning, however, is not determinate and coherent, but provisional. As Alcoff notes, "The phenomenal world constantly folds back on itself, adding to what has come before and what remains still in the background of the present moment" (110). As the perceptual field transforms through time, so too does the phenomenal world. See Alcoff, *Visible Identities*.

76. Merleau-Ponty, *Phenomenology of Perception,* 114.

77. Merleau-Ponty, *Phenomenology of Perception,* 245.

78. Merleau-Ponty, *Phenomenology of Perception,* 243.

79. Andrews, "Vision, Violence, and the Other," 169.

80. That said, many in the field also argue that phenomenology is particularly useful in feminist and critical race studies. Emily S. Lee, for instance, argues that "phenomenology, with Merleau-Ponty's appreciation for the particularities of embodiment, serves as an ideal framework for thinking about the meanings of the embodiments of race" (10). See Lee, Introduction.

81. Fanon, "The Fact of Blackness," 111. Markmann first translated this essay's title as "The Fact of Blackness," but the original French is "L'expérience vécu du Noir," which clearly references existential phenomenology. See Judy's analysis of this misleading translation in "Fanon's Body of Black Experience," 53–55. See also Fanon, "The Lived Experience of the Black Man," translated by Richard Philox.

82. Fanon, "The Fact of Blackness," 111.
83. Fanon, "The Fact of Blackness," 111–12.
84. Fanon, "The Fact of Blackness," xv.
85. Young, "Throwing like a Girl."
86. Young, *Throwing Like a Girl*, 14.
87. Weiss, *Body Images*, 166.
88. I use the phrase "nature-culture-power" borrowing in part from Donna Haraway's "naturecultures." In *The Companion Species Manifesto*, Haraway employs the term to signify "the implosion of nature and culture in the relentlessly historically specific, joint lives of dogs and people" (16). Here, Haraway is thinking in part of the history of breeding and therefore, as a biologist, of evolution and heritability. But she is also referring to the daily habits that develop between humans and dogs, the patterns of affection and of work that come to shape each. "Historical specificity and contingent mutability rule all the way down into nature and culture, into naturecultures," she writes. "There is no foundation; there are only elephants supporting elephants all the way down" (12). There exists a cohistory of dogs and people, an "ontological choreography," to borrow Charis Cussins Thompson's phrase (qtd. on Haraway 8). Our bodies come into being through these histories. To "naturecultures," I add "power" to highlight how the materialization of bodies emerges within contexts of power differentials and inequalities that shape those very bodies. See Haraway, *The Companion Species Manifesto*.
89. Merleau-Ponty, *Phenomenology of Perception*, xv.
90. Merleau-Ponty, *Phenomenology of Perception*, xv.
91. Oksala, *Feminist Experiences*, 163.
92. Smyth, *Merleau-Ponty's Existential Phenomenology*, 145.
93. Smyth, *Merleau-Ponty's Existential Phenomenology*, 63, 64.
94. Heinämaa, "Anonymity and Personhood," 125.
95. Heinämaa, "Anonymity and Personhood," 125.
96. Qtd. in Smyth, *Merleau-Ponty's Existential Phenomenology*, 148.
97. This reading overlaps with Rudolf Bernet's. Bernet argues that Merleau-Ponty's phenomenological reduction is not a reduction of the world to one's understanding of it, but rather a reduction to "natural life." See Bernet, "The Subject in Nature."
98. Such an understanding of the anonymous, prepersonal body departs from others. Several feminist scholars (such as Sharon Sullivan) read this body as either troubling in its alleged neutrality or promising in that it brings attention to how our bodies inform experience in noncultural, nonlinguistic ways (such as Carol Bigwood). In a series of articles, Silvia Stoller defends Merleau-Ponty, arguing

that his phenomenology is compatible with poststructuralist feminism, and contending that with anonymity, Merleau-Ponty does not refer to a neutral ground of embodied experience. Instead, she reads that body as the condition "for the possibility of difference" (2000; 178). This reading actually shares some overlap with Bigwood's analysis, which frames the perceptual body an "indeterminate constancy" in that it is not "an a priori closed to historical change and cultural variation but a kind of a priori that continually opens us to them" (66). In other words, this body is a potential for the experience of the world and for changing with that world. In contrast to Bigwood, and reading alongside Smyth and Heinämaa, I treat the anonymous body not only as an a priori that opens us to historical change but itself as a historical materialization of nature-culture-power. The anonymous body can be understood as the material form nature-culture-power takes in (and as) us, by no effort of our own and independent of how we consciously understand ourselves (though it certainly affects this understanding). See Sullivan, "Domination and Dialogue," Bigwood, "Renaturalizing the Body," Stoller, "Reflections," and Stoller, "Expressivity and Performativity."

99. Alcoff, *Visible Identities*, 10.

100. Alcoff, "Toward a Phenomenology of Racial Embodiment," 272. Alcoff is drawing on Grosz, *Volatile Bodies*.

101. Lee, Introduction, *Living Alterities*, 7.

102. Lee, Introduction, *Living Alterities*, 7.

103. Lee, Introduction, *Living Alterities*, 7.

104. See also Mills, "Materializing Race." Mills argues that while there is no biological basis for race, race is material in that "our bodies [...] have learned to see other bodies [...] through a [...] socio-politically materially originating normative cognitive apparatus [...] that has now become [...] materially embedded and which continues, through a fused physical and sociopolitical corporeality, to influence us today" (38). That cognitive apparatus was developed in the period of European expansion, and it differentiates humans into persons and subpersons.

105. Coates, *Between the World and Me*, 115.

106. Coates, *Between the World and Me*, 10.

107. Coates, *Between the World and Me*, 14.

108. Coates, *Between the World and Me*, 90.

109. Coates, *Between the World and Me*, 92.

110. Weate, "Fanon, Merleau-Ponty and the Difference of Phenomenology," 179.

111. Weate, "Fanon, Merleau-Ponty and the Difference of Phenomenology," 176.

112. Coates, *Between the World and Me*, 116.

113. Qtd. in Alcoff, *Visible Identities*, 110.

114. Alcoff, *Visible Identities*, 111. This balance is also central to Fanon's *Black Skin, White Masks*. Fanon recognizes the weight of history, yet looks toward the present and the future. As Jeremy Weate highlights in his reading of Fanon, "The body-image of the black subject is spliced asunder by history," the "historico-racial schema," a white myth that ascribes meaning to blackness. This becomes especially problematic as the myth is "naturalised as a condition of skin" (Weate 174). The historical becomes essentialized: "[H]istorical construction and contingency is effaced and replaced with the facticity of flesh" (Weate 174). Faced with this reification, Fanon ends *Black Skin, White Masks* arguing that both white and black men ought to "refuse to let themselves be sealed away in the materialized Tower of the Past" (qtd. in Weate 176). He continues, "The body of history does not determine a single one of my actions" (qtd. in Weate 179–80). The sedimentation of history might shape the anonymous body, but it does not define the lived, actual body. In other words, the lived body is constituted, but not determining. See Weate, "Fanon, Merleau-Ponty and the Difference of Phenomenology."

115. Foucault, Forward to the English Translation, *The Order of Things*, xix.

116. Others have made this argument. Coole contends that Merleau-Ponty "did not conform to the phenomenological subjectivism that Foucault condemn" (6). Alcoff refers to "Merleau-Ponty's non-foundationalist account of lived experience" (272). Hass argues, "Merleau-Ponty is emphatic that the living body is not to be grasped as a transcendental subject. For while the living body does set up in advance a field of meanings and a global situation in keeping with its possible movements and projects, this carnal power is not divorced from existence and contingency" (84). See Alcoff, "Toward a Phenomenology of Racial Embodiment," Hass, *Merleau-Ponty's Philosophy*, and Coole, *Merleau-Ponty*.

117. Merleau-Ponty, *Phenomenology of Perception*, xii. To be clear, the masculinism of this passage is Merleau-Ponty's, not mine. I explore the gendered aspect of his writing more thoroughly in the book's first chapter.

118. For more on the intersubjective reading of phenomenology (especially of Husserl), see Oksala, *Feminist Experiences*, 101–5. See also Oksala, *Foucault on Freedom* and Al-Saji, "Bodies and Sensings." Oksala concludes, "The historicity of the body-subject in Merleau-Ponty's phenomenology of the body means that that the body-subject is fundamentally constituted in history" (Oksala, *Foucault on Freedom*, 134). Al-Saji adds: touch is not "first self-given only to be afterwards molded by social relations" (Al-Saji 35). Instead, nature-culture-power are formative of sensation itself.

119. Fanon, *The Wretched of the Earth*, 4.

120. Fanon, *The Wretched of the Earth*, 15.

121. See Puar's critique of multiculturalism, diversity, and intersectionality in "'I Would Rather Be a Cyborg than a Goddess.'"

122. For work on the privilege of ignorance, see the essays collected in Sullivan and Tuana's *Race and Epistemologies of Ignorance*. See also Sedgwick, *Epistemology of the Closet*, 4–8.

123. Sandoval, *Methodology of the Oppressed*, 4.

124. This framing responds to Rey Chow's argument in *The Age of the World Target*, where she reads poststructuralism, with its insistence on finding difference *within* Continental philosophy, as self-referential. In contrast to such a method, I turn outside, though I recognize that I frame this "outside" in relation to the inside, which is to say, that this exteriority is not simply "exterior" at all. See Chow, *The Age of the World Target*, 45–70.

125. See Scott, "The Evidence of Experience" and Thrift, *Non-Representational Theory*, 6–8.

126. Cavarero, *For More than One Voice*; Irigaray, *Speculum,* and Irigaray, *An Ethics of Sexual Difference*.

127. Cavarero, *For More than One Voice*, 9.

128. As Rosi Braidotti, drawing on Adrienne Rich, puts it, "I believe that the redefinition of the female feminist subject starts with the revaluation of the bodily roots of subjectivity and the rejection of the tradition vision of the knowing subject as universal, neutral, and consequently gender-free. This 'positional' or situated way of seeing the subject is based on the understanding that the most important location or situation is the rooting of the subject into the spatial frame of the body. The first and foremost of location in reality is one's own embodiment." See Braidotti, "Toward a New Nomadism," 161.

129. Ortega, *In-Between*, 2.

130. Sedgwick and Frank, "Shame in the Cybernetic Fold."

131. Massumi, "The Autonomy of Affect."

132. Williams, *Marxism and Literature*. That said, something resembling structures of feeling have been an interest in feminist theory for some time. Feminists have long been interested in how feelings are shared across populations and in how these feelings are both indicative of social problems and important resources for change. Betty Friedan's 1963 *The Feminine Mystique* provides a good example. Friedan begins by analyzing the "problem with no name": "a strange stirring, a sense of dissatisfaction, a yearning that women suffered in the middle of the twentieth century in the United States" (15). See Friedan, *The Feminine Mystique*. See also Nash, "Practicing Love." Nash argues that long before the "affective turn," black feminists articulated a political feeling of love.

133. See, for instance, Berlant, *The Female Complaint*; Berlant, "Love: A Queer Feeling"; Berlant, *Cruel Optimism*; Cvetkovich, "Public Feelings"; Cvetkovich, *An Archive of Feeling*; Cvetkovich, *Depression*; Muñoz, "Feeling Brown"; Muñoz, "Feeling Brown, Feeling Down"; Love, *Feeling Backwards*; and Gould, *Moving Politics*. See also Puar's helpful mapping of affect studies in *Terrorist Assemblages*, 206–7.

134. I borrow this taxonomy of the "affective turn" from Puar's *Terrorist Assemblages*, 207.

135. Nash, "Practicing Love," 17.

136. Scott, *Extravagant Abjection*, 32–94.

Chapter 1

1. Although this is a consistent theme across feminist thought, I am thinking especially here of Judith Butler's chapter, "Beside Oneself: On the Limits of Sexual Autonomy" in *Undoing Gender*, 17–39 as well as *The Psychic Life of Power*. Both these texts focus on our dependence, as human living beings, on human others, and yet each text elides our dependence on more-than-human forces, such as temperature

2. Extensive literature about class, poverty, and the cold does exist. See, for instance, work based in the UK on fuel poverty, such as Boardman, *Fuel Poverty*. While the cold figures centrally in literature on poverty, phenomenological descriptions of poverty tend to overlook the significance of the sensation. For instance, Simon J. Charlesworth's *A Phenomenology of the Working Class*, while mentioning the experience of the cold several times, does not explore the sensation to consider how feeling cold affects one's sense of spatiality and embodiment, as I will argue.

3. Fanon, *Black Skin, White Masks*, trans. Philox, 112.

4. Fanon, *Black Skin, White Masks*, trans. Philox, 112.

5. Fanon, *Black Skin, White Masks*, trans. Philox, 112.

6. Fanon, *Black Skin, White Masks*, trans. Philox, 113.

7. Fanon, *Black Skin, White Masks*, trans. Philox, 113–14.

8. Bartky, *Femininity and Domination*, 27.

9. See, for a specific example, Laura Briggs's discussion of the medical experiments conducted by J. Marion Sims, whose 1852 paper, "On the Treatment of Vesico-Vaginal Fistula," taken to be the foundation of gynecology, involved him conducting twenty-nine experimental, unsuccessful surgeries, without anesthesia, on a slave, Anarcha. Briggs, "The Race of Hysteria," 262.

10. See Routledge, "In These Latitudes." I borrow the term "local biologies" from Lock and Nguyen, "Local Biologies."

11. Quoted in Deleuze, *Spinoza*, 17–18.

12. Fanon, *Peau Noire*, 112.

13. See Bennett's discussion of the minerality of bones in *Vibrant Matter*, 10–12.

14. This is one of Butler's projects in *Precarious Life*.

15. Deutscher, "Beauvoir's *Old Age*," 289–90.

16. Kruks, "Beauvoir's Time," 301.

17. Pandya, "The Borderlines."

18. Ahmed, *Cultural Politics of Emotion*, 63.

19. Ahmed, *Cultural Politics of Emotion*, 6.

20. Muñoz, "Feeling Brown," 70.

21. Muñoz, "Feeling Brown," 70.

22. Muñoz, "Feeling Brown," 70.

23. Muñoz, "Feeling Brown," 70.

24. Massumi, *Parables for the Virtual*, 28.

25. Massumi, *Parables for the Virtual*, 28.

26. Massumi, *Parables for the Virtual*, 28.

27. Massumi, *Parables for the Virtual*, 29.

28. The following chapter will analyze Massumi's work (and Deleuze's) in greater detail.

29. Puar, *Terrorist Assemblages*, 207.

30. Leys, "The Turn to Affect."

31. Leys, "The Turn to Affect," 457.

32. Massumi, *Parables for the Virtual*, 29.

33. See Irigaray, "The Invisibility of the Flesh"; Butler, "Sexual Ideology"; Sullivan, "Domination and Dialogue"; Grosz, "Merleau-Ponty and Irigaray"; Young, "Throwing Like a Girl"; and Weate, "Fanon, Merleau-Ponty and the Difference of Phenomenology."

34. In effect, Grosz argues that Merleau-Ponty "anticipates Derridean deconstruction" by refusing dualisms and finding spaces between binary pairs. See Grosz, "Merleau-Ponty and Irigaray," 146.

35. Pandya, "The Borderlines of Culture and Identity," 249.

36. Pandya, "The Borderlines of Culture and Identity," 249.

37. When Pandya includes the autobiographical in her text, she provides a sense of herself—in Adriana Cavarero's terms, a sense of her corporeal, unique, vulnerable condition. Rather than writing of "flesh in general," as Cavarero critiques

Merleau-Ponty, rather than avoiding singularity through a return to generalization, Pandya writes as a "phenomenology of one's uniqueness and the materiality of singular bodies" (Cavarero 2008 144). See Cavarero and Bertolino, "Beyond Ontology and Sexual Difference."

38. Pandya, "The Borderlines of Culture and Identity," 242.
39. Ortega, *In-Between*, 60.
40. Ortega, *In-Between*, 60.
41. Ortega, *In-Between*, 60.
42. Pandya, "The Borderlines of Culture and Identity, 248.
43. Pandya, "The Borderlines of Culture and Identity, 248.
44. Pandya, "The Borderlines of Culture and Identity, 248.
45. Pandya, "The Borderlines of Culture and Identity, 248.
46. Caverero and Bertolino, "Beyond Ontology," 162.
47. Caverero and Bertolino, "Beyond Ontology," 162.
48. Pandya, "The Borderlines of Culture and Identity," 248.
49. Pandya, "The Borderlines of Culture and Identity," 249.
50. Pandya, "The Borderlines of Culture and Identity," 249.
51. Pandya, "The Borderlines of Culture and Identity," 249.
52. Pandya, "The Borderlines of Culture and Identity," 252.
53. Pandya, "The Borderlines of Culture and Identity," 252.
54. Pandya, "The Borderlines of Culture and Identity," 252.
55. Pandya, "The Borderlines of Culture and Identity," 249.
56. Laplanche and Pontalis, *The Language of Psychoanalysis*, 205.
57. Fuss, *Identification Papers*, 2.
58. Fuss, *Identification Papers*, 2.
59. For a particularly helpful reading of the body-subject, see Okasala, "Female Freedom," 209–28.
60. Feerick's *Strangers in Blood* argues that in England, premodern notions of race were articulated in terms of blood and soil. In the late sixteenth and seventeenth centuries, a popular image of the English "social body was that of a multi-limbed tree sprouting from a land mass, one expressing a deep attachment to English soil. Like other 'natural' growths, this trope suggested that the social body was in part constituted by its rootedness in England, that is possessed attributes uniquely derived from that soil" (17). English blood emerged from England's soil. Colonization, Feerick argues, destabilized this imaginary: "Here bodily systems of blood began to unravel in profoundly unpredictable ways" (20). Lines of race were viewed as fixed, but migration was understood as transforming blood. Responding to this tension, writers revisited the centrality of blood and opened a

space for modern notions of race to emerge, such as those connected to skin color. The Canadian discourse that I trace here carries vestiges of this history. The settler colony links the Canadian social body to the land and its climate, but likewise imagines only particular bodies as suited to its geography.

61. Quoted in Berger, "The True North," 5.

62. Quoted in Berger, "The Truth North," 6.

63. Quoted in Berger, "The Truth North," 7.

64. Quoted in Filipczak, *Hot Dry Men*, 8.

65. Lo, "Passing Recognition," 325.

66. Also relevant is literature on whiteness as property: Harris, "Whiteness as Property," Lipsitz, *The Possessive Investment*. See also Moreton-Robinson's "'I Still Call Australia Home.'"

67. Qtd. in Day, *Alien Capital*, 24. See also Veracini, *Settler Colonialism*, 3.

68. Day, *Alien Capital*, 24.

69. Quoted in Berger, "The Truth North," 14.

70. Quoted in Walker, "*Race*," 255.

71. For more on the triangulation of settler colonialism, see Day, *Alien Capital*, 18–25.

72. Kant, "Of the Different Human Races," 8–22.

73. Kant, "Of the Different Human Races," 20.

74. It may seem as though Kant's connection between race and climate would suggest that those he characterizes as "native Americans" would be better acclimated to North America than those from the old world. However, Kant argues that "native Americans" have not "yet fully acclimated" themselves to the region (16). This is "confirmed" by a supposed "suppressed growth of hair on all parts of the body except the head" (16). Although "they" are not acclimated, "they" nonetheless have suffered the "natural" effects of the cold: "they" have a "half-extinguished life power" (17). This contradictory logic, claiming to describe a fact, also attempts to legitimize as natural the genocide and expropriation of settler colonialism.

75. Kelley and Trebilcock, *The Making of The Mosaic*, 316–80.

76. Grace, *Canada and the Idea of North*, 71–72.

77. For more about energy or heat poverty in Canada, see Cairney, "Energy Poverty."

78. Merleau-Ponty, *Phenomenology of Perception*, 330.

79. Merleau-Ponty, *Phenomenology of Perception*, 291.

80. Massumi, *Parables for the Virtual*, 2.

81. Young's "Throwing Like a Girl" brilliantly and beautifully demonstrates this argument.

82. Irigaray makes this argument in "The Invisibility of the Flesh."
83. Merleau-Ponty, *Phenomenology of Perception*, 330.
84. Merleau-Ponty, *Phenomenology of Perception*, 296.
85. Bartky, *Femininity and Domination*, 27.
86. Emphasis added; Fanon, *Black Skin, White Masks*, 110.
87. Emphasis added; Fanon, *Black Skin, White Masks*, 110.
88. Emphasis added; Fanon, *Black Skin, White Masks*, 109.
89. Fanon, *Black Skin, White Masks*, 109.
90. Fanon, *Black Skin, White Masks*, 111.
91. Bartky, *Femininity and Domination*, 27.
92. The understanding of territory that I am drawing on here comes from Gilles Deleuze and Félix Guattari's "1838: Of the Refrain," a chapter of *A Thousand Plateaus*. In this text, Deleuze and Guattari describe territories as spaces marked by repeated, expressive signatures. They give plenty examples from the animal world: the territory produced through the urine of a rabbit, the territory of the brown stagemaker who "lays down landmarks each morning by dropping leaves it picks from its tree, and then turning them upside down so the paler underside stands out against the dirt" (315). Ultimately, the chapter argues that there is something particular about the audible as opposed to the visual that makes it a preferred medium for the production of territory. Perhaps sound is especially linked to territory because sound fills spaces. Rooms, streets, cities, and trains can be tied together by the noises that imbue them.
93. Cavarero, *For More than One Voice*, 37. Cavarero argues that "our ears are always open, even when we sleep. With respect to sounds, therefore, we are in a position of passivity. They can strike us without our being able to foresee or control them" (37).
94. Bartky, *Femininity and Domination*, 27.
95. Fanon, *Black Skin, White Masks*, 98.
96. However, what counts as cold or hot may depend, at least within a range of temperatures, on what one is used to, such that what may feel cold for me may not feel cold for you.
97. Merleau-Ponty, *Phenomenology of Perception*, 218.
98. Butler, *The Psychic Life of Power*, 8.
99. Press Association, "Oxford University Changes Dress Code to Meet Needs of Transgender Students," *The Guardian* (July 29, 2012).
100. In fact, in 2013, *The Guardian* found that 25.7 percent of white students were admitted to the university, compared to 17.2 percent of students of color. In the field of medicine, white students were twice as likely to be admitted, even when

they had the same grades as their peers of color. In 2011, of the 3,186 students admitted, only thirty-two were black. This was "the highest number in 10 years." See Parel and Ball, "Oxford University," and Vasagar, "Black Student Intake."

Chapter 2

1. As this chapter will detail, some important examples of this trend include Massumi's *Parables for the Virtual*, Saldanha, "Politics and Difference), and Puar, *Terrorist Assemblages*.

2. See Polan, "Francis Bacon," 239–40, Vauday, "Écrit à vue." For Merleau-Ponty's analysis of Cézanne, see his "Cézanne's Doubt."

3. Deleuze, *Francis Bacon*, 31.

4. Deleuze, *Francis Bacon*, 37. My translation.

5. Deleuze, *Francis Bacon*, 37. My translation.

6. This is not to say that one can smell underwater. The point, rather, is that smell becomes different; the nose no longer takes in air, and the sense of smell effaces into touch and taste, until, that is, the swimmer returns to the surface: salty air, inhaled, the smell of seaweed tinged with sunscreen.

7. Grosz, *Chaos, Territory, Art*, 3.

8. See Stewart's definition of affect in *Ordinary Affects*: "They're things that happen. They happen in impulses, sensations, expectations, daydreams, encounters, and habits of relating . . ." (2).

9. Deleuze and Guattari, *What Is Philosophy?*, 169.

10. Deleuze and Guattari, *What Is Philosophy?*, 177.

11. Massumi, *Parables for the Virtual*, 36.

12. Massumi, *Parables for the Virtual*, 36 (italics in original).

13. Deleuze and Guattari, *What Is Philosophy?*, 173.

14. Hemmings, "Invoking Affect," 552.

15. Hemmings, "Invoking Affect," 552.

16. Deleuze, "The Shame and the Glory," 123.

17. Deleuze, "The Shame and the Glory," 124.

18. Deleuze, "The Shame and the Glory," 124.

19. Massumi also does not insist on affect's connection to art. He gives the example, for instance, of Ronald Reagan's speeches, focusing on the jerkiness of his spoken language and movements: "at each jerk, at each cut into the movement, the potential is there for the movement to veer off in another direction, to become a different movement" (40). This mode of speaking gives viewers a sense of potentiality. Massumi writes, "Reagan transmitted vitality, virtuality, tendency, in . . .

interruption . . . His means were affective. . . . [A]ffective, as opposed to emotional" (40–41). However, there is nothing particularly aesthetic to Reagan's performance. Massumi, *Parables for the Virtual*.

20. Puar, *Terrorist Assemblages*, 212.
21. Puar, *Terrorist Assemblages*, 212.
22. Puar, *Terrorist Assemblages*, 212.
23. Puar, *Terrorist Assemblages*, 215.
24. Puar, "'I Would Rather Be a Cyborg than a Goddess,'" 49–66.
25. Puar, "'I Would Rather Be a Cyborg than a Goddess,'" 49. Puar's concern with theories that start with the subject involves several arguments. First, drawing on Norma Alarcón, she questions whether subjectivity is in effect a position of privilege, and she wonders whether feminists are "going to make subjects of the whole world" (62–63). Next, drawing on Rey Chow, she develops a reading of intersectionality as, ironically, functioning to recenter white women: intersectionality comes to mark difference from white women, such that white women are again posited as the implicit point of reference. To focus on subjects, in this case, is to continually find difference-from, and yet this difference comes to take the same form over and again, always in reference to the one. And finally, building on new materialist feminists, Puar is worried by the implicit distinctions between nature and culture, as well as the privileging of language and meaning in subject-oriented approaches.
26. See the debate in Benhabib et. al. *Feminist Contentions*, especially Benhabib's "Subjectivity, Historiography, and Politics," 107–26. See also Nussbaum's infamous "The Professor of Parody." For a different, though overlapping response, see Moya, "Postmodernism."
27. Puar "'I Would Rather Be a Cyborg than a Goddess,'" 63.
28. Puar "'I Would Rather Be a Cyborg than a Goddess,'" 60.
29. Puar "'I Would Rather Be a Cyborg than a Goddess,'" 60.
30. Puar "'I Would Rather Be a Cyborg than a Goddess,'" 61.
31. This argument need not be understood as necessarily returning to Judith Butler's understanding that change is possible because norms can never be fully inhabited. In Butler's reading, norms are repeated, which introduces the possibility of difference. To see how Saba Mahmood provides a different understanding of transformation, see Clare, "Agency" and Mahmood, *Politics of Piety*.
32. Massumi, *Parables for the Virtual*, 30.
33. Massumi, *Parables for the Virtual*, 30.
34. Saldanha, "Politics and Difference," 293.
35. Saldanha, "Politics and Difference," 294.

36. Alcoff, "Toward a Phenomenology of Racial Embodiment," 271. Alcoff's attention to the subjective is not, she is clear, to deny the importance of an objectivist account of race, an analysis of how race functions at a "macro-level" through "economic, political, and cultural structures" (271).

37. Alcoff, "Toward a Phenomenology of Racial Embodiment," 271.

38. Alcoff, "Toward a Phenomenology of Racial Embodiment," 273.

39. Walsh, "The Immersive Spectator," 173.

40. Walsh, "The Immersive Spectator," 175.

41. Walsh, "The Immersive Spectator," 174.

42. Walsh, "The Immersive Spectator," 174.

43. My mother's statement is similar but different from the claim that I would never be happy—a frequent parental refrain in these moments, one that Ahmed writes about in *The Promise of Happiness*, 18.

44. Young, "Throwing like a Girl," 146.

45. Charlotte Pinsonnault, e-mail message to author, June 2, 2013.

46. Charlotte Pinsonnault, e-mail message to author, June 2, 2013.

47. Trudeau, "On Bilingualism," 135–43.

48. Charlotte Pinsonnault, email message to author, June 2, 2013.

49. Mortimer-Sandilands, "Unnatural Passions?"

50. Mortimer-Sandilands, "Unnatural Passions?"

51. Mortimer-Sandilands, "Unnatural Passions?"

52. Hill and National Gallery of Canada, *The Group of Seven*.

53. Frye, *The Bush Garden*.

54. Atwood, *Survival*.

55. Gould, "The Idea of North."

56. Ahmed, "A Phenomenology of Whiteness," 158.

57. Ahmed, "A Phenomenology of Whiteness," 159.

58. Whereas cities did not have formal bylaws prohibiting particular groups from living in certain spaces, the property around lakes were managed. For instance, until the 1960s, many lakeside hotels around Québec's major cities explicitly banned Jews. However, there did exist Jewish farming communities north of Montreal that, beginning especially in the 1920s and 1930s, opened their doors to urban Jews in order to supplement their income. These communities became popular vacation spots, and particular hotels and summer camps catering to Jewish customers opened in these regions. See MacLeod and Poutanen, "Upstairs for Hebrew," 34.

59. Dominion Bureau of Statistics, *Census of Canada, 1961*, tables 38–15 and 38–16.

60. US Department of Commerce, *Census of Population: 1960*.

61. Charlotte Pinsonnault, email message to author, June 2, 2013.
62. Ahmed, "A Phenomenology of Whiteness," 154.
63. United States Department of the Interior, *Cape Cod National Seashore*, 2–3.
64. United States Department of the Interior, *Cape Cod National Seashore*, 13.
65. The Mashpee Wampanoag Tribal Council was fully incorporated in 1974. See Peters, *The Wampanoags of Mashpee*, 50. Notwithstanding, in the 1960s, there existed an active, self-identified Mashpee Indian community on Cape Cod.
66. United States Department of the Interior, *Cape Cod National Seashore*, 4.
67. Kennedy, "Remarks of the President on Signing S. 857."
68. Kennedy, "Remarks of the President on Signing S. 857."
69. Edelman, *No Future*, 31.
70. Krahulik, "Cape Queer," 185–212.
71. National Park Service, "Official Report," 28.
72. National Park Service, "Official Report,"120.
73. United States Department of the Interior, *Cape Cod National Seashore*, 4.
74. United States Department of the Interior, *Cape Cod National Seashore*, 4..
75. Krahulik, "Cape Queer," 203.
76. Dresser, *African Americans on Martha's Vineyard.*
77. United States Department of the Interior, *Cape Cod National Seashore*, 8.
78. United States Department of the Interior, *Cape Cod National Seashore*, 8, 4.
79. Thoreau, *Cape Cod*, 215.
80. Buell, *The Environmental Imagination*, 117.
81. Buell, *The Environmental Imagination*, 117.
82. Baldwin explores this discourse of nature as life giving. In an essay about the Canadian feminist Flora MacDonald Denison, Baldwin explores how Denison understood wilderness as a "life giving" (897)—both to those who spend time there, and to the nation itself, a nation (and wilderness) imagined as "curiously devoid of difference" (885). Baldwin, "Wilderness and Tolerance."
83. Thank you to Sergey Dolgopolski for sharing this reading with me.
84. Cf. Razack, who asserts, "Want a nice view? A lovely hiking trail? A sustainable resource? Call a colonizer" (265). My contention is that a colonizer could not produce a nice view. She is not that powerful. Razack, "Colonization."
85. Fitzgerald, Fenster, Argow, and Buynevich, "Coastal Impacts." See also Fitzgerald and Montello, "Backbarrier."
86. For more on the "view-from-above," see chapter 6 in this book.
87. See Moxley, "The Abundance." Moxley explains that in "recent decades, gray seals ... recovered from exploitation, depletion and partial extirpation in the Northwest Atlantic" (abstract). For other reports on the seals, see Repanshek, "Some Long Missing Species" and Bidgood, "Thriving in Cape Cod's Waters." See

134   notes to chapter three

also Lafond, "Dynamics of Recolonization." Lafond focuses on increasing population of gray seals on Muskeget Island, just south of Cape Cod.

88. Skomal, Chisholm, and Correia, "Implications of Increasing Pinniped Populations."

89. For important autobiographical writing that has shaped feminist theorizing, see Rich, "Notes toward a Politics of Location," Lorde, *Sister Outsider,* Williams, *The Alchemy,* Pratt, "Identity." My introduction already cited important critiques of autobiography, notably Thrift, *Non-Representational Theory,* 6–8 and Scott, "The Evidence of Experience," 773–97.

90. See Haraway, "Situated Knowledges," Harding, *Whose Science,* and Rich, "Notes toward a Politics of Location."

91. Rich, "Notes toward a Politics of Location," 212.

92. Rich, "Notes toward a Politics of Location," 213.

93. Rich, "Notes toward a Politics of Location," 213.

94. For an elaboration of this argument, see Butler, *Giving an Account of Oneself,* 3–40.

95. hooks, "Writing Autobiography," in *Women, Autobiography, Theory: A Reader,* ed. Sidonie Smith and Julia Watson (Madison: University of Wisconsin Press, 1998), 429.

96. hooks, "Writing Autobiography," 429.

97. Oksala, *Feminist Experiences,* 5.

98. Alcoff, "Toward a Phenomenology of Racial Embodiment," 267.

99. Wiltse, *Contested Waters,* 209.

100. A few such pools had once existed. One, which was not a municipal facility, required membership to a club whose only requirement was whiteness. This pool shut down following the Civil Rights Act of 1964—it seemed better for white people not to swim than to swim in a nonsegregated space (Hoffman). This follows the trend Wiltse traces in his social history of swimming pools in America. During the 1920s until the early 1950s, tens of millions of Americans enjoyed public swimming pools. After racial desegregation, many of these pools shut down. This represents, as Wiltse writes, "[A] mass abandonment of public space and effectively resegregated swimming" (183). See also Hoffman, Interview with Diane Hoffman.

Chapter 3

1. I am thinking in particular of Foucault's *History of Sexuality,* vol. 1, where he writes, "The rallying point for the counterattack against the deployment of sexuality ought not to be sex-desire, but bodies and pleasures" (157). Also important is his interview "Sex, Power, and the Politics of Identity." Against Foucault,

however, I include the term *desire* here, thinking of Butler's "Imitation and Gender Insubordination," and I include the *erotic*, referencing Lorde's "The Uses of the Erotic."

2. Holland, *The Erotic Life of Racism*, 9. Holland's definition of "the erotic" is purposefully broad and references Audre Lorde's "The Uses of the Erotic." Holland explains that her understanding of the erotic "does not anchor itself in the psychoanalytic but rather fluctuates between dictionary definitions of the words 'desire' and 'erotic'" (120). "Desire" is object oriented (a desire for X). The "erotic" indexes a wider field of embodied experience.

3. See, for instance, Reddy, *Freedom with Violence*, Hanhardt, *Safe Space*; Puar, *Terrorist Assemblages*.

4. Bersani, "Is the Rectum a Grave?" 222.

5. See, for instance, Muñoz, "Thinking beyond Antirelationality," 825.

6. See Nash, *The Black Body in Ecstasy* and Miller-Young, *A Taste for Brown Sugar*. For a reworking of queer studies that asks scholars to neither idealize nor simply critique nonnormative sex, see Amin, *Disturbing Attachments*.

7. Lorde, "The Uses of the Erotic," 58.

8. Lorde, "The Uses of the Erotic," 58.

9. Foucault, "Sex, Power, and the Politics of Identity," 165.

10. Foucault, *History of Sexuality*, vol. 1, 157.

11. I do not, however, focus on the question of the autobiographical in *A Question of Power*. For provocative readings on "autobiography" in *A Question of Power*, see Elder "Bessie Head" and Balseiro, "Between Amnesia and Memory."

12. "Coloured" is the designation given under South African apartheid to those who were not "White," "African," or "Indian."

13. Head, *A Question of Power*, 26; hereafter page numbers are cited parenthetically in the text.

14. Nkosi, *Tasks and Masks*.

15. Ibrahim, *Bessie Head*, 134.

16. Counihan, "The Hell of Desire," 80.

17. Talahite, "Cape Gooseberries," 155.

18. Munro, *South Africa*, 168.

19. Currier and Migraine-George, "Queer Studies," 290.

20. Currier and Migraine-George, "Queer Studies," 289.

21. Weheliye, *Habeas Viscus*, 7.

22. Johnson, *Bessie Head*.

23. Coundouriotis, "An 'Internationalism of the Planted Earth,'" 20.

24. Holland, *The Erotic Life of Racism*, 43. I purposely pair these two texts, one theoretical and the other literary, to highlight my approach to Head's

autobiographical novel. While recognizing that the text is, in part, a piece of fiction, I am primarily interested in the ideas, concepts, or logic that it develops.

25. Hoad, Introduction, 16–18.

26. I write "biological" following the cultural norm that distinguishes between "biological" and "adoptive" parents. But, given that biological connections develop between "adoptive" parents and their children, as well as given practices of surrogacy, I am aware that this norm clearly begs for revision. See Pitts-Taylor, *The Brain's Body*, 95–117.

27. Jolly, "'Intersecting Marginalities,'" 116; Balseiro, "Between Amnesia and Memory," 18.

28. To clarify, while both Dan and Sello are "real" people in the village, they mostly appear in the novel as dreamlike or ghostly figures, and the relationship between the person and the figure remains unclear. The reader, like Elizabeth herself, is never sure whether the real-life Sello sends the ghostly Sello to her, whether the two are in fact one, or whether it is just a coincidence that they look like one another and have the same name. When I use the words "Dan," "Sello," or "Medusa," I am referring to the figures, but this does not mean that, as figures, these entities are not forceful. As Hershini Bhana puts it, "In the novel, Dan, Sello, Medusa . . . have a material presence, exist. . . . They violate Elizabeth's body, shatter her nerves, drag her to the abyss of obscenity and insanity in an almost ritualistic re-enactment of the terrors perpetuated by hegemonic constructions of a violent gendering and racialization" (Bhana 37). Bhana, "Reading Ghostly Desire," 37.

29. Coundouriotis, "An 'Internationalism of the Planted Earth,'" 37–38.

30. For influential analyses of this discourse, see Gilman, "Black Bodies" and Hammonds, "Toward a Genealogy."

31. Lorde, "The Uses of the Erotic," 49.

32. Talahite, "Cape Gooseberries," 146.

33. Lorde, "The Uses of the Erotic," 50.

34. Lorde, "The Uses of the Erotic," 50.

35. Lorde, "The Uses of the Erotic," 50.

36. Lorde, "The Uses of the Erotic," 50.

37. Lorde, "The Uses of the Erotic," 51.

38. Lorde, "The Uses of the Erotic," 53.

39. Lorde, "The Uses of the Erotic," 52.

40. Munro, *South Africa*, 168; Tucker, "A 'Nice-Time Girl.'"

41. For more on "death worlds" see Mbembe, "Necropolitics."

42. Rose, "On the 'Universality' of Madness," 404.

43. Ahuja, "Abu Zubaydah and the Caterpillar," 144.

44. Duggan, "Redefining the Pure."
45. Oksala, *Foucault on Freedom*, 141. Oksala is reading Merleau-Ponty here.
46. See especially the important work in critical race theory in the Crenshaw, et al., *Critical Race Theory*.
47. See Head, *A Woman Alone*, 95.
48. Weheliye, *Habeas Viscus*, 24.
49. Weheliye, *Habeas Viscus*, 22.
50. Nixon, "Refugees and Homecomings," 115–23.
51. Sample, "Space," 29.
52. Sharpe, *Monstrous Intimacies*, 76.
53. Sample, "Space," 29. It was after Botswana's independence in 1966, and after the publication of *A Question of Power*, that the country's mining industry, featuring especially diamonds, developed. See Campbell and Tlou, *History of Botswana*.
54. See Brown, *The Creative Vision of Bessie Head*, 15–16; Morton, Ramsay and Mgadla, *Historical Dictionary of Botswana*, 173–77.
55. See, for instance, Chow, "The Politics of Admittance." See also Halberstam, *The Queer Art of Failure*. In this text, Halberstam draws on Hartman's influential *Scenes of Subjectivity* to figure a form of feminism that uses passivity, self-destruction, and refusal. This "shadow feminism," suggests Halberstam, constitutes an attempt to rethink liberty in ways "that are unimaginable to those who offer freedom as the freedom to become a master" (145). While *A Question of Power* does not exemplify such a form of feminism, and Head herself was insistent that she was not a feminist, the form of belonging that it figures can be understood in line with aspects of this "shadow feminism."
56. Cvetkovich, *Depression*, 152.

Chapter 4

1. Fanon, *Towards the African Revolution*, 65.
2. Fanon, *The Wretched of the Earth*, 3–4.
3. Laplanche and Pontalis, *The Language of Psychoanalysis*, 450. Ranjana Khanna traces how Freud drew on the nationalist and colonialist discourses of archeology and anthropology to shape his understandings of the topography of selfhood. Khanna argues that, with the rise of fascism, Freud's national identity was called into question and he lost faith in the "'advance' of civilization." His concept of the self changed accordingly, moving away from the "notion of an archeologically conceived ego" (38). Freud could no longer draw on the colonialist, nationalist

discourses to imagine the self. Khanna, *Dark Continents*. See also Kuspit, "A Mighty Metaphor."

4. Lacan, "The Mirror Stage," 4, 5.
5. Wolman, "Human Space," 27.
6. Wolman, "Human Space," 25.
7. Akhtar, Prologue, 2.
8. Butler, *The Psychic Life of Power*, 2.
9. Barad, *Meeting the Universe Halfway*, 66.
10. This question overlaps with Elizabeth Wilson's work in "Gut Feminism." Wilson argues that "too often, it is only when anatomy or physiology or biochemistry are removed from the analytic scene . . . that it has been possible to generate a recognizably feminist account of the body" (70). Her analysis draws on Sandor Ferenczi to analyze the gut as sentient and affective. Though centering embodiment, my analysis here is interested in more-than-human forces outside of the body in their traffic with psychic life, as opposed to biology's affective role.
11. Foucault, *Discipline and Punish*.
12. Fanon, *The Wretched of the Earth*, 182.
13. Fanon, *The Wretched of the Earth*, 56.
14. Fanon, *Toward the African Revolution*, 15–16.
15. Foucault, *Discipline and Punish*, 222.
16. Gates, "Critical Fanonism," 467. See also Pellegrini, *Performance Anxieties*, 105.
17. Fanon, *Black Skin, White Masks*, trans. Richard Philcox, 180.
18. Frantz Fanon, *Black Skin, White Masks*, trans. Richard Philcox, 143.
19. Fanon, *Black Skin, White Masks*, trans. Richard Philcox, 148.
20. Fanon, *Black Skin, White Masks*, trans. Richard Philcox, 150.
21. Fanon, *Black Skin, White Masks*, trans. Richard Philcox, 152.
22. Fanon, *Black Skin, White Masks*, trans. Richard Philcox, 152.
23. Fanon, *Black Skin, White Masks*, trans. Richard Philcox, 165.
24. Fanon, *Black Skin, White Masks*, trans. Richard Philcox, 165.
25. Fanon, *Black Skin, White Masks*, trans. Richard Philcox, 188.
26. Scholarship in indigenous studies often argues that Indigeneity should not be understood as a racial formation, since such an understanding of Indigeneity reduces indigenous existence to a biopolitical question of population and frames indigenous nations as minorities within settler colonial nation-states, rather than as sovereign nations. My argument in this chapter suggests that race and racism do not only involve biopolitical questions, however, but questions concerning appropriation and land, as well. This framework can allow us to understand how Indigeneity

has been racialized without dismissing indigenous sovereignty in the first place. For example, Mark Rifkin writes of the problem of conceiving the Seneca nation as a racial identity. This transposes "questions of place (geopolitics) . . . into those of race (biopolitics)" (71). See Rifkin, *When Did the Indians Become Straight?*, 71. See also Deloria, "American (Indian) Studies," 670–71. *American Quarterly* 55, no. 4 (December 2003): 670–1; Smith, "American Studies without America," 309–15, Justice, "The Necessity of Nationhood."

27. Fanon, *The Wretched of the Earth*, 19.
28. Fanon, *The Wretched of the Earth*, 4.
29. Fanon, *The Wretched of the Earth*, 4.
30. Fanon, *The Wretched of the Earth*, 3.
31. Fanon, *The Wretched of the Earth*, 4.
32. Fanon, *The Wretched of the Earth*, 15.
33. Fanon, *The Wretched of the Earth*, 15.
34. Fanon, *The Wretched of the Earth*, 16.
35. Fanon, *Les damnés de la terre*, 19.
36. Du Bois, *The Souls of Black Folk*.
37. Khanna, *Dark Continents*, 175.
38. Fanon, *Black Skin, White Masks*, 167.
39. Fanon, *Black Skin, White Masks*, 151.
40. Scott, *Extravagant Abjection*, 32–94.
41. Scott, *Extravagant Abjection*, 69.
42. Scott, *Extravagant Abjection*, 65.
43. Scott, *Extravagant Abjection*, 61.
44. Qtd. in Scott, *Extravagant Abjection*, 61.
45. Scott, *Extravagant Abjection*, 68.
46. Scott, *Extravagant Abjection*, 70.
47. Scott, *Extravagant Abjection*, 68.
48. Scott, *Extravagant Abjection*, 70–71.
49. Scott, *Extravagant Abjection*, 90.
50. Scott, *Extravagant Abjection*, 76. Scott's italics.
51. Scott, *Extravagant Abjection*, 63.
52. Fanon, *Black Skin, White Masks*, 188.
53. Fanon, *The Wretched of the Earth*, 9. Following Philcox's translation, I use the term *land* here; however, in Fanon's original French text, the term he uses is *terre*, which can be translated either to "land" or to "earth." I will therefore use these two terms, *land* and *earth*, interchangeably. That said, within Anglo-American traditions, "land" is most often used within discourses concerning property and the

nation-state, whereas as "earth" figures in more ecological writing or writing concerned with "nature."

54. Fanon, *The Wretched of the Earth*, 8.

55. Fanon, *The Wretched of the Earth*, 8. For a reading of the importance of land in the American, black nationalist tradition, see Kelley, *Freedom Dreams*, 124–26. Kelley explains how "many critics ... are quick to dismiss the land question as impractical or even impossible"; however, land is central: it is "space, territory on which people can begin to reconstruct their lives" (125).

56. Sekyi-Otu, *Fanon's Dialectic of Experience*, 4.

57. Sekyi-Otu, *Fanon's Dialectic of Experience*, 5.

58. Fanon, *The Wretched of the Earth*, 9.

59. Fanon, *The Wretched of the Earth*, 232.

60. Fanon, *The Wretched of the Earth*, 9.

61. Fanon, *The Wretched of the Earth*, 9.

62. Fanon, *The Wretched of the Earth*, 9.

63. Marx, "The *Grundisse*," 226.

64. Marx, "The *Grundisse*," 227.

65. Marx, "The *Grundisse*," 226.

66. Marx, "Economic and Philosophic Manuscripts of 1844," 72.

67. Fanon, *The Wretched of the Earth*, 141.

68. Fanon, *The Wretched of the Earth*, 141.

69. Fanon, *The Wretched of the Earth*, 134.

70. Marx, "Economic and Philosophic Manuscripts of 1844," 115.

71. Marx, "Economic and Philosophic Manuscripts of 1844," 115.

72. Marx, "Economic and Philosophic Manuscripts of 1844," 72.

73. Marx, "Economic and Philosophic Manuscripts of 1844," 115.

74. Renault, "Corps à corps."

75. Fanon, *Toward the African Revolution*, 13.

76. Fanon, "The 'North African Syndrome,'" 13.

77. Freud, *Beyond the Pleasure Principle*, 76.

78. Freud, *Beyond the Pleasure Principle*, 61.

79. Fanon, *A Dying Colonialism*, 65.

80. Wenzel, "Stratigraphy and Empire," 174–75.

81. Fanon, *A Dying Colonialism*, 66.

82. Frantz and Azoulay, "La socialthérapie," 96.

83. Allen, *Frantz Fanon's Clinical Studies*, 90.

84. See especially Chow, "The Politics of Admittance," 34–56 and Pile, "The Troubled Spaces," 260–78.

85. Irigaray, *Speculum*, 133.

86. Irigaray, *Speculum*, 133.
87. Irigaray, *Speculum*, 134.
88. Irigaray, *Speculum*, 133.
89. Foucault, *The Order of Things*, 422.
90. Foucault, *The Order of Things*, 422.

Chapter 5

1. See, for instance, Crutzen, "Geology of Mankind," 23. This text popularized the term, yet the term has not yet been formally recognized by the International Commission on Stratigraphy. Crutzen in fact introduced the word earlier in Crutzen and Stoermer, "The Anthropocene." Other important publications include Steffen et al., "The Anthropocene," and Zalasiewicz et al., "Are We Now Living in the Anthropocene?"

2. Will Steffen, et al, "The Anthropocene," 843, 842.

3. Petition created by CJ Cuomo, available at http://petitions.moveon.org/sign/against-the-official-2.

4. In a conversation with Natalie Jeremijenko, Hannah makes a similar point. See Hannah, "Natalie Jeremijenko's New Experimentalism," 199.

5. Chakrabarty, "The Climate of History" and Chakrabarty, "Postcolonial Studies."

6. Chakrabarty, "The Climate of History," 217.

7. See Malm and Hornborg, "The Geology of Mankind?" and Haraway, "Anthropocene, Capitalocene, Plantationocene, Chtulucene."

8. Nixon, Interview with Marzec and Carruth, 300.

9. Malm and Hornborg, "The Geology of Mankind?," 67.

10. Haraway, *Staying with the Trouble*, 49. See also Lightfoot, et al. This essay explores how, while European colonists encountered landscapes that had *already* been shaped, to different degrees, by humans, colonialism quickly transformed many environments. The essay focuses in particular on changes in Alta and Baja California between the 1600s and early 1800s, and draws attention to the early modern world prior to industrialization. Kawa takes a different approach. He argues that the dominant narrative of the Anthropocene is Eurocentric in that it does not consider how people across the globe have contributed to changing the planet. Kawa argues that the Anthropocene has "a much deeper foundation" than European industrialization in pre-Columbian, Amazonian large-scale agriculture (ix). Kawa especially looks at the production of "*terra preta*," a particularly fertile form of soil in Amazonia. See Kawa, *Amazonia in the Anthropocene*.

11. Haraway, *Staying with the Trouble*, 33.

12. Haraway, *Staying with the Trouble*, 55.

13. Haraway, *Staying with the Trouble*, 55.

14. Kawa, *Amazonia in the Anthropocene* also identifies this irony and seeks to rethink the Anthropocene in a way that decenters humans. He explains: "I argue that any discussion of the Anthropocene requires not only a deeper awareness of the human influence on the planet but also greater attention toward planetary responses to human action" (ix).

15. Ahuja, "Species in a Planetary Frame," 29.

16. Chen, *Animacies*, 2.

17. Haraway explains that while the term is misleading and insufficient, she will continue to use it sparingly but strategically because it is recognizable and institutionalized. I follow suit. See Haraway, *Staying with the Trouble*, 47

18. Alaimo, "Your Shell on Acid," 90.

19. Alaimo, "Your Shell on Acid," 90.

20. Crutzen and Stoermer, "The Anthropocene," 17.

21. Steffen, et al. "The Anthropocene," 842.

22. Schellnhuber, "'Earth System' Analysis," 1020.

23. Schellnhuber, "'Earth System' Analysis," 1020.

24. "Amsterdam Declaration on Global Change."

25. "Amsterdam Declaration on Global Change."

26. It is worth noting that the term *ecosystem* actually preexists wide interest in "system theory." The term was introduced in Tansley, "The Use and Abuse of Vegetational Concepts and Terms." Tansley posited an "ecosystem" as an object of study that highlights organisms in their physical environments. Organisms and their environments together form "ecosystems." He claimed that "ecosystems" are one category of the "multitudinous physical systems of the universe, which range from the universe as a whole down to the atom" (299–300).

27. Chisholm, "General System Theory," 45.

28. Qtd. in Chisholm, "General System Theory," 46.

29. The link to structuralism here is obvious. For Saussure, signifiers have meaning only in reference to other signifiers. The relations between signifiers form a structure: language. See Saussure, *Course in General Linguistics*.

30. Lövbrand, Stripple, and Wilman, "Earth System Governmentality," 7.

31. Lawton, "Earth System Sciences," 1965.

32. Lawton, "Earth System Sciences," 1965.

33. Clifford and Richards, "Earth System Science," 379–83.

34. In effect, Schellnhuber first argues that there are three ways, but he later contends that one of these methods is not feasible. Schellnhuber, "'Earth System' Analysis," 1020.

35. O'Neil and Steenman-Clark, "The Computational Challenges of Earth-System Science."

36. An exception is Walker, "Earth System Science and the Western Worldview." Walker concludes, "Earth system science may yet teach us that ... predictive ability is unattainable. Earth system science may be the first natural science to introduce humility into the western worldview" (369).

37. Pitman, "On the Role of Geography," 140.

38. See Lawton, "Earth System Science," 1965 and Schellnhuber, "'Earth System' Analysis," 1020.

39. Schellnhuber, "'Earth System' Analysis," 1019.

40. As I will explain in the following section, this image, as well as Pitman's phrase, explicitly link ESS to the space program and the visual politics embedded within.

41. Zerilli, "This Universalism," 5.

42. Schor, "The Crisis," 46.

43. Schor, "The Crisis," 44.

44. Schor, "The Crisis," 46.

45. Cosgrove, *Apollo's Eye*, xi.

46. Other scholars have also begun to trace these connections. See especially DeLoughrey, "Satellite Planetarity" and Marzec, "Militarized Ecologies."

47. Doel, "Constituting the Postwar Earth Sciences."

48. Doel, "Constituting the Postwar Earth Sciences," 644.

49. Doel, "Constituting the Postwar Earth Sciences," 644.

50. Carruth and Marzec, "Environmental Visualization in the Anthropocene," 205.

51. DeLoughrey comes to the same conclusion in "Satellite Planetarity." She writes, "our evidence for and understanding of the Anthropocene has been produced by the very military technologies that brought us the Cold War" (274).

52. Cosgrove, *Apollo's Eye*, 259.

53. Tellingly, visitors today who enter the Kennedy Space Center, a tourist destination in Northern Florida that attempts to build support for NASA, first encounter a large fountain and commemoration to Kennedy and this speech. On this fountain, tourists read the engraved sentence: "The eyes of the world now look into space, to the moon and to the planets beyond, and we have vowed that we shall not see it governed by a hostile flag of conquest, but by a banner of freedom and peace." Kennedy's statements about American leadership are not included. This is a vision of the universal that hides the center of power it calls for.

54. Cosgrove, *Apollo's Eye*, xi.

55. Cosgrove, *Apollo's Eye*, xi.

56. See Kaplan, "Mobility and War," Kaplan, "The Balloon Prospect," and Jazeel, "Spatializing Difference," 78.

57. Oliver, *Earth and World*, 20.

58. "Vision," International Geosphere-Biosphere Programme.

59. "Future Earth Secretariat Announced," International Geosphere-Biosphere Programme.

60. Schellnhuber, "'Earth System' Analysis," 1023.

61. Schellnhuber, "'Earth System' Analysis," 1022.

62. Haraway, *Staying with the Trouble*, 49.

63. I draw the term *survivance* (a form of resistant survival) from Vizenor, *Manifest Manners*.

64. Surrallés, "Intimate Horizons," 135.

65. Surrallés, "Intimate Horizons," 144.

66. Viveiros de Castro, "Cosmological Deixis," 470.

67. Viveiros de Castro, "Cosmological Deixis," 478.

68. Viveiros de Castro, "Cosmological Deixis," 470.

69. Viveiros de Castro, "Cosmological Deixis," 469.

70. Viveiros de Castro, "Cosmological Deixis," 470.

71. Viveiros de Castro, "Cosmological Deixis," 470.

72. Deleuze and Guattari, *What Is Philosophy?*, 164.

73. Deleuze and Guattari, *What Is Philosophy?*, 164.

74. Viveiros de Castro, "Cosmological Deixis," 470.

75. Lorimer also develops a multinatural approach to the Anthropocene, focusing on biodiversity conservation in particular. See Lorimer, "Multinatural Geographies." See also Latour, "From Multiculturalism to Multinaturalism," 9. Latour does not write specifically about the Anthropocene here, however. But he locates in the environmental movement's mononaturalism its political limit: "It is their *mono*-naturalism that renders them unable to be the ones who monitor our collective experiments. They might expand to renew the whole of politics, but only when they are ready to swallow not only multiculturalism but also multinaturalism" (9).

76. Some environmental scientists largely agree with this conclusion. Clifford and Richards, for instance, argue that "ESS downplays the significance of spatial diversity and differentiation, and the local needs for environmental science." They continue, "The world is highly differentiated ... [E]xcessive emphasis on its global functioning can divert attention from that diversity and its inequalities" (382). On the basis of such arguments, Clifford and Richards argue that funding agencies ought not simply put resources into ESS but also continue to support

environmental sciences. Jäger, a policy consultant who works on environmental issues, also agrees. She writes of the need to collaborate with "'local' stakeholders and decision makers," arguing for the need of "placed-based" and "highlight contextualized" science and technology (24). See Clifford and Richards, "Earth System Science" and Jäger, "Sustainability Science."

77. Chakrabarty, *Provincializing Europe*, 63.
78. Chakrabarty, *Provincializing Europe*, 63.
79. Chakrabarty, *Provincializing Europe*, 63.
80. Chakrabarty, *Provincializing Europe*, 63. In this passage, Chakrabarty is quoting Marx, *Theories of Surplus Value*, 468.
81. Chakrabarty, *Provincializing Europe*, 66.
82. Chakrabarty, *Provincializing Europe*, 67.
83. Baucom also makes this argument in "The Human Shore," 10.
84. Chakrabarty, "The Climate of History," 221.
85. Benjamin, "Theses on the Philosophy of History," 262, 256.
86. Chakrabarty, *Provincializing Europe*, 66.
87. Chakrabarty, "The Climate of History," 220.
88. Chakrabarty, "The Climate of History," 220.
89. Chakrabarty, "Postcolonial Studies," 12.
90. Clark, *Ecocriticism on the Edge*, 38.
91. Clark, *Ecocriticism on the Edge*, 38.
92. Clark, *Ecocriticism on the Edge*, 38.
93. Boes, "Beyond Whole Earth," 162.
94. Boes, "Beyond Whole Earth," 162.
95. Clark, *Ecocriticism on the Edge*, 39.
96. Heise, *Sense of Place and Sense of Planet*, 8.
97. Heise, *Sense of Place*, 49.
98. Heise, *Sense of Place*, 49.
99. Heise, *Sense of Place*, 47.
100. Heise, *Sense of Place*, 55.
101. Both Braidotti and Alaimo make similar arguments. See Braidotti, "Four Theses on Posthuman Feminism," 40 and Alaimo, "Your Shell on Acid," 90.
102. Heise, *Sense of Place*, 62.
103. To be fair, Heise does understand eco-cosmopolitanism as something to be sensed: as her subtitle indicates, she is keen to develop a "*sense* of the planet" (italics added). But Heise does not write about the significance of how something akin to sensation remains important in her project. Heise also recognizes what I too see as a central challenge for environmental thought: how to create "a vision of the global

that integrates allegory—still a mode that is hard to avoid in representations of the whole planet—into a more complex formal framework able to accommodate social and cultural multiplicity" (21).

104. Abram, *The Spell of the Sensuous*, 50.

105. Weston, *Animate Planet*, 115.

106. Weston, *Animate Planet*, 124.

107. Weston, *Animate Planet*, 129.

108. Ahuja, "Species in a Planetary Frame," 29.

109. Wilson, "Will Wilson: AIR."

110. Qtd. in Haraway, *Staying with the Trouble*, 100.

111. Qtd. in Haraway, *Staying with the Trouble*, 100.

112. Silko, "Landscape," 1005.

113. Silko, "Landscape," 1005.

114. Weisiger, *Dreaming of Sheep*, 4.

115. Weisiger, *Dreaming of Sheep*, xv.

116. Roffman, "Will Wilson," 39.

117. Weisiger, *Dreaming of Sheep*, 47.

118. Passalacqua, Introduction, xii. For more on colonialism, resistance, and the history of photography of the Diné in particular, see Faris, *Navajo and Photography*. See also Vizenor, *Fugitive Poses*, 145–66.

119. For more on Curtis's photography and for indigenous readings of this photography, see Tsinhnahjinnie, "When Is a Photograph Worth a Thousand Words?" and Lyman, *The Vanishing Race*.

120. Qtd. in Passalacqua, Introduction, xvii.

121. This aesthetic can also be read in line with Silko's description of how Pueblo landscape avoids realism. Silko explains, "The ancients did not presume to tamper with what had already been created. [...] A 'lifelike' rendering of an elk is too restrictive. Only the elk *is itself*" (1005, 1006). Similarly, one might say that only the place Wilson portrays is itself. Therefore, he is not reproducing it or capture it so much as render something else. See Silko, "Landscape."

122. Vizenor, *Fugitive Poses*, 160.

123. Vizenor, *Fugitive Poses*, 154.

124. I am borrowing here from Passalacqua's reading of Zig Jackson's photograph, "Kennecott Copper Mine, Tooele, Utah" (2000). Passalacqua writes: "The size and scope of the open-put strip mine—one of the largest in the world—is almost incomprehensible. Jackson sits at the edge as witness to the devastation as political protagonist by photographing and exhibiting it" (xvii). In Passalacqua, Introduction.

125. Wilson, Artist Statement, 54.

126. Wilson, Artist Statement, 54.
127. Boes, "Beyond Whole Earth," 162.
128. Abram, *The Spell of the Sensuous*, 268.
129. Benjamin, "Theses on the Philosophy of History," 257.
130. For an explanation of the concept of intra-action, see Barad, *Meeting the Universe Halfway*, 33.

Bibliography

Abram, David. *The Spell of the Sensuous: Perception and Language in a More-Than-Human World.* New York: Vintage Books, 1997.
Ahmed, Sara. *Cultural Politics of Emotion.* New York: Routledge, 2004.
———. "A Phenomenology of Whiteness." *Feminist Theory* 8, no. 2 (2007): 149–68.
———. *The Promise of Happiness.* Durham, NC: Duke University Press, 2010.
———. *Queer Phenomenology: Orientations, Objects, Others.* Durham, NC: Duke University Press, 2006.
———. "Some Preliminary Remarks on the Founding Gestures of 'New Materialism.'" *European Journal of Women's Studies* 15, no. 1 (2008): 23–39.
Ahuja, Neel. "Abu Zubaydah and the Caterpillar," *Social Text* 29, no. 106 (2011): 127–49.
———. *Bioinsecurities: Disease Interventions, Empire, and the Government of Species.* Durham, NC: Duke University Press, 2016.
———. "Species in a Planetary Frame: Eco-cosmopolitanism, Nationalism, and *The Cove.*" *Tamkang Review* 42, no. 2 (June 2012): 13–31.
Akhtar, Salman. Prologue. In *The Geography of Meaning: Psychoanalytic Perspectives on Place, Space, Land, and Dislocation*, edited by Maria Teresa Savio Hooke and Salman Akhtar, 1–9. London: International Psychoanalytical Association, 2007.
Alaimo, Stacy. "Your Shell on Acid: Material Immersion, Anthropocene Dissolves." In *Anthropocene Feminism*, edited by Richard Grusin, 89–120. Minneapolis: University of Minnesota Press, 2017.
Alaimo, Stacy, and Susan Hekman. "Introduction: Emerging Models of Materiality in Feminist Theory." In *Material Feminisms*, edited by Stacy Alaimo and Susan Hekman, 1–22. Bloomington: University of Indiana Press, 2008.
———, editors. *Material Feminism.* Bloomington: University of Indiana Press, 2008.
Alarcón, Norma. "The Theoretical Subject(s) of *This Bridge Called My Back* and Anglo-American Feminism." In *The Second Wave: A Reader in Feminist Theory*, edited by Linda Nicholson, 288–99. New York: Routledge, 1997.

Alcoff, Linda Martín. "Merleau-Ponty and Feminist Theory on Experience." In *Chiasm: Merleau-Ponty's Notion of Flesh*, edited by Fred Evans and Leonard Lawlor, 251–71. Albany: State University of New York Press, 2000.

———. "Toward a Phenomenology of Racial Embodiment." In *Race*, edited by Robert Bernasconi, 267–83. New York: Blackwell Books, 2002.

———. *Visible Identities: Race, Gender, and the Self.* New York: Oxford University Press, 2006.

Allan, Richard P. "Climate Change: Human Influence on Rainfall." *Nature* 40 (February 17, 2011): 344–45.

Allen, Mazi A. Frantz Fanon's Clinical Studies. PhD Dissertation, Graduate School of Binghamton University State University of New York, 2011.

Al-Saji, Alia. "Bodies and Sensings: On the Uses of Husserlian Phenomenology for Feminist Theory." *Continental Philosophy Review* 43 (2010): 13–37.

Amin, Kadji. *Disturbing Attachments: Genet, Modern Pederasty, and Queer History.* Durham, NC: Duke University Press, 2017.

"Amsterdam Declaration on Global Change." *Challenges of a Changing Earth: Global Change Open Science Conference.* Amsterdam. July 13, 2001.

Andrews, Jorella. "Vision, Violence, and the Other: A Merleau-Pontean Ethics." In *Feminist Interpretations of Maurice Merleau-Ponty*, edited by Dorothea Olkowski and Gail Weiss, 167–82. University Park: Pennsylvania State University Press, 2006.

Associated Press. "Oxford University Changes Dress Code to Meet Needs of Transgender Students." *The Guardian* (July 29, 2012).

Atwood, Margaret. *Survival: A Thematic Guide to Canadian Literature.* Toronto, ON: Anansi Press, 1972.

Baldwin, Andrew. "Wilderness and Tolerance in Flora MacDonald Denison: Towards a Biopolitics of Whiteness." *Social and Cultural Geography* 11, no. 8 (2010): 883–901.

Balseiro, Isabel. "Between Amnesia and Memory: Bessie Head and Her Critics." In *Emerging Perspectives on Bessie Head*, edited by Huma Ibrahim, 17–24. Trenton, NJ: Africa World Press, 2004.

Barad, Karen. *Meeting the Universe Halfway: Quantum Physics and the Entanglement of Matter and Meaning.* Durham, NC: Duke University Press, 2007.

Bartky, Sandra Lee. *Femininity and Domination: Studies in the Phenomenology of Oppression.* New York: Routledge, 1990.

Baucom, Ian. "The Human Shore: Postcolonial Studies in an Age of Natural Science." *History of the Present: A Journal of Critical History* 2, no. 1 (Spring 2012): 1–23.

de Beauvoir, Simone. *Memoires d'une jeune filles rangée*. Paris: Gallimard, 2008.
———. "A Review of *The Phenomenology of Perception* by Maurice Merleau-Ponty." In *Simone de Beauvoir: Philosophical Writings*, edited by Margaret A. Simons, Marybeth Timmermann, and Mary Beth Mader, 151–64. Champaign: University of Illinois Press, 2014.
Benhabib, Seyla. "Subjectivity, Historiography, and Politics." In *Feminist Contentions,* 107–26. London: Routledge, 1995.
Benjamin, Walter. "Theses on the Philosophy of History." In *Illuminations*, edited by Hannah Arendt, translated by Harry Zohn, 253–64. New York: Schocken Books, 2007.
Bennett, Jane. *Vibrant Matter: A Political Ecology of Things*. Durham, NC: Duke University Press, 2010.
Berger, Carl. "The True North Strong and Free." In *Nationalism in Canada*, edited by Peter Russell, 3–26. Toronto, ON: McGraw Hill, 1966.
Bergthaller, Hannes. " 'Trees Are What Everyone Needs:' *The Lorax*, Anthropocentrism, and the Problem of Mimesis." In *Nature in Literary and Cultural Studies*, edited by Catrin Gersdorf and Sylvia Mayer, 155–75. Amsterdam: Editions Rodopi, 2006.
Berlant, Lauren. *Cruel Optimism*. Durham: Duke University Press, 2011.
———. *The Female Complaint: The Unfinished Business of Sentimentality in American Culture*. Durham, NC: Duke University Press, 2008.
———. "Love: A Queer Feeling." In *Homosexuality & Psychoanalysis*, edited by Tim Dean and Christopher Lane, 432–52. Chicago: University of Chicago Press, 2001.
Bernet, Rudolf. "The Subject in Nature: Reflections on Merleau-Ponty's *Phenomenology of Perception*." In *Merleau-Ponty in Contemporary Perspectives*, edited by P. Burdke and J. van Der Veken, 53–68. Doredretch, The Netherlands: Kluwer, 1993.
Bersani, Leo. "Is the Rectum a Grave?" *October* 43 (Winter, 1987): 197–222.
Bhana, Hershini. "Reading Ghostly Desire: Writing the Edges of Bessie Head's *A Question of Power*," In *Emerging Perspectives on Bessie Head*, edited by Huma Ibrahim, 52–73. Trenton, NJ: Africa World Press, 2004.
Bidgood, Jess. "Thriving in Cape Cod's Waters, Gray Seals Draw Fans and Foes." *New York Times* (August 17, 2013).
Bigwood, Carol. "Renaturalizing the Body (With the Help of Merleau-Ponty)." *Hypatia* 6, no. 3 (Autumn, 1991): 54–73.
Boardman, Brenda. *Fuel Poverty: From Cold Homes to Affordable Warmth*. London: Earthscan, 2010.

Boes, Tobias. "Beyond Whole Earth: Planetary Mediation and the Anthropocene." *Environmental Humanities* 5 (2014): 155–70.

Borrows, John. "Sovereignty's Alchemy: An Analysis of *Delgamuukw v. British Columbia*." *Osgoode Hall Law Journal* 37, no. 3 (1999): 537–96.

Braidotti, Rosi. "Four Theses on Posthuman Feminism." In *Anthropocene Feminism*, edited by Richard Grusin, 21–48. Minneapolis: University of Minnesota Press, 2017.

———. "Toward a New Nomadism: Feminist Deleuzian Tracks; or, Metaphysics and Metabolism." In *Gilles Deleuze and the Theater of Philosophy*, edited by Constantin V. Boundas and Dorothea Olkowski, 159–86. New York: Routledge, 1994.

Braun, Bruce. *The Intemperate Rainforest: Nature, Culture, and Power on Canada's West Coast*. Minneapolis: University of Minnesota Press, 2002.

———. "Producing Vertical Territory: Geology and Governmentality in Late Victorian Canada." *Cultural Geographies* 7, no. 1 (2000): 7–46.

———, and Sarah J. Whatmore, editors. *Political Matter: Technoscience, Democracy, and Public Life*. Minneapolis: University of Minnesota Press, 2010.

Briggs, Laura. "The Race of Hysteria: 'Overcivilization' and the 'Savage' Woman in Late Nineteenth-Century Obstetrics and Gynecology." *American Quarterly* 52, no. 2 (2000): 246–73.

Brown, Bill. "Thing Theory." *Critical Inquiry* 28, no. 1 (Autumn 2001): 1–22.

Brown, Coreen. *The Creative Vision of Bessie Head*. Madison, NJ: Fairleigh Dickinson University Press, 2003.

Buell, Lawrence. *The Environmental Imagination: Thoreau, Nature Writing, and the Formation of American Culture*. Cambridge, MA: Harvard University Press, 1995.

Butler, Judith. *Bodies that Matter: On the Discursive Limits of "Sex."* New York: Routledge, 1993.

———. *Giving and Account of Oneself*. New York: Fordham University Press, 2005.

———. "Imitation and Gender Insubordination." In *Inside/Out: Lesbian Theories, Gay Theories*, edited by Diana Fuss, 13–31. New York: Routledge, 1991.

———. *Precarious Life: The Power of Mourning and Violence*. New York: Verso, 2004.

———. *The Psychic Life of Power: Theories of Subjection*. Palo Alto, CA: Stanford University Press, 1997.

———. "Sexual Ideology and Phenomenological Description: A Feminist Critique of Merleau-Ponty's *Phenomenology of Perception*." In *The Thinking Muse:*

Feminism and Modern French Philosophy, edited by J. Allen and Iris Marion Young, 85–100. Bloomington: Indiana University Press, 1989.

———. *Undoing Gender*. New York: Routledge, 2004.

Cairney, Kristen Meredith Forbes. "Energy Poverty as Ideological Poverty in Canada." *Esurio: Journal of Hunger and Poverty* 1, no. 1 (2008): 21–27.

Campbell, Alec, and Thomas Tlou. *History of Botswana*. Gaborone, Bostwana: Macmillan, 1997.

Cantrell, Carol H. "'The Locus of Compossibility': Virginia Woolf, Modernism, and Place." *Interdisciplinary Studies in Literature and Environment* 5, no. 2 (1998): 25–40.

Carruth, Allison, and Robert P. Marzec. "Environmental Visualization in the Anthropocene: Technologies, Aesthetics, Ethics." *Public Culture* 26, no. 2 (2014): 205–11.

Cavarero, Adriana. *For More than One Voice: Toward a Philosophy of Vocal Expression*. Translated by Paul. A Kottman. Stanford, CA: University of Stanford Press, 2005.

———, and Elisabetta Bertolino. "Beyond Ontology and Sexual Difference: An Interview with the Italian Feminist Philosopher Adriana Cavarero." *differences: A Journal of Feminist Cultural Studies* 19, no. 1 (2008): 128–67.

Césaire, Aimé. "Letter to Maurice Thorez." *Social Text* 28, no. 2 (Summer 2010): 145–52.

Chakrabarty, Dipesh. "The Climate of History: Four Theses." *Critical Inquiry* 35, no. 2 (Winter 2009): 197–222.

———. "Postcolonial Studies and the Challenge of Climate Change." *New Literary History* 43, no. 1 (Winter 2012): 1–18.

———. *Provincializing Europe: Postcolonial Thought and Historical Difference*. Princeton, NJ: Princeton University Press, 2000.

Charlesworth, Simon J. *Phenomenology of the Working Class*. Cambridge, UK: Cambridge University Press, 2000.

Chen, Mel. *Animacies: Biopolitics, Racial Mattering and Queer Affect*. Durham, NC: Duke University Press, 2012.

Chisholm, Michael. "General System Theory and Geography." *Institute of British Geographers: Transactions* 42 (1967): 45–52.

Chow, Rey. *The Age of the World Target: Self-Referentiality in War, Theory, and Comparative Work*. Durham, NC: Duke University Press, 2006.

———. "The Politics of Admittance: Female Sexual Agency, Miscegenation, and the Formation of Community in Frantz Fanon." In *Frantz Fanon: Critical*

Perspectives, edited by Anthony C. Alessandrini, 34–56. London: Routledge, 1999.

Clare, Stephanie. "Agency, Signification, Temporality." *Hypatia: A Journal of Feminist Philosophy* 24, no. 4 (2009): 50–62.

Clark, Timothy. *The Cambridge Introduction to Literature and the Environment.* Cambridge, UK: University of Cambridge Press, 2011.

———. *Ecocriticism on the Edge: The Anthropocene as a Threshold Concept.* London: Bloomsbury, 2015.

Clifford, Nick, and Keith Richards. "Earth System Science: An Oxymoron?" *Earth Surface Processes and Landforms* 30 (2005): 379–83.

Clough, Patricia, editor. *The Affective Turn: Theorizing the Social.* Durham, NC: Duke University Press, 2007.

Coates, Ta-Nehisi. *Between the World and Me.* New York: Spiegel & Grau, 2015.

Coole, Diana. *Merleau-Ponty and Modern Politics after Anti-Humanism.* Plymouth, UK: Rowman and Littlefield Publishers, 2007.

———, and Samantha Frost, editors. *New Materialisms: Ontology, Agency, and Politics.* Durham, NC: Duke University Press, 2010.

Cosgrove, Denis. *Apollo's Eye: A Cartographic Genealogy of the Earth in Western Imagination.* Baltimore, MD: Johns Hopkins University Press, 2001.

Coundouriotis, Eleni. "An 'Internationalism of the Planted Earth': The Literary Origins of Bessie Head's Idea of the Village." *Comparative Literature Studies* 48, no. 1 (2011): 20–43.

Counihan, Clare. "The Hell of Desire: Narrative, Identity, and Utopia in *A Question of Power*." *Research in African Literatures* 42, no. 1 (Spring 2011): 68–86.

Coupe, Laurence, editor. *The Green Studies Readers: From Romanticism to Ecocriticism.* London: Routledge, 2000.

Crenshaw, Kimberlé, Neil Gotanda, Gary Peller, and Kendall Thomas, editors. *Critical Race Theory: The Key Writings That Formed the Movement.* New York: New Press, 1995.

Cruikshank, Julie. "Invention of Anthropology in British Columbia's Supreme Court: Oral Tradition as Evidence in *Delgamuukw v. B.C.*" *BC Studies* 92 (Autumn 1992): 25–42.

Crutzen, Paul. "Geology of Mankind: The Anthropocene." *Nature* 415 (2002): 23.

———, and Eugene F. Stoermer. "The Anthropocene." *IGBP (International Geosphere-Biosphere Programme) Newsletter* 41 (2000): 17.

Currier, Ashley, and Thérèse Migraine-George. "Queer Studies/African Studies: An (Im)possible Transaction?" *GLQ: A Journal of Lesbian and Gay Studies* 22, no. 2 (April 2016): 281–305

Cvetkovich, Ann. *An Archive of Feeling: Trauma, Sexuality, and Lesbian Public Cultures.* Durham, NC: Duke University Press, 2003.

———. *Depression: A Public Feeling.* Durham, NC: Duke University Press, 2012.

———. "Public Feelings." *South Atlantic Quarterly* 106, no. 3 (Summer 2007): 459–68.

Daly, Richard. *Our Box Was Full: An Ethnography for the Delgamuukw Plaintiffs.* Vancouver: University of British Columbia Press, 2005.

Day, Iyko. *Alien Capital: Asian Racialization and the Logic of Settler Colonialism.* Durham, NC: Duke University Press, 2016.

Deleuze, Gilles. *Francis Bacon: Logique de la sensation.* Paris: Editions de la différence, 1984.

———. "The Shame and the Glory: T. E. Lawrence." In *Essays Critical and Clinical*, translated by Daniel W. Smith and Michael A. Greco, 115–25. Minneapolis: University of Minnesota Press, 1997.

———. *Spinoza: Practical Philosophy.* Translated by Robert Hurley. San Francisco, CA: City Lights Books, 1988.

———, and Félix Guattari. *A Thousand Plateaus.* Translated by Brian Massumi. London: Athlone Press, 1988.

———, and Félix Guattari. *What Is Philosophy?* Translated by Hugh Tomlinson and Graham Burchell. New York: Columbia University Press, 1994.

Deloria, Philip. "American (Indian) Studies: Can the ASA Be an Intellectual Home?" *American Quarterly* 55, no. 4 (December 2003): 669–80.

DeLoughrey, Elizabeth. "Satellite Planetarity and the Ends of the Earth," *Public Culture* 26, no. 2 (2014): 257–80.

Deutscher, Penelope. "Beauvoir's *Old Age.*" In *The Cambridge Companion to Simone de Beauvoir*, edited by Claudia Card, 286–304. Cambridge, UK: Cambridge University Press, 2003.

Doel, Ronald E. "Constituting the Postwar Earth Sciences: The Military's Influence on the Environmental Sciences in the USA after 1945." *Social Studies of Science* 33, no. 5 (October 2003): 635–66.

Dominion Bureau of Statistics. *Census of Canada, 1961, Series 1.2: Population, Ethnic Groups.* Ottawa: Queen's Printer and Controller Stationery, 1962. Tables 38–15 and 38–16.

Dresser, Tom. *African Americans on Martha's Vineyard: From Enslavement to Presidential Visit.* Charleston, SC: The History Press, 2010.

Dreyfus, Herbert, and Paul Rabinow. *Michel Foucault: Beyond Structuralism and Hermeneutics.* Chicago, IL: University of Chicago Press, 1982.

Du Bois, W. E. B. *The Souls of Black Folk.* New York: Dover Publications, 1994.

Duggan, Niamh. "Redefining the Pure—Sexual Retreat and Virtual Relation in Colette's *The Pure and The Impure.*" Presentation. National Women's Studies Association Annual Conference, Oakland, CA, November 9, 2012.

Edelman, Lee. *No Future: Queer Theory and the Death Drive.* Durham, NC: Duke University Press, 2004.

Elder, Arlene. "Bessie Head: The Inappropriate Appropriation of 'Autobiography.'" In *Emerging Perspectives on Bessie Head,* edited by Huma Ibrahim, 1–16. Trenton, NJ: Africa World Press, 2004.

Fanon, Frantz. *Black Skin, White Masks.* Translated by Richard Philox. New York: Grove Press, 2008.

———. *Les damnés de la terre.* Paris: Éditions La Découverte/Poche, 2002.

———. "The Fact of Blackness." In *Black Skin, White Masks,* translated by Charles L. Markmann, 109–40. New York: Grove Press, 1967.

———. "The Lived Experience of the Black Man." In *Black Skin, White Masks,* translated by Richard Philox, 89–119. New York: Grove Press, 2008.

———. *Peau Noire, Masques Blancs.* Paris: Les Éditions du Seuil, 1952.

———. *Toward the African Revolution.* Translated by Haakon Chevalier. New York: Monthly Review Press, 1964.

———. *The Wretched of the Earth.* Translated by Richard Philcox. New York: Grove Press, 2004.

———, and Jacques Azoulay. "La socialthérapie dans un service d'hommes musulmans: difficultés méthodologiqes." *Information psychiatrique* 30, no. 9 (1954): 1095–106.

Faris, James C. *Navajo and Photography: A Critical History of the Representation of an American People.* Albuquerque: University of New Mexico, 1996.

Feerick, Jean E. *Strangers in Blood: Relocating Race in the Renaissance.* Toronto, ON: University of Toronto Press, 2010.

Fielding, Helen, A. "Feminism." In *The Routledge Companion to Phenomenology,* edited by Sebastian Luft and Søren Overgaard, 518–27. Florence, KY: Taylor & Francis, 2013.

Filipczak, Zirka Z. *Hot Dry Men, Cold Wet Women: Theories of the Humors in Western European Art, 1575–1700.* New York: American Federation of Arts, 1997.

Fitzgerald, Duncan, Michael Fenster, Britt Argow, and Illya Buynevich. "Coastal Impacts Due to Sea-Level Rise." *Annual Review of Earth and Planetary Sciences* 36 (2008): 601–47.

———, and Todd M. Montello. "Backbarrier and Inlet Sediment Response to the Breaching of Nauset Spit and Formation of New Inlet, Cape Cod, MA."

In *Formation and Evolution of Multiple Tidal Inlet Systems*, edited by David G. Aubrey and Graham S. Giese, 158–85. Washington, DC: American Geophysical Union, 1993.

Foucault, Michel. *Discipline and Punish: The Birth of the Prison*. Translated by Alan Sheridan. New York: Vintage Books, 1995.

———. Forward to the English Translation. *The Order of Things: An Archeology of the Human Sciences*, ix–xiv. New York: Vintage, 1994.

———. *History of Sexuality*, vol.1. Translated by Robert Hurley. New York: Random House, 1990.

———. "Sex, Power, and the Politics of Identity." In *Ethics: Subjectivity and Truth, Essential Works of Foucault*, vol. 1, edited by Paul Rabinow, 163–73. New York: New Press, 1997.

Freud, Sigmund. *Beyond the Pleasure Principle*. Translated by James Strachey. London: Norton & Co., 1989.

Friedan, Betty. *The Feminine Mystique*. New York: W. W. Norton & Company, 1963.

Frye, Northrop. *The Bush Garden: Essays on the Canadian Imagination*. Toronto, ON: Anansi Press, 1971.

Fuss, Diana. *Identification Papers*. New York: Routledge, 1995.

"Future Earth Secretariat Announced." International Geosphere-Biosphere Programme. Accessed April 2017. www.igbp.net/about/vision.4.1b8ae20512db692f2 a6800017590.html.

Gates, Henry Louis. "Critical Fanonism." *Critical Inquiry* 17 (Spring 1991): 457–70.

Gifford, Terry. *Green Voices: Understanding Contemporary Nature Poetry*. London: Manchester University Press, 1995.

Gilman, Sander. "Black Bodies, White Bodies: Toward an Iconography of Female Sexuality in Late Nineteenth-Century Art, Medicine, and Literature." *Critical Inquiry* 12, no. 1 (1985): 204–42.

Gould, Deborah. *Moving Politics: Emotion and Act Up's Fight Against AIDS*. Chicago, IL: University of Chicago Press, 2009.

Gould, Glenn. "The Idea of North (1967)." *Solitude Trilogy*. CBC.

Grace, Sherrill E. *Canada and the Idea of North*. Montreal and Kingston, QC: McGill-Queen's University Press, 2001.

Grosz, Elizabeth. *Becoming Undone: Darwinian Reflection on Life, Politics, and Art*. Durham, NC: Duke University Press, 2011.

———. *Chaos, Territory, Art: Deleuze and the Framing of the Earth*. New York: Columbia University Press, 2008.

———. "Merleau-Ponty and Irigaray in the Flesh." In *Merleau-Ponty, Interiority and Exteriority, Psychic Life and the World*, edited by Dorothea Olkowski and James Morley, 145–66. Albany: State University of New York Press, 1999.

———. *Time Travels: Feminism, Nature and Power*. Durham, NC: Duke University Press, 2005.

———. *Volatile Bodies: Toward a Corporeal Feminism*. Bloomington: Indiana University Press, 1994.

Guerrero, Marie Anna Jaimes. "Civil Rights versus Sovereignty: Native American Woman in Life and Land Struggles." In *Feminist Genealogies, Colonial Legacies, Democratic Futures*, edited by M. Jacqui Alexander and Chandra Talpade Mohanty, 101–24. New York: Routledge, 1996.

Guthman, Julie, and Becky Mansfield. "The Implications of Environmental Epigenetics: A New Direction for Geography Inquiry on Health, Space, and Nature-Society Relations." *Progress in Human Geography* 37, no. 4 (2013): 486–504.

Haile III, James B. "Ta-Nehisi Coates's Phenomenology of the Body," *Journal of Speculative Philosophy* 31, no. 3 (2017): 493–503.

Halberstam, Judith. *The Queer Art of Failure*. Durham, NC: Duke University Press, 2011.

Hammonds, Evelynn. "Toward a Genealogy of Black Female Sexuality: The Problematic of Silence." In *Feminist Theory and the Body: A Reader*, edited by Janet Price and Margrit Shildrick, 93–104. New York: Routledge, 1997.

Hanhardt, Christina. *Safe Space: Gay Neighborhood History and the Politics of Violence*. Durham, NC: Duke University Press, 2013.

Hannah, Dehlia, and Natalie Jeremijenko. "Natalie Jeremijenko's New Experimentalism." In *Anthropocene Feminism*, edited by Richard Grusin, 197–220. Minneapolis: University of Minnesota Press, 2017.

Haraway, Donna J. "Anthropocene, Capitalocene, Plantationocene, Chtulucene: Making Kin." *Environmental Humanities* 6 (2015): 159–65.

———. *The Companion Species Manifesto: Dogs, People, and Significant Otherness*. Chicago, IL: Prickly Paradigm Press, 2003.

———. "Situated Knowledges: The Science Question in Feminism and the Privilege of Partial Perspectives." *Feminist Studies* 14, no. 3 (Autumn 1988): 575–99.

———. *Staying with the Trouble: Making Kin in the Chthulucene*. Durham, NC: Duke University Press, 2016.

Harding, Sandra. *Whose Science? Whose Knowledge?* Ithaca, New York: Cornell University Press, 1991.

Harris, Cheryl. "Whiteness as Property." *Harvard Law Review* 106, no. 8 (June 1993): 1707–91.
Hartman, Saidiya. *Scenes of Subjection: Terror, Slavery, and Self-Making in Nineteenth-Century America*. New York: Oxford University Press, 1997.
Hass, Lawrence. *Merleau-Ponty's Philosophy*. Bloomington: Indiana University Press, 2008.
Head, Bessie. *A Question of Power*. London: Heinemann, 1974.
———. *A Woman Alone: Autobiographical Writings*. Oxford, UK: Heinemann, 1990.
Heinämaa, Sara. "Anonymity and Personhood: Merleau-Ponty's Account of the Subject of Perception." *Continental Philosophy Review* 48 (2015): 123–42.
Heise, Ursula K. *Sense of Place and Sense of Planet: The Environmental Imagination of the Global*. New York: Oxford University Press, 2008.
Hemmings, Clare. "Invoking Affect: Cultural Theory and the Ontological Turn." *Cultural Studies* 19, no. 5 (September 2005): 548–67.
Hill, Charles, and National Gallery of Canada. *The Group of Seven: Art for a Nation*. Ottawa, ON: McClelland & Stewart, 1995.
Hoad, Neville. Introduction. In *Sex and Politics in South Africa*, edited by Neville Hoad, Karen Martin and Graeme Reid, 14–27. Cape Town, South Africa: Double Storey Books, 2005.
Hoffman, Barnett. *StoryCorps*. By Diane Hoffman. October 5 and 6, 2007. http://nbfpl.org/story.html.
Holland, Sharon Patricia. *The Erotic Life of Racism*. Durham, NC: Duke University Press, 2012.
hooks, bell. "Writing Autobiography." In *Women, Autobiography, Theory: A Reader*, edited by Sidonie Smith and Julia Watson, 429–32. Madison: University of Wisconsin Press, 1998.
"Hot Storms Bring Big Rainfall Swings." *Nature* (June 11, 2015): 130–31.
Howes, David. "Introduction: Empires of the Senses." In *Empire of the Senses: The Sensual Culture Reader*, edited by David Howes, 1–20. New York: Berg, 2005.
Ibrahim, Huma. *Bessie Head: Subversive Identities in Exile*. Charlottesville: University Press of Virginia, 1996.
Irigaray, Luce. *An Ethics of Sexual Difference*. Translated by Carolyn Burke and Gillian C. Gill Ithaca, NY: Cornell University Press, 1993.
———. "The Invisibility of the Flesh: A Reading of Merleau-Ponty, *The Visible and the Invisible*, 'The Intertwining—The Chiasm.' " In *An Ethics of Sexual Difference*, translated by Carolyn Burke and Gillian C. Gill, 127–53. London: Continuum, 2005.

———. *Speculum: Of the Other Woman*. Translated by Gillian C. Gill. Ithaca, NY: Cornell University Press, 1985.

Jackson, Gabrielle Bennet. "Skill and Critique of Descartes in Gilbert Ryle and Maurice Merleau-Ponty." In *Merleau-Ponty at the Limits of Art, Religion, and Perception*, edited by Kascha Semonovitch and Neal DeRoo, 63–78. New York: Continuum International Publishing Group, 2010.

Jäger, Jill. "Sustainability Science." In *Earth System Science in the Anthropocene*, edited by Eckart Ehlers and Thomas Krafft, 19–26. New York: Springer, 2006.

Jameson, Fredric. *The Prison-House of Language: A Critical Account of Structuralism and Russian Formalism*. Princeton, NJ: Princeton University Press, 1975.

Jazeel, Tariq. "Spatializing Difference beyond Cosmopolitanism: Rethinking Planetary Futures." *Theory Culture Society* 28 (2011): 75–97.

Johnson, Joyce. *Bessie Head: The Road of Peace of Mind, A Critical Appreciation*. Newark: University of Delaware Press, 2008.

Jolly, Rosemary. "'Intersecting Marginalities': The Problem of Homophobia in South African Women's Writing." In *Cross-Addressing: Resistance Literature and Cultural Borders*, edited by John C. Hawley, 107–20. Albany: State University of New York Press, 1996,

Judy, Ronald A. T. "Fanon's Body of Black Experience." In *Fanon: A Critical Reader*, edited by Lewis R Gordon, T. Denean Sharpley-Whiting, and Renée T. White, 53–73. Cambridge, MA: Blackwell Publishers, 1996.

Justice, Daniel Heath. "The Necessity of Nationhood: Affirming the Sovereignty of Indigenous National Literatures." In *Moveable Margins: The Shifting Spaces of Canadian Literatures*, edited by Chelva Kanaganayakam, 143–59. Toronto, ON: TSAR, 2006.

Kant, Immanuel. "Of the Different Human Races" (1775). In *The Idea of Race*, edited by Robert Bernasconi and Tommy L. Lott, 8–22. Indianapolis, IN: Hackett Publishing Company, 2000.

Kaplan, Caren. "Mobility and War: The Cosmic View of U.S. Air Power," *Environment and Planning A* 38, no. 2 (2006): 395–407.

———. "The Balloon Prospect: Aerostatic Observation and the Emergence of Militarized Aeromobility." In *From Above: War, Violence, and Verticality*, edited by Peter Adey, Mark Whitehead, and Alison J. Williams, 19–40. London: Hurst, 2013.

Kaplan, Jonathan. "When Socially Determined Categories Make Biological Realities: Understanding Black/White Health Disparities in the U.S." *The Monist* 93, no. 2 (2010): 281–97.

Kawa, Nicholas C. *Amazonia in the Anthropocene: People, Soils, Plants, Forests.* Austin: University of Texas Press, 2016.

Kelley, Ninette, and Michael Trebilcock. *The Making of The Mosaic: A History of Canadian Immigration Policy.* Toronto, ON: University of Toronto Press, 2010.

Kelley, Robin D. G. *Freedom Dreams: The Black Radical Imagination.* Boston, MA: Beacon Press, 2002.

Kennedy, John F. "Remarks of the President on Signing S. 857, An Act to Provide for the Establishment of the Cape Cod National Seashore." Washington, DC, Office of the White House Press Secretary. August 7, 1962.

Khanna, Ranjana. *Dark Continents: Psychoanalysis and Colonialism.* Durham, NC: Duke University Press, 2003.

Kirby, Vicky. *Quantum Anthropologies: Life at Large.* Durham, NC: Duke University Press, 2011.

Krahulik, Karen Christel. "Cape Queer? A Case Study of Provincetown, Massachusetts." *Journal of Homosexuality* 52, no. 1–2 (2006): 185–212.

Kruks, Sonia. "Beauvoir's Time/Our Time: The Renaissance in Simone de Beauvoir Studies." *Feminist Studies* 31, no. 2 (Summer 2005), 286–309.

———. *Retrieving Experience: Subjectivity and Recognition in Feminist Politics.* Ithaca, NY: Cornell University Press, 2001.

Kuspit, Donald. "A Mighty Metaphor: The Analogy of Archaeology and Psychoanalysis." In *Sigmund Freud and Art*, edited by Lynn Gamwell and Richard Wells, 133–52. London: Freud Museum, 1989.

Kuzawa, Christopher and Elizabeth Sweet. "Epigenetics and the Embodiment of Race: Developmental Origins of US Racial Disparities in Cardiovascular Health." *American Journal of Human Biology* 21, no. 1 (2009): 2–15.

Lacan, Jacques. "The Mirror Stage as the Formative of the Function of the I." In *Écrits*, edited and translated by Alan Sheridan, 1–8. London: Travistock Publications, 1977.

Laplanche, Jean, and Jean-Bertrand Pontalis. *The Language of Psychoanalysis.* Translated by Donald Nicholson-Smith. New York: W. W. Norton and Company, 1973.

Latour, Bruno. "From Multiculturalism to Multinaturalism: What Rules of Method for the New Socio-Scientific Experiments?" *Nature and Culture* 6, no. 1 (Spring 2011): 1–17.

Lawton, John. "Earth System Sciences." *Science* 292, no. 5524 (June, 15, 2001): 1965.

Le Doeuff, Michèle. *Hipparchia's Choice: An Essay Concerning Women, Philosophy, Etc.*, translated by Trista Selous. New York: Columbia University Press, 2007.

Lee, Emily S. "Introduction." In *Living Alterities: Phenomenology, Embodiment, and Race*, edited by Emily S. Lee, 1–18. Albany: State University of New York Press, 2014.

Levin, David Michael. "Singing the World: Merleau-Ponty's Phenomenology of Language." *Philosophy Today* 42, no. 3 (Fall 1998): 319–36.

Leys, Ruth. "The Turn to Affect: A Critique." *Critical Inquiry* 37, no. 3 (Spring 2011): 434–72.

Lightfoot, Kent G., Lee M. Panich, Tsim D. Schneider, and Sara L. Gonzalez. "European Colonialism and the Anthropocene: A View from the Pacific Coast of North America." *Anthropocene* (2013): e1–e15.

Lipsitz, George. *The Possessive Investment in Whiteness*. Philadelphia, PA: Temple University Press, 1998.

Lo, Marie. "Passing Recognition: *Obasan* and the Borders of Asian American and Canadian Literary Criticism." *Comparative American Studies* 5, no. 3 2007: 307–32.

Lock, Margaret and Vinh-Kim Nguyen. "Local Biologies." In *An Anthropology of Biomedicine*, 319. Oxford, UK: Wiley-Blackwell, 2010.

Lorde, Audre. *Sister Outsider: Essays and Speeches*. Berkeley, CA: Crossing Press, 1984.

———. "The Uses of the Erotic: The Erotic as Power." In *Sister Outsider: Essays and Speeches*, 53–59. Berkeley, CA: Crossing Press, 1984.

Lorimer, Jamie. "Multinatural Geographies for the Anthropocene." *Progress in Human Geography* 36, no. 5 (2012): 593–612.

Lövbrand, Eva, Johannes Stripple, and Bo Wilman, "Earth System Governmentality: Reflections on science in the Anthropocene." *Global Environmental Change* 19 (2009): 7–13.

Love, Heather. *Feeling Backwards: Loss and the Politics of Queer History*. Cambridge, MA: Harvard University Press, 2001.

Lyman, Christopher M. *The Vanishing Race and Other Illusions: Photographs of Indians by Edward S. Curtis*. Washington, DC: Smithsonian Institution Press, 1982.

MacLeod, Roderick, and Mary Anne Poutanen. "Upstairs for Hebrew, Downstairs for English: The Jewish Community of Ste-Sophie, Quebec and Strategies for Public Education, 1914–1952." *Canadian Jewish Studies/Études juives canadiennes* 10 (2002): 29–52.

Mahmood, Saba. *Politics of Piety: The Islamic Revival and the Feminist Subject*. Princeton, NJ: Princeton University Press, 2008.

Malabou, Catherine. *What Should We Do with Our Brains?* New York: Fordham University Press, 2008.
Malm, Andreas, and Alf Hornborg. "The Geology of Mankind? A Critique of the Anthropocene Narrative." *The Anthropocene Review* 1, no. 1 (April 2014): 62–69.
Marx, Karl. "The *Grundisse*." In *The Marx-Angels Reader*, 2nd ed., edited by Robert C. Tucker, 221–93. New York: W. W. Norton & Company, 1978.
———. "Economic and Philosophic Manuscripts of 1844." In *The Marx-Angels Reader*, 2nd ed., edited by Robert C. Tucker, 66–125. New York: W. W. Norton & Company, 1978.
———. *Theories of Surplus Value*, vol. 3. Moscow, USSR: Progress Publishers, 1978.
Marzec, Robert P. "Militarized Ecologies: Visualizations of Environmental Struggle in the Brazilian Amazon." *Public Culture* 26, no. 2 (2014): 233–55.
Massumi, Brian. "The Autonomy of Affect," *Cultural Critique* 31 (Autumn 1995): 83–109
———. *Parables for the Virtual: Movement, Affect, Sensation.* Durham, NC: Duke University Press, 2002.
Mbembe, Achille. "Necropolitics." Translated by Libby Meintjes. *Public Culture* 15, no. 1 (2003): 11–40.
Merleau-Ponty, Maurice. "Cézanne's Doubt." In *Sense and Non-Sense*, 9–25. Evanston, IL: Northwestern University Press, 1964.
———. *Phenomenology of Perception*. Translated by Colin Smith. New York: Routledge and Kegan Paul, 1970.
Miller-Young, Mireille. *A Taste for Brown Sugar: Black Women in Pornography.* Durham, NC: Duke University Press, 2014.
Mills, Charles W. "Materializing Race." In *Living Alterities: Phenomenology, Embodiment, and Race*, edited by Emily S. Lee, 19–41. Albany: State University of New York Press, 2014.
Mohanty, Chandra Talpade. *Feminism without Borders: Decolonizing Theory, Practicing Solidarity.* Durham, NC: Duke University Press, 2003.
Moreton-Robinson, Aileen. "'I Still Call Australia Home': Indigenous Belonging and Place in a White Postcolonising Society." In *Uprootings/Regroundings: Questions of Home and Migration*, edited by Sara Ahmed, 23–40. London: Berg Publishing, 2003.
Morris, Aldon D. *The Origins of the Civil Rights Movement: Black Communities Organizing for Change.* New York: The Free Press, 1984.
Mortimer-Sandilands, Catriona. "Unnatural Passions?: Notes Toward a Queer Ecology." *Invisible Culture: An Electronic Journal for Visual Culture* 9 (2005).

Morton, Fred, Jeff Ramsay, and Part Themba Mgadla. *Historical Dictionary of Botswana*. Lantham, MD: Scarecrow Press, 2008.

Moya, Paula. "Postmodernism, 'Realism,' and the Politics of Identity: Cherríe Moraga and Chicana Feminism." In *Feminist Genealogies, Colonial Legacies, Democratic Futures*, edited by M. Jacqui Alexander and Chandra Talpade Mohanty, 125–50. New York: Routledge, 1997.

Moxley, Jerry. The Abundance and Behavioral Ecology of Cape Cod Gray Seals Under Predation Risk from White Sharks. PhD Dissertation, Duke University, 2016.

Muñoz, José Esteban. "Feeling Brown: Ethnicity and Affect in Ricardo Bracho's *The Sweetest Hangover (and Other STDs)*." *Theatre Journal* 52, no. 1 (2000): 67–79.

———. "Feeling Brown, Feeling Down: Latina Affect, the Performativity of Race, and the Depressive Position." *Signs* 31, no. 3 (Spring 2006): 675–88.

———. "Thinking beyond Antirelationality and Antiutopianism in Queer Critique." *PMLA* 121 (2006): 825–26.

Munro, Brenna M. *South Africa and the Dream of Love to Come: Queer Sexuality and the Struggle for Freedom*. Minneapolis: University of Minnesota Press, 2012.

Musser, Amber Jamilla. *Sensational Flesh: Race, Power, and Masochism*. New York: New York University Press, 2014.

Nash, Jennifer. *The Black Body in Ecstasy: Reading Race, Reading Pornography*. Durham, NC: Duke University Press, 2014.

———. "Practicing Love: Black Feminism, Love-Politics, and Post-Intersectionality." *Meridians* 11, no. 2 (2011): 1–24.

National Park Service in the Matter of Cape Cod National Seashore Advisory Committee. "Official Report of Proceedings before the U.S. Department of the Interior." Washington, DC: February 16, 1962. http://archive.org/stream/capecodnationals2311unit#page/n0/mode/2up.

Nixon, Rob. Interview with Robert P. Marzec and Allison Carruth. *Public Culture* 26, no. 2 (2014): 281–300.

———. "Refugees and Homecomings: Bessie Head and the End of Exile." In *Travellers' Tales: Narratives of Home and Displacement*, edited by George Roberston, Melinda Mash, Lisa Tickner, Jon Bird, Barry Curtis, and Tim Putnam, 115–23. New York: Routledge, 1994.

———. *Slow Violence and the Environmentalism of the Poor*. Cambridge, MA: Harvard University Press, 2013.

Nkosi, Lewis. *Tasks and Masks: Themes and Styles of African Literature*. Harlow, UK: Longman, 1981.

Nussbaum, Martha. "The Professor of Parody." *New Republic* 220, no. 8 (February 1999): 37–45.
Okasala, Johanna. "Female Freedom: Can the Lived Body Be Emancipated?" In *Feminist Interpretations of Maurice Merleau-Ponty*, edited by Dorothea Olkowski and Gail Weiss, 209–28. University Park: Pennsylvania State University Press, 2006.
———. *Feminist Experiences: Foucauldian and Phenomenological Investigations.* Evanston, IL: Northwestern University Press, 2016.
———. *Foucault on Freedom.* Cambridge, UK: Cambridge University Press, 2005.
———. "Post-Structuralism: Michel Foucault." In *The Routledge Companion to Phenomenology*, edited by Sebastian Luft and Soren Overgaard, 528–39. Florence, KY: Taylor & Francis, 2013.
Oliver, Kelly. *Earth and World: Philosophy after the Apollo Missions.* New York: Columbia University Press, 2015.
O'Neil, Alan, and Louis Steenman-Clark. "The Computational Challenges of Earth-System Science." *Philosophical Transactions: Mathematical, Physical and Engineering Sciences* 360, no. 1795 (June 15, 2002), 1267–75.
Oppermann, Serpil. "Theorizing Ecocriticism: Toward a Postmodern Ecocritical Practice." *Interdisciplinary Studies in Literature and Environment* 13, no. 2 (Summer 2006): 103–28.
Ortega, Mariana. *In-Between: Latina Feminist Phenomenology, Multiplicity, and the Self.* Albany: State University of New York Press, 2016.
Pandya, Rashmika. "The Borderlines of Culture and Identity." In *Intertwinings: Interdisciplinary Encounters with Merleau-Ponty*, edited by Gail Weiss, 241–64. Albany: State University of New York Press, 1998.
Parel, Kurien, and James Ball. "Oxford University Accused of Bias Against Ethnic Minority Applicants." *The Guardian* (February 26, 2013).
Passalacqua, Veronica. Introduction. In *Our People, Our Land, Our Images: International Indigenous Photographers*, edited by Hulleah J. Tsinhnahjinnie and Veronica Passalacqua, xi–xxi. Berkeley, CA: Heydey Books, 2006.
Pellegrini, Ann. *Performance Anxieties: Staging Psychoanalysis, Staging Race.* New York: Routledge, 1997.
Peters, Russell M. *The Wampanoags of Mashpee: An Indian Perspective on American History.* Somerville, MA: Media Action, 1987.
Phillips, Dana. "Ecocriticism, Literary Theory, and the Truth of Ecology." *New Literary History* 30, no. 3 (Summer 1999): 577–602.
Pile, Steven. "The Troubled Spaces of Frantz Fanon." In *Thinking Space*, edited by Mike Crang and Nigel Thrift, 260–78. New York: Routledge, 2000.

Pitman, A. J. "On the Role of Geography in Earth System Science." *Geoforum* 36 (2005): 137–48.

Pitts-Taylor, Victoria. "Neurobiology and the Queerness of Kinship." In *The Brain's Body: Neuroscience and Corporeal Politics*, 95–117. Durham, NC: Duke University Press, 2016.

Polan, Dana. "Francis Bacon: The Logic of Sensation." In *Gilles Deleuze and the Theater of Philosophy*, edited by Constantin V. Boundas and Dorothea Olkowski, 229–54. New York: Routledge, 1994.

Pratt, Minnie Bruce. "Identity: Skin Blood Heart." In *Yours in Struggle: Three Feminist Perspective on Racism and Anti-Semitism*, with Elly Bulkin and Barbara Smith, 11–63. Brooklyn, NY: Long Haul Press, 1984.

Puar, Jasbir K. "'I Would Rather Be a Cyborg than a Goddess': Becoming-Intersectional in Assemblage Theory." *philoSOPHIA* 2, no. 1 (2012): 49–66.

———. *Terrorist Assemblages: Homonationalism in Queer Times*. Durham, NC: Duke University Press, 2007.

Razack, Sherene H. "Colonization: The Good, the Bad, and the Ugly." In *Rethinking the Great White North: Race, Nature, and the Historical Geographies of Whiteness in Canada*, edited by Andrew Baldwin, Laura Cameron, and Audrey Kobayashi, 264–71. Vancouver: University of British Columbia Press, 2011.

Reddy, Chandan. *Freedom with Violence: Race, Sexuality, and the US State*. Durham, NC: Duke University Press, 2011.

Renault, Matthieu. "'Corps à corps': Frantz Fanon's Erotics of National Liberation." *Journal of French and Francophone Philosophy: Revue de la philosophie française et de langue française* 19, no. 1 (2011): 49–55.

Repanshek, Kurt. "Some Long Missing Species Returning to Cape Cod National Seashore." *National Park Traveler* (March 8, 2015).

Rich, Adrienne. "Notes toward a Politics of Location." In *Blood, Bread, and Poetry: Selected Prose 1979–1985*, 210–32. New York: W. W. Norton & Company, 1986.

Rifkin, Mark. *When Did the Indians Become Straight?* New York: Oxford University Press, 2011.

Roffman, Seth. "Will Wilson's Auto Immune Response Lab." *Green Fire Times* (August 1, 2011): 39.

Rose, Jacqueline. "On the 'Universality' of Madness: Bessie Head's *A Question of Power*." *Critical Inquiry* 20, no. 3 (Spring 1994): 401–18.

Routledge, Karen. *In These Latitudes: American and Inuit Stories of Survival, 1850–1922*. Dissertation. Rutgers University, 2011.

Roy, Deboleena, and Banu Subramanian. "Matter in the Shadows: Feminist New Materialism and the Practices of Colonialism." In *Mattering: Feminism,*

Science, and Materialism, edited by Victoria Pitts-Taylor, 23–42. New York: New York University Press, 2016.

Saldanha, Arun. "Politics and Difference." In *Taking-Place: Non-Representational Theories and Geography*, edited by Ben Anderson and Paul Harrison, 283–303. Farnham, UK: Ashgate Publishing, 2010.

———, "Reontologising Race: The Machinic Geography of Phenotype." *Environment and Planning D: Society and Space* 24 (2006): 9–24.

Sample, Maxine. "Space: An Experiential Perspective: Bessie Head's *When Rain Clouds Gather.*" In *Critical Essays on Bessie Head*, edited by Maxine Sample, 25–45. Westport, CT: Praeger, 2003.

Sandoval, Chela. *Methodology of the Oppressed*. Minneapolis: University of Minnesota Press, 2002.

Saussure, Ferdinand de. *Course in General Linguistics*. Translated by Wade Baskin. New York: McGraw-Hill Book Co., 1966.

Schellnhuber, H. J. "'Earth System' Analysis and the Second Copernican Revolution." *Nature* 402 (December 2, 1999): C19–C23.

Schor, Naomi. "The Crisis of French Universalism." *Yale French Studies* 100 (2001): 43–64.

Scigaj, Leonard. *Sustainable Poetry: Four American Ecopoets*. Lexington: University Press of Kentucky, 1999.

Scott, Darieck. *Extravagant Abjection*. New York: New York University Press, 2010.

Scott, Joan W. "The Evidence of Experience." *Critical Inquiry* 17, no. 4 (Summer 1991): 773–97.

Sedgwick, Eve Kosofsky. *Epistemology of the Closet*. Berkeley: University of California Press, 1990.

———. *Touching Feeling: Affect, Pedagogy, Performativity*. Durham, NC: Duke University Press, 2003.

———, and Adam Frank. "Shame in the Cybernetic Fold: Reading Silvan Tomkins." *Critical Inquiry* 21, no. 2 (Winter 1995): 496–522.

Sekyi-Otu, Ato. *Fanon's Dialectic of Experience*. Cambridge, MA: Harvard University Press, 1996.

Sexton, Jared. "The Social Life of Social Death: On Afro-Pessimism and Black Optimism." *InTensions Journal* 5 (Fall/Winter 2011): 1–47.

Sharpe, Christina. *Monstrous Intimacies: Making Post-Slavery Subjects*. Durham, NC: Duke University Press, 2010.

Silko, Leslie Marmon. "Landscape, History and the Pueblo Imagination." *Antaeus* 57 (Autumn 1986): 83–94.

Skomal, Gregory B., John Chisholm, and Steven J. Correia. "Implications of Increasing Pinniped Populations on the Diet and Abundance of White Sharks off the Coast of Massachusetts." In *Global Perspectives on the Biology and Life History of the White Shark*, edited by Michael L. Domeler, 405–18. Boca Raton, FL: CRC Press, Taylor & Francis Group, 2012.

Smith, Andrea. "American Studies without America: Native Feminisms and the Nation State." *American Quarterly* 60, no. 2 (June 2008): 309–31.

Smyth, Bryan A. *Merleau-Ponty's Existential Phenomenology and the Realization of Philosophy*. London: Bloomsbury, 2014.

Spivak, Gayatri Chakravorty. "Can the Subaltern Speak?" In *Marxism and the Interpretation of Culture*, edited by Cary Nelson and Lawrence Grossberg, 271–313. London: Macmillan, 1988.

———. *Death of a Discipline*. New York City: Columbia University Press, 2003.

———. "Imperative to Re-imagine the Planet." In *An Aesthetic Education in the Era of Globalization*, 335–50. Cambridge MA: Harvard University Press, 2012.

———. "World Systems & the Creole." *Narrative* 14, no. 1 (January 2006): 102–12.

Steffen, Will, Jacques Grinevald, Paul Crutzen, and John McNeill. "The Anthropocene: Conceptual and Historical Perspectives." *Philosophical Transactions of the Royal Society A* 369 (2011): 842–67.

Stewart, Kathleen. *Ordinary Affects*. Durham, NC: Duke University Press, 2007.

Stoller, Silvia. "Expressivity and Performativity: Merleau-Ponty and Butler." *Continental Philosophy Review* 43 (2010): 97–110.

———. "Reflections on Feminist Merleau-Ponty Skepticism." *Hypatia* 15, no. 1 (Winter 2000): 175–82.

Subramaniam, Banu. *Ghost Stories for Darwin: The Science of Variation and the Politics of Diversity*. Chicago: University of Illinois Press, 2014.

Sullivan, Shannon. "Domination and Dialogue in Merleau-Ponty's *Phenomenology of Perception*." *Hypatia* 12, no. 1 (Winter 1997): 1–19.

———, and Nancy Tuana. *Race and Epistemologies of Ignorance: Perspectives on Literacy and Schooling*. Albany: State University of New York Press, 2007.

Surrallés, Alexandre. "Intimate Horizons: Person Perception and Space among the Candoshi." In *The Land Within: Indigenous Territory and the Perception of Environment*, edited by Alexandres Surrallés and Pedro García Hierro, 126–49. Copenhagen: International Work Group for Indigenous Affairs, 2005.

Talahite, Anissa. "Cape Gooseberries and Giant Cauliflowers: Transplantation, Hybridity, and Growth in Bessie Head's *A Question of Power*." *Mosaic: Journal for the Interdisciplinary Study of Literature* 38, no. 4 (2005): 141–56.

Tansley, Arthur. "The Use and Abuse of Vegetational Concepts and Terms." *Ecology* 16, no. 3 (July 1935): 299–306.

Thoreau, Henry David. *Cape Cod [1865]*. Princeton, NJ: Princeton University Press, 1988.

Thrift, Nigel. *Non-Representational Theory*. Abington, UK: Routledge, 2008.

Trudeau, Pierre Elliott. "On Bilingualism." In *The Essential Trudeau*, edited by Ron Graham, 135–43. Toronto, ON: McClelland & Stewart, 1998.

Tsing, Anna Lowenhaupt, Heather Anne Swanson, Elaine Gan, and Nils Bubandt. "Introduction: Haunted Landscapes of the Anthropocene." In *Arts of Living on a Damaged Planet*, edited by Anna Lowenhaupt Tsing, Tsing, Anna Lowenhaupt, Heather Anne Swanson, Elaine Gan, and Nils Bubandt, 1–15. Minneapolis: University of Minnesota Press, 2017.

Tsinhnahjinnie, Hulleah. "When Is a Photograph Worth a Thousand Words?" In *Native Nations: Journeys in American Photography*, edited by Jane Alison, 41–55. London: Barbican Art Gallery, 1999.

Tuana, Nancy. "Material Locations: An Interactionist Alternative to Realism/Social Constructivism." In *Engendering Rationalities*, edited by Nancy Tuana and Sandi Morgen, 221–43. Bloomington: Indiana University Press, 2001.

Tuck, Eve. "Suspending Damage: A Letter to Communities." *Harvard Educational Review* 79, no. 3 (Fall 2009): 409–27.

Tucker, Margaret. "A 'Nice-Time Girl' Strikes Back: An Essay on Bessie Head's *A Question of Power*." *Research in African Literatures* 20, no. 1 (Spring 1989): 170–81.

United States Department of Commerce. *Census of Population: 1960, Volume I: Characteristics of the Population, Part 1, United States Summary*. Washington, DC: U.S. Government Printing Office, 1964.

United States Department of the Interior. National Park Service. *Cape Cod National Seashore: A Proposal*. January 28, 1959.

Vasagar, Jeevan. "Black Student Intake at Oxford University Rises to 32." *The Guardian* (December 18, 2011).

Vauday, Patrick. "Écrit à vue: Deleuze-Bacon," *Critique* 426 (November 1982): 963–64.

Veracini, Lorenzo. *Settler Colonialism: A Theoretical Overview*. London: Palgrave Macmillan, 2010.

"Vision." International Geosphere-Biosphere Programme. Accessed April 2017. www.igbp.net/about/vision.4.1b8ae20512db692f2 a6800017590.html.

Viveiros de Castro, Eduardo. "Cosmological Deixis and Amerindian Perspectivism." *Journal of the Royal Anthropological Institute* 4, no. 3 (September 1998): 469–88.

Vizenor, Gerald. *Fugitive Poses: Native American Indian Scenes of Absence and Presence*. Lincoln: University of Nebraska Press, 1998.

———. *Manifest Manners: Narratives on Postindian Survivance*. Lincoln: University of Nebraska Press, 1999.

Walker, James. *"Race," Rights and the Law in the Supreme Court of Canada*. Toronto, ON: The Osgoode Society for Canadian Legal History and Wilfred Laurier University Press, 1997.

Walker, James C. G. "Earth System Science and the Western Worldview." *Chemical Geology Including Isotope Geoscience* 161 (1999): 365–71.

Walsh, Maria. "The Immersive Spectator: A Phenomenological Hybrid." *Angelaki* 9, no. 3 (December 2004): 169–85.

Weate, Jeremy. "Fanon, Merleau-Ponty and the Difference of Phenomenology." In *Race*, edited by Robert Bernasconi, 169–83. Malden, MA: Blackwell Publishers, 2001.

Weheliye, Alexander. *Habeas Viscus: Racializing Assemblages, Biopolitics, and Black Feminist Theories of the Human*. Durham, NC: Duke University Press, 2014.

Weisiger, Marsha. *Dreaming of Sheep in Navajo Country*. Seattle: University of Washington Press, 2009.

Weiss, Gail. *Body Images: Embodiment as Intercorporeality*. New York: Routledge, 1999.

Wenzel, Jennifer. "Stratigraphy and Empire: *Waiting for the Barbarians*, Reading under Duress." In *Anthropocene Reading: Literary History in Geologic Times*, edited by Tobias Menely and Jesse Oak Taylor, 167–83. University Park: Pennsylvania State University, 2017.

West, Cornel. "Ta-Nehisi Coates Is the Neoliberal Face of the Black Freedom Struggle." *The Guardian* (December 17, 2017).

Weston, Kath. *Animate Planet: Making Visceral Sense of Living in a High-Tech Ecologically Damaged World*. Durham, NC: Duke University Press, 2017.

Whatmore, Sarah, *Hybrid Geographies: Natures Cultures Spaces*. London: Sage Publications, 2002.

Wilderson, Frank III. *Red, White & Black*. Durham, NC: Duke University Press, 2010.

Willey, Angela. *Undoing Monogamy: The Politics of Science and the Possibilities of Biology*. Durham, NC: Duke University Press, 2016.

Williams, Patricia. *The Alchemy of Race and Rights: Diary of a Law Professor*. Cambridge MA: Harvard University Press, 1992.

Williams, Raymond. *Marxism and Literature*. Oxford, UK: Oxford University Press, 1977.

Wilson, Elizabeth. "Gut Feminism." In *differences: A Journal of Feminist Cultural Studies* 15, no. 3 (2004): 66–94.

———. *Psychosomatic: Feminism and the Neurological Body.* Durham, NC: Duke University Press, 2004.

Wilson, Will. Artist Statement. In *Our People, Our Land, Our Images: International Indigenous Photographers*, edited by Hulleah J. Tsinhnahjinnie and Veronica Passalacqua. Berkeley, CA: Heydey Books, 2006.

———. "Will Wilson: AIR." *Peters Projects.* 2017. http://www.petersprojects.com/will-wilson-air/.

Wiltse, Jeff. *Contested Waters: A Social History of Swimming Pools in America.* Chapel Hill: University of North Carolina Press, 2007.

Wolman, Thomas. "Human Space, Psychic Space, Analytic Space, Geopolitical Space." In *The Geography of Meaning: Psychoanalytic Perspectives on Place, Space, Land, and Dislocation*, edited by Maria Teresa Savio Hooke and Salman Akhtar, 23–45. London: International Psychoanalytical Association, 2007.

Wood Lafond, Stephanie A. "Dynamics of Recolonization: A Study of the Gray Seal (*Halichoerus Grypus*) in the Northeast U.S. PhD Dissertation, University of Massachusetts, December 2009.

Young, Iris Marion. *Throwing Like a Girl.* Bloomington: Indiana University Press, 1990.

———. "Throwing Like a Girl: A Phenomenology of Feminine Body Comportment Motility and Spatiality." *Human Studies* 3, no. 2 (April 1980): 137–56.

Zalasiewicz, Jan, Mark Williams, Alan Smith, Tiffany Barry, Angela Coe, Paul Brown, Patrick Brenchly, David Cantrill, Andrew Gale, Philip Gibbard, John F. Gregory, Mark W. Hounslow, Andrew C. Kerr, Paul Pearson, Robert Knox, John Powell, Colin Waters, John Marshall, Michael Oates, Peter Rawson, and Philip Stone. "Are We Now Living in the Anthropocene?" *GSA Today* 18, no. 2 (February 2008): 4–8.

Zerilli, Linda. "This Universalism Which Is Not One." *Diacritics* 28, no. 2 (Summer 1998): 3–20.

Index

Abram, David, xxiii–xxiv, 105, 114n12
academia, 20–21, 49, 92
aesthetics, 22, 23–24, 100, 106–11, 130–31n19
affect, xxxv–xxxvii, 21–43; and aesthetics, 23–24, 130–31n19; and belonging, 102; and biology, xxv, 138n10; distinct from emotion, 5–6, 32; and positionality, 24–28, 131n31; and sensation, xxxv–xxxvi, 4–6, 22, 26, 31–32; stereotypes of Latinx, 4–5; as transformative, 22–24, 26, 28; transmission between people, 31–32
Africa: Algeria, 65–66, 72–73, 76, 78–81; Botswana, xxxviii, 47, 49, 61–62, 137n53; South Africa, 47, 49–53, 58–59, 61
Age of the World Target, The (Chow), 124n124
Ahmed, Sara, 4, 36
Ahuja, Neel, 87, 106
AIR (Auto Immune Response) (exhibit), xxxviii, 89, 106–11
Alarcón, Norma, 131n25
Alcoff, Linda Martín, xxx, xxxi, 27, 42, 120n75, 123n116
Algeria, 65–66, 72–73, 76, 78–81
"Algeria Unveiled" (Fanon), 80
Algonquin Park, 33
Al-Saji, Alia, 123n118
Amazon (region), 97–100, 141n10, 142n14
Amerindians. *See* indigenous peoples and nations
Amsterdam Declaration (2001), 91
Andrews, Jorella, xxvii

animals: in Amazonian cosmology, 100; and belonging, 57; dogs, 121n88; humans as, 86; livestock reduction, 107–9; in racist speech, 58–59; seals, 40, 133–34n87; and territory, 40, 129n92
Animate Planet (Weston), 105–6
anonymous body, xxvii–xxxii, 27–28, 32, 40, 74, 121–22n98
Anthropocene, xxxviii, 85–113; in *AIR*, 106–11; contra indigenous views, 97–100, 141n10, 142n14; development of Earth System Science, 89–92; and forms of history, 101–2; and inequality, xvi, 86–87; phenomenological approach to, 89; and sensation, 102–6; universalism in, 88, 93–97, 103–4, 144–45n76; use of term, 85–88, 113n2, 142n17
"Anthropocene: Conceptual and Historical Perspectives, The" (Steffen et al.), 90
"'Anthropocene,' The" (Crutzen and Stoermer), 89–90
Antilles, 70
apartheid, 50–53, 56–57, 61–62, 63
Apollo program, 95–96
appropriation: alternatives to, 81–84; in decolonization, xxxviii, 75–81; and discipline, 69; and gender, 80–84; and psyche, 65–66, 69
Araweté, 99–100
art, 22, 23–24, 100, 106–11, 130–31n19
AS17-22727 (image of Earth), 95–96
assemblages, 25–26

173

174 index

Atwood, Margaret, 13, 33
autobiography: Clare's swimming, 21, 29–32, 34–36, 39–40, 42–43; philosophical value of, xxxiv, 40–42, 126–27n37, 135–36n24
Auto Immune Response (AIR) (exhibit), xxxviii, 89, 106–11
autonomous response, xxxv–xxxvi, xxxvii, 5–6, 21, 24, 26
"Autonomy of Affect, The" (Massumi), xxxv
Azoulay, Jacques, 80

Baldwin, Andrew, 133n82
Bantu Authorities Act (1951), 50
Bantu Building Workers Act (1951), 50
Bantu Homelands Citizens Act (1970), 51–52
Barad, Karen, 67
Bartky, Sandra, 2, 4, 16–18
de Beauvoir, Simone, xxiii, 3
becoming: and affect, xxxvii, 6, 21, 23, 26, 28; of body, xxi, 45; with natural world, 87, 109
belonging: and affect, 102; and inequality, 62–63; and kin, 51, 53–54; and race, 51, 53–54, 60–62; in space, 48–49, 51, 58–59; through sensation, 47–49, 54–57
Benjamin, Walter, 101, 111
Bentham, Jeremy, 67–68
Bernet, Rudolf, 121n97
Bertalanffy, Ludwig von, 91
Between the World and Me (Coates), xv–xvii, xxx–xxxi
Bhana, Hershini, 136
Bhopal disaster, xxii
Bigwood, Carol, 121–22n98
bilingualism, 31
biology: and affect, xxxv, 138n10; biological *vs.* adoptive parenthood, 135n26; psychic roots of illness, 78–79; and race, xxx, xxxvii, 10–14, 122n104, 128n60; reality of biological facts, 3–4; species-thinking, 86, 87; as system, 91. *See also* body
black feminism, xxxvi, 46
black nationalism, 140n55

blackness: and African identity, 51, 53, 58–59; objectification, 1, 16–18, xxvii–xxviii; psychic occupation of, 65–66, 70–75, 79–81; and sexuality, 46, 48, 50–54, 71; women of color, 46, 61, xxxiv. *See also* race
black power, 60, 73
Black Skin, White Masks (Fanon), 3–4, 16–18, 70–73, 123n114
black studies, 60–61
Blida-Joinville Psychiatric Hospital, 80–81
Bodies that Matter (Butler), xxiv
body: and affect, xxxv–xxxvi, xxxvii, 5–6, 22–24, 32; in Amazonian cosmology, 99–100; anonymous body, xxvii–xxxii, 27–28, 32, 40, 74, 121–22n98; as basis of sensation, xxvi, 60, 63; body-subject, xxxvii, 6, 10–11, 104, 118–19n54, 123n116, 123n118; and materialism, xxi–xxii, xxiv, 45, 67; and nature, xxxvii, 11–12, 109, 127–128n60; and pleasure, 45–48, 54; and power, 67, 69, 75; in space, 34–35, 41, 43, 74, 98, 124n128; virtual body, 14–15, 18, 23. *See also* biology; cold; objectification
body, social effects on: muscular tension, xxx–xxxi, 71–75, 79–81; and phenomenological approach, 15, 26–27; by pollution, 34; through history, xxvii–xxviii, xxix, xxx, 123n114; under white gaze, 17, 71
body image, xxvii–xxviii, xxx, 123n114
body-subject, xxxvii, 6, 10–11, 104, 118–19n54, 123n116, 123n118
Boes, Tobias, 103–4, 111
"Borderlines of Culture and Identity, The" (Pandya), xxxiii, xxxvii, 4, 7–10, 13–16
Botswana, xxxviii, 47, 49, 61–62, 137n53
bracketing (phenomenological reduction), xxviii–xxix, 42, 121n97
Braidotti, Rosi, 124n128
Braun, Bruce, xxiv
Briggs, Laura, 125n9
Bryan Smyth, xxix
Buell, Lawrence, xvii, 38

Bureau of Indian Affairs, 107–8
Bush Garden, The (Frye), 33
Butler, Judith: and affect, 131n31; *Bodies that Matter*, xxiv; on externality, xxiv; on psyche, 67, 69, 75; *Psychic Life of Power*, 19, 67, 69; on subject, 19, 25

California, 141n10
Camp Century (Cold Regions Research and Engineering Laboratory), 95
Canada: and climate, xxxvii, 9–14, 15–16, 35; indigenous land dispute, 116–17n41; national identity, xxxvii, 9–14, 15–16, 31–35
Canada First Movement, 44
Candoshi, 98–100
"Can the Subaltern Speak?" (Spivak), xxiv
Cape Cod (Thoreau), 38–39
Cape Cod, Massachusetts, 35–39, 133–34n87
capitalism, xvi, xviii, xix, 85–87, 101
Capitalocene, 87
Castro, Eduardo Viveiros de, 99–100
Cavarero, Adriana, xxxiv, 8, 126–27n37, 129n93
Chakrabarty, Dipesh, 86, 89, 101–2
de la Chambre, Marin Cureau, 11
Charlesworth, Simon J., 125n2
Chen, Mel, 87
Chisholm, Michael, 91
Chow, Rey, 124n124, 131n25
Chthulucene, 87
citizen science, 105
Civil Rights Act (1964), 38, 134n100
Clare, Stephanie, 21, 29–32, 34–36, 39–40, 42–43
Clark, Timothy, 89, 102–4
class, 13, 34–35, 97, 125n2
Clifford, Nick, 144–45n76
climate: and distribution of labor, 96–97; and national identity, xxxvii, 9–14, 15–16, 35
climate change: and colonialism, xxxviii, 87, 109, 141n10; and inequality, xvi, 86–87; and local experience, xv–xvi, xviii, 88, 102–6, 109, 111; and materialism, xxi. *See also* Anthropocene; Earth System Science
"Climate of History, The" (Chakrabarty), 101
clothing, 13, 19–20, 30
Coast Guard Beach, 36
Coates, Ta-Nehisi, xv–xviii, xxx–xxxi, 114n14
cold, 1–20, xxxvii; and affect, 4–6; and class, 125n2; and immigration, 7–10; in metaphor, 1–2, 9, 16–18; and national identity, 9–14, 35; and spatiality, 14–16, 19; and women's clothing, 19–20
Cold Regions Research and Engineering Laboratory (Camp Century), 95
Cold War, 95, 103
Collier, John, 108
colonialism: absence in Botswana, 61–62; and development of racial views, 127–28n60; effects on nature, xxi, xxxviii, 68–69, 87, 109, 141n10; effects on psyche, 70–75; and the globe, xix; in scholarship, 49, 98; and space, xxxiii, 50–54, 72–75, 80. *See also* decolonization; indigenous peoples and nations; settler colonialism
Companion Species Manifesto, The (Haraway), 121n88
consciousness, 77–78
conservation, 107–8, 144n75
context. *See* positionality
continental philosophy, xxvii. *See also* phenomenology
Coole, Diana, 123n116
Cosgrove, David, 95
cosmology, 97–100
Coundouriotis, Eleni, 54
Counihan, Clare, 47
Crutzen, Paul J., 89–90
culture: in Amazonian cosmology, 99–100; effects on experience, 15–16, 27–28, 70–71; effects on nature, xiv, xxvii–xxxii, xxxvi, 121n88; effects on space, 36, 50–54, 62–63; and identity, 11–13, 33–35, 73. *See also* body, social effects on

Currier, Ashley, 49
Curtis, Edward, 109–10
Cvetkovich, Ann, xxxv, 63

dance, 71, 73
Day, Iyko, 12
death, 78–79
decolonization: and appropriation, xxxviii, 75–81; and belonging, 60, 62–63; feminist approach to, 81–84; and geopower, 68–69; postcolonial scholarship, xxv, 86, 101–3, 104; use of colonial tools, 109
deconstruction, xvii, xxiv, xxv
Deleuze, Gilles, xxxvii, 5, 22–27, 100, 129n92
Delgamuukw v. B.C., 116–117n41
demographics of Shawinigan, Québec, 34
Denison, Flora MacDonald, 133n82
determinism, xxxi, xxxv, 11, 97, 105
Deutscher, Penelope, 3
developing world, 96–97
Diné (Navajo), 106–11
Discipline and Punish (Foucault), 67, 69
dogs, 121n88
double-bodiedness, 73
Dreamers, xvi
drought, 107, 109
Dying Colonialism, A (Fanon), 79

Earth. *See* Anthropocene; climate; Earth System Science
"'Earth System' Analysis and the Second Copernican Revolution" (Schellnhuber), 90
Earth System Science: development of, 89–92; universalism in, 88, 93–97, 103–4, 144–145n76. *See also* Anthropocene
eco-cosmopolitanism, 104–5, 145–46n103
ecocriticism, xvii, 102–3, 104
"Economic and Philosophic Manuscripts of 1844" (Marx), 77
ecosystems, 142n26
Edelman, Lee, 37
"1838 Of the Refrain" (Deleuze and Guattari), 129n92

embodiment. *See* body
emotion. *See* affect
England, 127–28n60
Enlightenment, 93
entanglement, xxvi–xxvii, 8, 22–23, 31, 86
environmentalism: concerning indigenous lands, 107–8, 109; and Earth System Science, 144–45n76; eco-cosmopolitanism, 104–5, 145–46n103; ecocriticism, 102–3, 104, xvii; and local experience, xv–xvi, xviii, 88, 102–6, 109, 111; national parks, 32–34, 36–39, aposa; planetarity, xix–xx, 87. *See also* Anthropocene; climate change
eroticism, 45–46, 54–55, 116n38, 135n2. *See also* sexuality
ethics, xxii, xxiv–xxv, 41, 100
ethnicity, 34. *See also* Jews; Latinx; race
Euclidean geometry, 98
eugenics, xxi
exclusion. *See* belonging
existentialism, xxviii, 16, 65
experience. *See* body; perception; sensation
externality, xxiv–xxvi, xxviii–xxix, xxxi–xxxii, 5–6, 65

Fairclough, Ellen, 13
Falconer, Robert Alexander, 12
family: in *AIR*, 108–9; in Clare's account, 29–30, 31–32, 34–36; and immigration, 9, 70; and love, 19; in *Question of Power*, 51, 53–54, 56, 58, 70
Fanon, Frantz, xxvii–xxviii, xxxii, xxxviii, 1; "Algeria Unveiled," 80; *Black Skin, White Masks*, 3–4, 16–18, 70–73, 123n114; *Dying Colonialism*, 79; "Lived Experience of the Black", xxvii–xxviii. *See also Wretched of the Earth, The* (Fanon)
"Feeling Brown: Ethnicity and Affect in Ricardo Bracho's *The Sweetest Hangover (and Other STDs)*" (Muñoz), 4–5
Feerick, Jean E., 127–28n60
Feminine Mystique, The (Friedan), 124n132
Femininity and Domination: Studies in the Phenomenology of Oppression (Bartky), 2, 16–18

feminism: and appropriation, 81–84; black feminism, xxxvi, 46; Head's attitude toward, 60; love-politics, xxxvi, 46; and positionality, 41–42, 124n128; scholarly approaches, xxviii–xxix, xxxiv, xxxv, 40–42; shadow feminism, 137n55; and structures of feeling, 124n132. *See also* gender; sexuality
fiction, 56–57, 135–36n24
Fielding, Helen, 117–18n44
Fink, Eugen, xxviii
first-person perspective. *See* autobiography
food, 76, 77, 81, 96–97, 99
For More than One Voice (Cavarero), 129n93
Foster, William, 11
Foucault, Michel, xxxi, xxxviii, 46, 67–69, 74–75, 83–84, 134–35n1
France, 78, 93–94
Frank, Adam, xxxv
French language, 30–31, 93–94
Freud, Sigmund, 66, 79, 137n3
Friedan, Betty, 124n132
Frye, Northrop, 33
Fuss, Diana, 10

Gates, Henry Louis, 70
gaze, 16–17, 67–68, 71
gender: and appropriation, 80–84; and cold, 11, 14, 19–20; in decolonization, 81–82; Head's treatment of, 60; and intersectionality, 131n25; objectification of women, 2, 19–20, 82; and positionality, 26, 124n128; and swimming, 29–30, 38–39; women of color, xxxiv, 46, 61; women's clothing, 19–20, 30. *See also* body; feminism; masculinity; queerness; sensation
"General System Theory and Geography" (Chisolm), 91
geology. *See* Anthropocene
geometry, 98
geopolitics, 69
geopower, xv, xxxii, xxxviii, 66, 67–69, 88
Gestalt psychology, xxvi, 118–19n54
Ghosh, Amitav, 106

Gitksan Nation, 116–17n41
globalization, xix, 96–97, 102
global south, 96–97
global subject, 90, 97
global system, Earth as. *See* Earth System Science
global warming. *See* climate change
globe, xix, 117n42
Globe, The (newspaper), 11
Gould, Glenn, 33
Grant, George, 13
Greek mythology, 96
Grinevald, Jacques, 90
Grosz, Elizabeth, 22–23, 126n34
Group Areas Act (1950), 50
Group of Seven (painters), 33
Grundrisse, The (Marx), 77
Guattari, Félix, 23–24, 100, 129n92
"Gut Feminism" (Wilson), 138n10

habit, xxx, xxxi, 28
Haile, James B., III, xviii
Halberstam, Judith, 137n55
Haliburton, Robert Grant, 11
Haraway, Donna, xx, 86, 88, 97, 105, 121n88, 142n17
Harvey, David, xxiv
Hass, Lawrence, 118–19n54, 123n116
Hatsoh, Tsékooh, 109
Head, Bessie, xxxiii, 61–62. See also *Question of Power, A* (Head)
hearing, 8, 17–18, 129n93
Hegel, 78
Hegel, Georg Wilhelm Friedrich, 76, 78
Heinämaa, Sara, xxix
Heise, Ursula, 104, 145–46n103
Hemmings, Clare, 24
Hindu mythology, 96
history: Chakrabarty's framework, 101–2; influence on body, xxvii–xxviii, xxix, xxx, 123n114; influence on perception, xxvi; materialist approach, 101, 111; military history, 95–96; of notions of race, 127–28n60

History of Sexuality (Foucault), 46, 134–35n1
hogan, 107, 109
Holland, Sharon Patricia, 45, 50, 135n2
Holocene, 85–86, 107
homosexuality. *see* queerness
hooks, bell, 41–42
Hornborg, Alf, xvi, 86
Howes, David, 118n44
Hungry Tide, The (Ghosh), 106
Husserl, Edmund, xxviii

Ibrahim, Huma, 47
idealism, xxviii, 6, 14
"Idea of North, The" (musical piece), 33
identity: and affect, xxxvi, 6, 25–28; in autobiography, 41–42; Canadian national identity, 10–14, 15–16, 31–35; connection with precolonial culture, 73; identity politics, 60; of immigrants, 9, 12–14; and inequality, 62–63; multiplicity of, xviii, 115n16; self-sovereignty, 46, 61, 63, 114–15n14; and space, 8, 62–63, 65; through others, 10, 19, 55; through proprietorship, 81–82; through sensation, 4, 7–10; and universalism, 60–61. *See also* belonging
imaginaries: of Earth, xx, 88–89, 93, 94, 102, 107; of nations, 31, 33, 36, 37, 39, 97
"Immersive Spectator: A Phenomenological Hybrid, The" (Walsh), 27–28
immigration, xxxvii, 7–10, 12–14, 70, 78
Immorality Law (1949), 50
"Imperative to Re-imagine the Planet" (Spivak), xix–xx
imperialism, 94–96. *See also* colonialism
In-Between (Ortega), 115n16
India, xxii
indigenous peoples and nations, xxv, xxxviii; Amazonians, 97–100, 141n10, 142n14; Araweté, 99–100; Candoshi, 98–100; Diné (Navajo), 106–11; Inuits, 2–3; Kant's views on, 128n74; land dispute, 116–17n41; Mashpee Wampanoag Tribe, 36, 133n65; and national parks, 33–34, 36; and race, 138–39n26; Tupi-Guarani, 99–100; Wet'suwet'en Nation, 116–17n41
intentionality, xxvi, xxxi, 6, 29–30
interdependence, 87
International Geosphere-Biosphere Programme, 96
International Union of Geological Sciences, 85
intersectionality, xxxvi, 25, 131n25
intersubjectivity, xxxi–xxxii, 123n118
Inuits, 2–3
Irigaray, Luce, xxxiv, 82
Islam, 72, 80–81
"I Would Rather Be a Cyborg than a Goddess" (Puar), 25, 131n25

Jackson, Gabrielle Bennet, xxvi, 120n75
Jäger, Jill, 144–45n76
Jameson, Fredric, xxiv, xxv
Jews, 35, 132n58
Jolly, Rosemary, 52
Jordan, June, xxxvi

Kant, Immanuel, 12–13, 128n74
Kawa, Nicholas C., 141n10, 142n14
Kelley, Robin D. G., 140n55
Kelly Oliver, 117n42
Kennedy, John F., 36, 38, 95, 143n53
Khama, Seretse, 62
Khanna, Ranjana, 137n3
King, William Lyon Mackenzie, 12
kinship. *See* family
Kruks, Sonia, 3

labor, 77, 78
Lacan, Jacques, 66
land, 62, 75–76, 79–81, 82, 116–17n41, 140n55. *See also* nature
landscape, 107, 146n121
language: and emotion, 5; French, 30–31, 93–94; gendered representation, 82; representation through, xvii, xviii, 82; sensory underpinnings of, xvii, xviii, 8, 18
Latinx, xxxiv, 4–5, 43, 115n16
Latour, Bruno, 144n75

Lawrence, T. E., 24
Lawton, John, 91
Lee, Emily, xxx
lesbianism, 29–30, 37–38. *See also* queerness
Leys, Ruth, 5–6
literature, xxxiv, 33, 49–50, 56–57, 135–36n24
"Lived Experience of the Black, The" (Fanon), xxvii–xxviii
Lo, Marie, 11
locality. *See* positionality
Lorde, Audre, xxxvi, 46, 55
love: family and, 19; politics and, xxxvi, 46; in *Question of Power*, 48, 53, 54, 57–59, 60
Lukács, György, xxix

Mair, Charles, 11
Malm, Andreas, xvi, 86
Marks, Laura, 28
marriage, mixed-race, 50, 62
Marx, Karl, xxix, 77, 78, 83, 101
Marxism and Literature (Williams), xxxv
masculinity: and climate, 11, 13–14, 15–16; and nature, 38–39; and objectification, 17, 82; and power, 52–53; and race, xvi, 51–52; and sexuality, 46
Mashpee Wampanoag Tribe, 33, 133n65
Massachusetts, 35–39, 133–34n87
Massey, Vincent, 13
Massumi, Brian, xxxv, xxxvi; assemblages, 25–26; autonomy of affect, xxxv, 5–6, 21; "Autonomy of Affect," xxxv; *Parables for the Virtual*, 25–26; power's influence on body, 15; vitality of affect, 23, 130–31n19
materialism: new materialism, xx–xxiv, 45, 116n38, 131n25; and positionality, 41; and power, 67–68; and psychoanalysis, 65–66, 71–75, 81; in queer theory, 45; in study of history, 101, 111
"Materializing Race," 122n104
McEachern, Allan, 116–117n41
McNeill, John, 90
meaning, xxiii, xxvii, xxviii
medicine, 78–79, 80, 92

Merleau-Ponty, Maurice. *See* phenomenology, Merleau-Ponty's theory; *Phenomenology of Perception* (Merleau-Ponty)
metaphor: Angel of History, 111; cold as, 1–2, 9, 16, 18; for experience of racism, xvi–xvii, 16, 18; likeness to lived experience, xviii, 2, 18; of muscular tension, 73–74; of ocean, 83–84; in psychoanalysis, 66; in racist speech, 58–59
Methodology of the Oppressed (Sandoval), xxxiii
Migraine-George, Thérèse, 49
military, 39, 95–96, 103
Mills, Charles W., 122n104
mining, 34, 85, 87, 146n124
molar/molecular differences, 27, 32, 40
Montreal, Québec, 31
Moore, Jason, 86
more-than-human world, xv, 113n2. *See also* Anthropocene; body; nature; sensation; space
Moreton, W. L., 13
Moreton-Robinson, Aileen, 12
Mortimer-Sandilands, Catriona, 33
MoveOn (advocacy group), 85
Moxley, Jerry, 133n87
Muir, John, 32
Muñoz, José Esteban, xxxv, 4–5
Munro, Brenna, 48, 54
muscular tension, xxx–xxxi, 71–75, 79, 81
music, 33
Muslims, 72, 80–81
Musser, Amber Jamilla, xxi
mythology, 96

NASA, 95–96
Nash, Jennifer, xxxvi, 124n132
nationalism, xxv–xxvi; black nationalism, 140n55; in Canada, xxxvii, 9–14, 15–16, 31, 31–35; and Freud, 137n3
national parks, 32–34, 36–39
Native Americans. *See* indigenous peoples and nations
Native Land Act (1913), 50
nature: and body, xxxvii, 11–12, 109, 127–28n60; effects of colonialism, xxi, xxxviii,

68–69, 87, 109, 141n10; national parks, 32–34, 36–39; sensory experience of, 57, 68, 102–106, 109, 111, 145–46n103; species-thinking, 86, 87; as universal, 99, 133n82. *See also* Anthropocene; climate
nature-culture-power, xxvii–xxxii, xxxvi, 121n88
Nauset Spit, Cape Cod, 39, 42
Navajo (Diné), 106–111
Negro myth, 72–73
Negrophobia, 71
New Brunswick, New Jersey, 43
new materialism, xx–xxiv, 45, 116n38, 131n25
Nixon, Rob, 86
Nkosi, Lewis, 47
North Africa, 65, 72–73, 78–81
"'North African Syndrome,' The," 78
"Notes toward a Politics of Location" (Rich), 41

objectification: in Anthropocene view, 92; of people of color, xxvii–xxviii, 1, 16–18; of women, 2, 19–20, 82
obliteration of psyche, 72, 74
occupation. *See* colonialism; psychic occupation
ocean: and climate change, 85, 91; in metaphor, 83–84; swimming in, 21, 22, 36, 39. *See also* swimming
Oedipus complex, 66, 70
"Of the Different Human Races" (Kant), 12
Oksala, Johanna, 42, 123n118
Old Age (de Beauvoir), 3
Oliver, Kelly, 96
Ontario, 33
"On the Concept of History" (Benjamin), 101, 111
ontology, xx–xxi, xxiv, 98–99
Order of Things, The (Foucault), 83–84
Ortega, Mariana, xxxiv, 7, 115n16
otherness, xxiv–xxvi, 10, 14, 19, 55
outer space, 95–96, 143n53
Oxford University, 19–20, 129–30n100

painting, 22, 33

Pandya, Rashmika, xxxiii, xxxvii, 4; "Borderlines of Culture and Identity," xxxiii, xxxvii, 4, 7–10, 13–16; and identity, 7–10, 13–14; and spatiality, 14–16; use of autobiography, 126–27n37
panopticon, 67–68
Parables for the Virtual (Massumi), 25–26
Paradis, Charles, 13
Parkin, George, 12
Passalacqua, Veronica, 109, 146n124
Pass Laws (1952), 52
people of color (POC). *See* blackness; race
perception: in Amerindian thought, 99–100; human *vs.* global scale, xxxviii, 103, 106, 111; primacy of, xxii–xxvii, 120n75; *vs.* sensation, xxiii, 118–19n54; shaped by race, xxxi, 27. *See also* sensation
petition, 85–86
phenomenological reduction, xxviii–xxix, 42, 121n97
phenomenology: and Amazonian cosmology, 100; anonymous body, xxvii–xxxii, 27–28, 32, 40, 74, 121–22n98; and Anthropocene, 89, 105; and materialism, xxii–xxvii, 71–75; and objectification, 16–17; of race, xxx–xxxi, 6, 27, 42; scholarly value of, 6, 117–18n44
phenomenology, Merleau-Ponty's theory: anonymous body, xxvii–xxxii, 74, 121–22n98; language, 18; phenomenological reduction, xxviii–xxix, 42, 121n97; primacy of perception, xxii–xxvii, 120n75; spatiality, 14–15, 74; transcendental consciousness, xxviii, xxix, xxxi, 116n123, 123n116
Phenomenology of Perception (Merleau-Ponty), xxii–xxvii, xxxvii, 7, 14–15, 114n12, 118–19n54. *See also* phenomenology, Merleau-Ponty's theory
Philadelphia, Pennsylvania, xv
philosophy, xxvii, xxxii–xxxiv, 124n124. *See also* phenomenology
photography, xxxviii, 106–10, 146n124
Pitman, A. J., 92
place. *See* space

planetarity, xix–xx, 87
pleasure: in queer studies, 45–46; in *Question of Power*, 54–60; sensual *vs.* sexual, xxxvii–xxxviii, 46–47, 48, 54–55, 135–36n1; and swimming, 30, 31–32
Points System (1967), 13
politics: and climate change, 109; geopolitics, 69; identity politics, 60; and love, xxxvi, 46; of scholarly approaches, xx, xxiv–xxv, xxvii, xxxiii, 41; and subjectivity, 25–26
"Politics and Difference" (Saldanha), 27
pools, 42–43, 134n100
pornography, 55
positionality, 117n42; and affect, 24–28, 131n31; and Anthropocene, 88, 103–7, 110–12, 144–45n76; changing context, xxi–xxii, 32; context of sensation, xx, xxvi–xxviii, 118–19n54; and environmentalism, xv–xvi, xviii, 88, 102–6, 109, 111; and feminism, 41–42, 124n128; in *Question of Power*, 61–62; in time, xxvii; view-from-nowhere, 92, 94, 98–99, 104, 107
posthumanism, 83
poststructuralism, xvii, xx, xxiv, xxv, 121–22n98, 124n124
potentiality, xxxvi, 23, 49
poverty, 13, 125n2
power: and autobiography, 42; black power, 60, 73; in Earth science, 94–95, 96–97, 106; and French universalism, 94; geopower, xv, xxxii, xxxviii, 66, 67–69, 88; influence on body, xxvii–xxviii, xxx, 15; and knowledge, xxvii, 97; and masculinity, 52–53; nature-culture-power, xxvii–xxxii, xxxvi, 121n88; and punishment, 67–68, 69; and sexuality, 46, 48–49, 54; and sleep, 59
prepersonal body. *See* anonymous body
Prevention of Illegal Squatting Act (1951), 50
primacy of perception, xxii–xxvii, 120n75
Princeton, New Jersey, 43
problem of universals, 93
property, 77, 81–84
Provincetown, Massachusetts, 37–38
Provincializing Europe (Chakrabarty), 101, 102

Psychic Life of Power, The (Butler), 19, 67, 69
psychic occupation, 65–66, 70–75, 79–81
psychoanalysis, 10, 65–66, 70–75, 81
Puar, Jasbir, 5, 25–26, 131n25
public pools, 42–43, 134n100

Québec, 31, 34–35, 132n58
Queer Art of Failure, The (Halberstam), 137n55
queerness: in apartheid laws, 50–51; lesbianism, 29–30, 37–38; of Provincetown, 37–38; queer studies, xxxv, 45–46; in *Question of Power*, 51–52, 53, 57, 63; and race, 51–52, 63
Question of Power, A (Head), xxxvii–xxxviii, 45–63, 136n28; homosexuality in, 51–52, 53, 57, 63; race in, 50–53; scholarship on, 47–49; sensual pleasure in, 54–60; summary, 47

race: apartheid, 50–53, 56–57, 61–62, 63; and belonging, 51, 53–54, 60–62; and biology, xxx, xxxvii, 10–14, 122n104, 128n60; college admission rates, 129–30n100; damage-centered approach, 114n14; defined by climate, 11–14, 15–16; and history, 123n114, 127–28n60; and indigenous peoples and nations, 138–39n26; and metaphor, xvi–xvii, 16, 18, 58–59; mixed-race marriage, 50, 62; and national parks, 32–33; phenomenology of, xxx–xxxi, 6, 27, 42; and queer studies, 45; segregation, 34, 38, 42, 132n58; and sexuality, 46, 47–48, 50–54, 63, 71. *See also* blackness; body; Jews; Latinx; sensation; whiteness
rain, xvi–xvii
rape, 24
Reagan, Ronald, 130–131n19
realism, xvii, 110, 146n121
Renault, Matthieu, 78
representation: and affect, xxxv, 5–6; in art, 23–24; of Earth, 82, 88, 89–91, 94, 97–102; legal impact of, 116–17n41; and materialism, xx–xxi; through language, xvii, xviii, 82

reproductive futurism, 37
Rice University, 95
Rich, Adrienne, 41
Richards, Keith, 144–45n76
Rose, Jacqueline, 56–57
Roy, Deboleena, xxi–xxii

Saldanha, Arun, 27
Saltonstall, Leverett, 37–38
Sandoval, Chela, xxxiii
Sartre, Jean-Paul, ix, 16
Sassure, Ferdinand de, 142n29
Schellnhuber, H. J., 90, 92
science. *See* climate change; Earth System Science
Scott, Darieck, xxxviii, 73–74
Scott, Joan, xxxiv
seals, 40, 133–134n87
Sedgwick, Eve Kosofsky, xxv, xxxv
segregation: apartheid, 50–53, 56–57, 61–62, 63; globally, 71; in Quebec, 34, 132n58; in United States, 38, 42
Sekyi-Otu, Ato, 76
selfhood. *See* identity
sensation: and affect, xxxv–xxxvi, 4–6, 22, 26, 31–32; in Amazonian cosmology, 99–100; belonging through, 47–49, 54–57; body as basis of, xxvi, 60, 63; differential capacity for, 2–3, 125n9; identity through, 4, 7–10; and language, xvii, xviii, 8, 18; of nature, 57, 68, 102–106, 109, 111, 145–146n103; vs. perception, xxiii, 118–19n54; scholarly value of, xx–xxi, 5, 45, 117–118n44; sensual *vs.* sexual, xxxvii–xxxviii, 46–47, 48, 54–55, 135–36n1; sight, xxvi, 55; smell, 130n6; sound, 8, 17–18, 129n93; temperature, 8–9, 15–16; touch, 8, 29. *See also* cold; phenomenology; pleasure
settler colonialism, xxi, xxxiii, xxxviii; in Algeria, 65–66, 76; in Canada, 11–14, 31, 32–33, 35; in United States, 32–33, 36–39, 109
Seven Pillars of Wisdom: A Triumph (Lawrence), 24

"Sex, Power, and the Politics of Identity" (Foucault), 46
sexuality: eroticism, 45–46, 54–55, 116n38, 135n2; and power, 46, 48–49, 54; and race, 46, 47–48, 50–54, 63, 71; sensual *vs.* sexual, xxxvii–xxxviii, 46–47, 54–55, 59–60, 134–35n1. *See also* queerness
shadow feminism, 137n55
Shawinigan, Québec, 34–35
sight, xxvi, 55
Silko, Leslie Marmon, 107, 146n121
Sims, J. Marion, 125n9
"Situated Knowledges" (Haraway), 105
situatedness. *See* positionality
Skin of the Film, The (Marks), 28
sleep, 59–60
smell, 130n6
"Solitude Trilogy" (musical piece), 33
sound, 8, 17–18, 129n93
South Africa, 6, 47, 49–53, 58–59
sovereignty: of indigenous peoples and nations, xxxviii, 109, 138–39n26; and nature, 39, 69; of self, 46, 61, 63, 114–15n14
space: belonging in, 48–49, 51, 58–59; and cold, 14–16, 19; and colonialism, xxxiii, 50–54, 72–75, 80; and identity, 8, 62–63, 65; and immigration, 7–10; indigenous views of, 98–100; outer space, 95–96, 143n53; in psychoanalysis, 66; public spaces, 42–43, 134n100; and selfhood, 8, 62–63; social construction of, 36, 50–54, 62–63; urban *vs.* rural, xv, 61–62. *See also* imaginaries; positionality; segregation; territory
species-thinking, 86, 87
Speculum: Of the Other Woman (Irigaray), 82
Spell of the Sensuous, The (Abram), 114n12
Spinoza, Baruch, 3
spiritual unity, 99
Spivak, Gayatri, xxiv, xix–xx
Steffen, Will, 90
Stern, Erich, 72
Stewart, Kathleen, 23
Stoermer, Eugene, 89–90
Stoller, Silvia, 121–122n98

Strangers in Blood (Feerick), 127–128n60
Street Corner Society (Whyte), 27
structuralism, 142n29
structures of feeling, xxxv–xxxvi, 124n132
Studies on Hysteria (Freud), 66
subjectivity: as analytic basis, xv, xxxiv, 19, 25–26, 131n25; body-subject, xxxvii, 6, 10–11, 104, 118–19n54, 123n116, 123n118; global subject, 90, 97; intersubjectivity, xxxi–xxxii, 123n118; and masculinity, 82; and territory, 66. *See also* identity; positionality
Subramaniam, Banu, xxi–xxii
Surrallés, Alexandre, 98, 100
Survival: A Thematic Guide to Canadian Literature (Atwood), 33
swimming, xxxvii, 21–43; Clare's account, 21, 29–32, 34–36, 39–40, 42–43; public pools, 42–43, 134n100
systems theory, 91, 142n26. *See also* Earth System Science

Talahite, Anissa, 47, 54
Tansley, Arthur, 142n26
temperature, 8–9, 15–16. *See also* cold
territory: and animals, 40, 129n92; and Canadian identity, 33–34; and objectification, 17–18, 20; psychic occupation, 65–66, 70–75, 79–81; and sound, 17–18, 129n92
terror, 73–74
Terrorist Assemblages (Puar), 25
Thoreau, Henry David, 38–39
Thousand Plateaus, A (Deleuze and Guattari), 129n92
Thrift, Nigel, xxxiv
"Throwing Like a Girl" (Young), xxviii
time, xxvii, 74, 80, 103
Tomkins, Silvan, xxxv
touch, 8, 29
"Toward a Phenomenology of Racial Embodiment" (Alcoff), 27
transcendental consciousness, xxviii, xxix, xxxi, 116n123, 123n116

transformation: affect as, 22–24, 26, 28; of Earth, 39–40, 68–69, 77–78, 81, 83; and materialism, xxi; phenomenological approach as, 42; of psyche, 72. *See also* Anthropocene
Trudeau, Pierre Elliott, 31
Tsing, Anna, 106–7
Tuana, Nancy, xv
Tuck, Eve, 114n14
Tucker, Margaret, 55
Tupi-Guarani, 99–100

Undoing Monogamy (Willey), 116n38
United States: census, 34; during Cold War, 95, 103; environmentalism in, 32–33, 104, 107–8, 109; national parks in, 32–33, 35–39; segregation in, 38, 42
universalism: in Clare's autobiography, 42; contra identity-based views, 60–61; Earth system view as, 88, 93–97, 103–4, 144–45n76; in epistemology, 103–4; of French language, 94; of history, 101, 111; of human species, 2–3, 86, 88; in multiculturalism, 98–99; nature as, 99, 133n82; of Western canon, xxxiii; whiteness as, xxvii–xxviii, xxxiv, 70
universal love, 57–59, 60
University of Toronto, 12
Upper Canada College, 12
"Use and Abuse of Vegetational Concepts and Terms, The" (Tansley), 142n26
"Uses of the Erotic: The Erotic as Power, The" (Lorde), 46

Veracini, Lorenzo, 12
view-from-nowhere, 92, 94, 98–99, 104, 107
violence: and colonialism, xxxii, 71–72, 74–75; and differential sensation, 2, 125n9; domestic, 25–26; metaphor for, xvii; in *Question of Power*, 47, 50, 58–59; against self, xxv
virtual body, 14–15, 18, 23
vitality, xxxviii, 23, 39, 66, 71, 75, 130–31n19
Vizenor, Gerald, 110

Walker, Alice, xxxvi
Walsh, Maria, 27–28
warmth, 8–9
water. *See* ocean; swimming
Weate, Jeremy, xxxi
Weheliye, Alexander, 49, 60–61
Weisiger, Marsha, 108
Weiss, Gayle, xxviii
West, Cornel, 114n14
Weston, Kath, 105–6
Wet'suwet'en Nation, 116–17n41
What Is Philosophy? (Deleuze and Guattari), 23–24
whiteness: and affect, 4–5; as assumed universal, xxvii–xxviii, xxxiv, 70; and attitudes toward POC, 17, 71; and intersectionality, 131n25; in national identity, 11–16, 32–34; of Oxford University, 19–20, 129–30n100; in philosophical canon, xxvii; and privilege, 36. *See also* race

White Paper (1966), 13
Whyte, William Foote, 27
wilderness, 32–34, 133n82. *See also* nature
Willey, Angela, 116n38
Williams, Raymond, xxxv
Williams, Ruth, 62
Wilson, Elizabeth, 138n10
Wilson, Will, xxxviii, 89, 106–11
Wiltse, Jeff, 42, 134n100
wind, xvii–xviii, 9
Winnicott, Donald, 66
Wirth, Conrad, 37
women. *See* gender
Wretched of the Earth, The (Fanon), xxxii, xxxviii; on appropriation, 76–80; on land, 75–76; on psyche, 71–75
"Writing Autobiography" (hooks), 41–42
Wynter, Sylvia, 61

Young, Iris Marion, xxviii, 29–30

www.ingramcontent.com/pod-product-compliance
Lightning Source LLC
Chambersburg PA
CBHW060952230426
43665CB00015B/2161